Building Websites with OpenCms

Matt Butcher

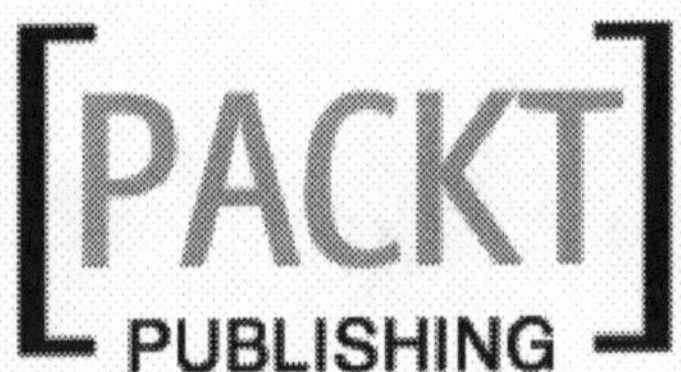

Building Websites with OpenCms

First edition: June 2004

Published by Packt Publishing Ltd.
32 Lincoln Road
Olton
Birmingham, B27 6PA, UK.

ISBN 1-904811-04-3

www.packtpub.com

Cover Design by www.visionwt.com

Credits

Author
Matt Butcher

Technical Reviewers
Olli Arro
Paul D Bain
Alex Epshteyn
Stephan Hartmann
Harald Gottlicher

Layout
Niranjan Jahagirdar

Commissioning Editor
Douglas Paterson

Technical Editor
Niranjan Jahagirdar

Indexer
Ashutosh Pande

Proofreader
Chris Smith

Cover Designer
Helen Wood

About the Author

Matt Butcher is the Principal Consultant for Aleph-Null, Inc., a systems integrator located in Colorado, USA. Specializing in open-source software, Matt has worked on a wide variety of projects, including embedding Linux in set-top boxes and developing advanced search engines based on artificial intelligence and medical informatics technologies. Matt is involved in several Open Source communities, including OpenCms, Gentoo Linux, and RT (Request Tracker). In addition to his software development, Matt has worked as a freelance journalist covering areas of interest to the Open Source community. When Matt is not working, he enjoys exploring Colorado with his wife and his two daughters.

When I first started working with Open Source developers, I thought it was all about the software. After years of work with some fantastic people from many nations and walks of life, I realize that the software is an added benefit, but it is really all about the people and the community.

Thanks to Olli Arro, Joachim Arrasz, Paul D. Bain, Alex Epshteyn, Harald Gottlicher, Stephan Hartmann, Niranjan Jahagirdar, Douglas Paterson, and Ernesto De Santis, each of whom contributed (directly or indirectly) more to this book than I could describe here. Thanks also to Rene van't Veen for the SQL Server query.properties patch and Geoff Winkless for his SQL Server stored procedures.

I'd also like to thank the members of the OpenCms developers' list who have proved an invaluable resource in all of my OpenCms projects, and especially in writing this book.

And, of course, Alexander Kandzior and the OpenCms developers for building a great product around which an even greater community has formed.

Thanks to JP and Jonathan Marsden from Global Resources for Computing for initially allowing me to contribute the OpenCms Lucene module, and for providing me flexible work during the writing of this book.

Also, thanks to Dr. Wes Munsil and Janet Siebert for lending technical expertise as well as their encouragement.

Special thanks to Angie, Annabelle, and Claire for their encouragement.

Table of Contents

Introduction

OpenCms is an open-source enterprise-grade content management system based on Java and XML technology, and is designed specifically for creating and maintaining websites. It provides a full set of tools for dealing with content creation, editorial workflow, publishing, and versioning.

In this book we will take you through the process of constructing an OpenCms website, showing you how to work with OpenCms, customize and extend your system with Java libraries and classes, JSP pages, and XML templates, and how to administer and deploy your OpenCms solution.

Like many of the open-source content management systems, OpenCms is daunting on first use, but its power and flexibility reward the investment in learning to use it. This book exists to ease you into getting the most from OpenCms.

What This Book Covers

Chapter 1 gives us an introduction to OpenCms, its features, and its history. *Chapter 2* walks us through the process of installing and configuring OpenCms. We look at installing OpenCms with its setup wizard, securing and troubleshooting the installation, and configuring the client.

Chapter 3 explores the OpenCms Workplace; this is the primary interface for managing the contents of your OpenCms repository, and includes tools for editing, project management, workflow, publishing, and server administration. In this chapter, we cover various aspects of working in the OpenCms Workplace, including managing projects, using modules, permissions, editing and publishing documents, creating new pages, and customizing the Workplace.

In *Chapter 4* we turn our attention to customizing the site. We look at developing the look and feel of published content, adding dynamic elements, and controlling resources. This includes topics such as working with templates, using OpenCms JSP tag libraries, creating JSP scriptlets, and managing FlexCache directives.

Chapter 5 takes us into the heart of OpenCms, looking at the mechanisms that drive the content management system. We look at resource types, content definitions, the Virtual File System (VFS), and the class structure of OpenCms.

In *Chapter 6* we look at OpenCms modules; these provide a mechanism for extending the functionality of OpenCms. Modules are designed to be easily distributed among

OpenCms installations, and can provide functional elements ranging from portable content to sophisticated applications that interact with content in OpenCms. We take an in-depth look at developing modules, covering topics such as creating a module, adding templates, content, and JSP pages to the module, adding custom Java classes and libraries, and exporting and deploying your module.

Chapter 7 tackles some advanced features of the OpenCms module mechanism. We cover creating an administration point for a module, using JSPs to produce administration screens, and creating a custom launcher class.

In *Chapter 8* we return to the administrative aspect of managing OpenCms, and examine the issues surrounding the deployment of an OpenCms solution. We cover static exports, user authentication and management, and other administrative tasks such as backup, recovery, and performance tuning.

There are two appendices that cover building OpenCms from its sourcecode, and installing, configuring, and using the OpenCms Lucene Module to improve the searching of your site.

What You Need for Using This Book

To use this book, you will of course need OpenCms. This is freely downloadable from `http://www.opencms.org/opencms/en/download/opencms.html`.

OpenCms has its own requirements for installation: Java 2 SDK version 1.4 or higher, Apache Tomcat 4.x, and MySQL 3.23.x or higher.

You will find details of where to download these applications from in Chapter 2, but each is freely available.

A sound knowledge of Java, JSP, and XML will help you get the most out of this book.

Conventions

In this book you will find a number of styles of text that distinguish between different kinds of information. Here are some examples of these styles, and an explanation of their meaning.

There are three styles for code. Code words in text are shown as follows: "Rather than get the contents of `myFile` with the `getContents()` method, we construct a new `CmsXmlControlFile` object".

If we have a block of code, it will be set as follows:

```
CmsJspActionElement cms = new CmsJspActionElement( pageContext,
                                                   request,
                                                   response );
```

```
String myFileName = "/playground/index.html";
CmsObject cmso = cms.getCmsObject();
CmsFile myFile = cmso.readFile( myFileName );
```

When we wish to draw your attention to a particular part of a code block, the relevant lines will be made bold:

```
CmsJspActionElement cms = new CmsJspActionElement( pageContext,
                                                   request,
                                                   response );
String myFileName = "/playground/index.html";
CmsObject cmso = cms.getCmsObject();
CmsFile myFile = cmso.readFile( myFileName );
```

New terms and **important words** are introduced in a bold-type font. Words that you see on the screen—in menus or dialog boxes, for example—appear in the text as follows: "Clicking the Next button moves you to the next screen".

> Tips, suggestions, or important notes appear in a box like this.

Any command-line input and output is written as follows:

```
mysql> create table books (name char(100), author char(50));
Query OK, 0 rows affected (0.03 sec)
```

Reader Feedback

Feedback from our readers is always welcome. Let us know what you think about this book, what you liked or may have disliked. Reader feedback is important for us to develop titles that you really get the most out of.

To send us general feedback, simply drop an e-mail to `feedback@packtpub.com`, making sure to mention the book title in the subject of your message.

If there is a book that you need and would like to see us publish, please send us a note in the Suggest a title form on `www.packtpub.com` or e-mail `suggest@packtpub.com`.

If there is a topic that you have expertise in and you are interested in either writing or contributing to a book, see our author guide on `www.packtpub.com/authors`.

Customer Support

Now that you are the proud owner of a Packt book, we have a number of things to help you to get the most from your purchase.

Downloading the Example Code for the Book

Visit `http://www.packtpub.com/support`, and select this book from the list of titles to download any example code or extra resources for this book. The files available for download will then be displayed.

> The downloadable files contain instructions on how to use them.

Errata

Although we have taken every care to ensure the accuracy of our contents, mistakes do happen. If you find a mistake in one of our books—maybe a mistake in text or code—we would be grateful if you could report this to us. By doing this you can save other readers from frustration, and also help to improve subsequent versions of this book.

If you find any errata, report them by visiting `http://www.packtpub.com/support`, selecting your book, clicking on the Submit Errata link, and entering the details of your errata. Once your errata have been verified, your submission will be accepted and the errata added to the list of existing errata. The existing errata can be viewed by selecting your title from `http://www.packtpub.com/support`.

Questions

You can contact us at `questions@packtpub.com` if you are having a problem with some aspect of the book, and we will do our best to address it.

1

Introduction to OpenCms

The purpose of this chapter is to provide a brief introduction to OpenCms and the concepts and technologies it employs. In this chapter, we will cover:

- The concept of a Content Management System (CMS)
- The features of OpenCms
- The history and community surrounding OpenCms
- A technical overview of the OpenCms project

What Is a Content Management System?

The exact definition of a CMS is somewhat slippery, as the range of CMS systems is broad and the functionalities of each differ markedly. At the core, however, a content management system provides a framework for creating, managing, and publishing documents and texts. In more practical terms, a content management system handles the process of creating and maintaining a collection (large or small) of documents.

While CMS systems in general deal with a wide variety of types of collections, ranging from memos to marketing material, web-based collections are the most high profile. To that end, many CMS systems, including OpenCms, focus on web-based management (also called Web Content Management or WCM) and delivery of content.

Three Essential Components

There are three essential components to an enterprise-class CMS:

- Editorial workflow
- Publishing
- Versioning

Editorial workflow refers to the process of preparing a piece of content for production. In the simplest case, this may simply involve one person writing a document, proofing it, and perhaps also revising it. However, in a larger context, the process may involve multiple authors writing content that is then edited by a team of editors and producers. A manager may assign a topic to an individual author who then writes a document. Once the author is done with the document, a team of editors reviews and corrects it, occasionally handing it back to the author for revision. Once this iterative process is complete, the editors submit the document to a producer, who makes decisions about whether the content is to be distributed, and if so, when. A good CMS must handle both the simple and the complex cases of editing. Once a document is written, it must be published.

Publishing is the next step in the life of the document. Publishing the document makes it accessible to potential readers. Some collections of content, such as the numerous chapters in a manual, are all published *together*. Other content, such as a news article or a press release, may be published on its own without requiring simultaneous publishing of other material. Sometimes images need to be published along with a particular document. Sometimes the document may require a certain amount of dynamic information (such as stock quotes or live images) to be incorporated. All of these possibilities mandate an effective publishing mechanism. A document's life cycle is not complete once it's published—it now enters version control.

Versioning becomes important once a document has been published. Authors and editors may make corrections or add updated information, and these changes may require their own editorial cycle before they can be published. Changes to the document should not be immediately incorporated into the published version, but must remain in the editorial stage while the currently published version remains available. Even after the changes are published, circumstances may require that the update be 'backed out' and the prior version restored. This process of revising and updating a document while preserving a record of changes is called versioning.

What Is OpenCms?

OpenCms is an open-source enterprise-grade content management system designed specifically for maintaining websites. It provides a full set of tools for dealing with content creation, editorial workflow, publishing, and versioning.

OpenCms is released under the **Lesser GNU Public License** (**LGPL**), which is an **Open Source Initiative** (**OSI**) certified open-source license created by the Free Software Foundation. Since OpenCms is released as open source, its source code is available from the OpenCms website.

The LGPL dictates that the source code for OpenCms must be made freely available. The source code for any changes made to it must also be made freely available.

However, external components, such as modules, wrappers, or JSP files, are not restricted by the LGPL, and can use different licenses (including proprietary, 'closed-source' licenses). This gives the application developer the power to decide how many restrictions should be placed on the code.

> For more information on the LGPL, see the following websites:
>
> OpenCms: `http://www.opencms.org/`
> The Free Software Foundation's LGPL License:
> `http://www.gnu.org/licenses/licenses.html#LGPL`
> The Open Source Initiative: `http://www.opensource.org/`

Features

OpenCms is a web application. It runs on a web server and is accessed and used via a web browser. The following list discusses its features:

- **Browser-based interface**: The only tool CMS users need, be they system administrators, authors, editors, or project managers, is a web browser. The OpenCms developers designed OpenCms to behave in a way similar to a normal Windows application, making it easier for the beginner to learn.
- **WYSIWYG editing tool**: Authors and editors need not learn HTML to create content. OpenCms uses an ActiveX control to provide a rich graphical user interface (GUI) for composing content (effectively limiting the WYSIWYG editor to IE5+ browsers). Users familiar with word processing should easily acclimate to the OpenCms composer.
- **Role-based workflow**: OpenCms has a sophisticated role-based workflow for managing the entire process of content creation.
- **Permissions model**: Using a combination of UNIX-like permissions and roles, OpenCms provides methods for setting and restricting assets available to CMS users.
- **Sophisticated publishing**: OpenCms provides project and file-based publishing. Additionally, it performs link and dependency checking to ensure that all of the necessary files are published together. Content can be exported from the CMS and deployed on other systems, or OpenCms itself can serve content to the public.
- **System administration**: OpenCms administration is also browser-based. Tasks ranging from scheduling tasks to manually flushing caches can be done via the browser.

- **Online help**: Open-source projects are often criticized for the lack of documentation. OpenCms, however, does not suffer from that problem. While the help module is optional, it provides context-sensitive help throughout OpenCms. Additionally, there are tutorial modules that can provide developer help and reference within OpenCms.
- **Module-based framework**: OpenCms provides a module mechanism for adding functionality to the system. Modules ranging from online documentation (tutorials and references) to advanced content handling (calendars, news, search engines, etc.) are available as add-on software.

History

Alexander Kandzior began tinkering with content management software in 1994. By 1998, the pieces began to come together into a single content management system. In March 2000, the OpenCms Group, a loose collection of individuals working on the system, released OpenCms under an open-source license.

Under the auspices of the OpenCms Group, a number of companies and individuals contributed to the formation of OpenCms, but by the time OpenCms reached version 5.0 in 2002, some of the original members of the group were ready to move on to new projects. The OpenCms Group was dissolved.

Wanting to continue the development of his code, Alexander Kandzior started a new company, Alkacon Software, which took the reins of the OpenCms project. Alkacon Software now maintains the project, providing the roadmap and release cycle, as well as contributing code to OpenCms. To fund ongoing development of OpenCms, Alkacon provides support contracts, training, and consulting services.

Alexander and the Alkacon team are a visible presence in the community, and Alexander often contributes help and advice on the public OpenCms developer's list.

The OpenCms Community

Like many open-source projects, OpenCms has a lively community of developers and users. Many software developers contribute code directly to OpenCms. Others create add-on modules to provide additional services and features. Many more simply use the product. All three of these groups participate on mailing lists and forums surrounding OpenCms.

With many active contributors, the **opencms-dev** mailing list is a great resource for help installing, configuring, and developing OpenCms. In addition to providing help, the list is also a useful source of code and new modules.

> To join the **opencms-dev** mailing list, go to:
> `http://www.opencms.org/opencms/en/development/mailinglist.html`
>
> The list archives are available at: `http://www.opencms.org/opencms/en/development/mailinglist-archive.html`

Also, the 'unofficial' **OpenCms forums** hosted by Synyx oHG provides an online forum for discussion. The forum has a section for HowTos, and sample code generated by members of the community. Finally, the **OpenCms Modules and Tutorials** section mentions the `al-arenal.de` website. While `opencms.org` hosts completed modules on its website, developers will often release beta modules, modifications of existing modules, and 'semi-formal' documentation on this unofficial OpenCms website.

> These 'unofficial' sites provide useful information on OpenCms:
>
> The OpenCms Forums: `http://synyx.de/board/`
> OpenCms Modules and Tutorials: `http://opencms.al-arenal.de/`
> Online OpenCms demo: `http://demo.comundus.com/`

The Purpose of This Book

This book is intended to provide detailed information for those interested in developing and deploying OpenCms-based sites. It is assumed that the reader is familiar with installing software and managing either Windows 2000 or Linux/UNIX. Because much of this book is dedicated to writing HTML, Java Server Pages, and Java code, having a working knowledge of these technologies is necessary.

Technical Overview

OpenCms is written in Java. It makes use of industry-standard XML (eXtensible Markup Language), and uses Java DataBase Connectivity (JDBC) to store data in a relational database. Built in Java, OpenCms can run on different platforms, including numerous versions of UNIX and Linux, and Windows.

Hardware-wise, OpenCms is designed for scalability. It will run on hardware ranging from small laptops (I've run it on a Pentium III 733 Toshiba Tecra laptop with 256 MB RAM and Red Hat 8) to a distributed collection of servers.

Being a web-based application, OpenCms runs as a Java servlet inside a servlet container such as Apache Tomcat or BEA WebLogic. For data storage, it can use a number of SQL databases, including MySQL, Microsoft SQL Server, and Oracle.

At one time, OpenCms required developers to learn a proprietary XML schema for developing templates, but in version 5.0, OpenCms has changed direction and now uses Java Server Pages; we'll get into the details of the system later. Here is a brief summary of how each of these components works (and how they all work together).

The Web Server and Java Servlets

The web server handles incoming connections. As it sees connections intended for OpenCms, it hands them off to the servlet container for processing. The servlet container manages one or more Java servlets. Unlike a CGI script, which runs only for the amount of time it takes to process a single request, a servlet stays running until the server explicitly stops it (which usually only happens when the server shuts down). The job of the servlet container is to provide the runtime environment for the servlets.

While it is possible to run OpenCms on the command line, it is almost always run as a servlet.

The Database

OpenCms uses a database for persistent data storage. Information about file types, templates, and publishing is stored in the database, as is all the content. OpenCms supports a couple of major SQL-based databases, including MySQL, Microsoft SQL Server, and Oracle. Developers are working on ports to PostgreSQL and other databases.

OpenCms uses JDBC to connect the Servlet to the database during startup. Content is managed inside the database, though it can be exported from the database into static files during a publishing cycle.

Pages, Templates, and Java Server Pages

Content is stored in the database in the form of XML files. Layout information and processing code is also stored in the database, but not in the same XML document as the content. When a page is requested, the content is pulled out of the database and put into a template. Any special processing needed is run, and the results are sent back to the requester (usually a web browser) in the form of a complete HTML file.

Templates and custom code are written in two languages: XML Template, a simple XML-based language developed by the OpenCms team, and Java Server Pages, a standardized language for embedding Java processing instructions inside of an HTML or XML document. While XML Template is still used in OpenCms 5, it will be phased out and replaced by the more flexible and mature JSP technology in future releases.

Bringing it Together

Each of these pieces functions together for each request. A typical response to a document (we'll call it `test.html`) might look like this:

1. The web browser requests `test.html`.
2. The web server recognizes that the request must be handled by OpenCms; it passes it off to the OpenCms Servlet request handler.
3. OpenCms retrieves information about `test.html` (including the content) from the database.
4. OpenCms puts the content for `test.html` into its template, adding all of the necessary layout elements and interpreting any JSP or XML template code that it needs for fulfilling the request.
5. Once OpenCms has created the complete HTML document, the document is returned to the browser.
6. The web browser interprets the HTML, runs any JavaScript that it finds, and displays the `test.html` page.

Summary

By now, you should be familiar with the basics of OpenCms—its uses, history, and key components. The next chapter will cover the installation of OpenCms, and subsequent chapters will discuss the use of and development on OpenCms.

Bringing it Together

2

Installing OpenCms

This chapter walks through the process of installing and configuring OpenCms. In the last chapter, I mentioned that OpenCms can run on a wide range of platforms and configurations; this chapter focuses on the two most common platforms: Linux/MySQL/Tomcat and Windows 2000/MySQL/Tomcat. Generally speaking, installation on other platforms is similar enough for these instructions to suffice. In this chapter, we will cover:

- Prerequisites for installing OpenCms
- Obtaining OpenCms
- Deploying the `opencms.war` file
- Installing OpenCms with the Setup Wizard
- Securing the installation
- Configuring the client
- Troubleshooting the installation

Prerequisites

OpenCms will need a configured database and a functioning servlet engine. We will use MySQL for the database and Tomcat for the servlet engine. Since OpenCms uses the **ISO 8859-1** character set, I will explain how to configure Tomcat to use that character set as default. Additionally, I will cover the registry settings that Windows installations require.

To install these packages on Linux, you will need to be root unless your system administrator has configured your system in a way that you can install these packages a different way (such as using `sudo`).

In Windows 2000, you will need to install the software as the Administrator user.

Configuring the MySQL Database

MySQL (`http://www.mysql.com`) is an open-source relational database server maintained by MySQL AB. While OpenCms supports other databases, including Oracle and MS SQL Server, MySQL runs on Windows *and* Linux, is free, and is the database on which OpenCms developers work.

OpenCms 5.0 can use either the 3.23.x or the 4.0.x version of MySQL. On Linux, if you are comfortable with MySQL, you may prefer to get the latest release from the MySQL website. However, if you are new to MySQL it is best to use the version your distribution contains (for example, at the time of this writing, Red Hat still used 3.23.x, while Gentoo used 4.0.x). That way, you can rely on your Linux vendor to provide updates and fixes.

On Windows, it is best to use the newest stable release from the MySQL website (at press time, 4.0.18 was the latest release).

MySQL on Linux

There are a couple of ways to install MySQL on a machine running Linux. You may decide to build the database from the source code, or you may download and install the binary provided by MySQL. Most Linux distributions provide a MySQL package (and often, it is installed already)—this is usually the best version to install.

> OpenCms does not require that the database be on the same machine as the servlet engine. OpenCms simply needs access to the database over the network (via JDBC).

To install the database, consult the documentation for your Linux distribution and that on the MySQL website `http://www.mysql.com/documentation/index.html`.

Many Linux distributions turn off network-based database connections by default, so you may need to manually enable the network-based server. Usually, this simply involves editing the `/etc/my.cnf` file. In the `[mysqld]` section, add the line `port=3306`. Consider the following relevant portion of my `my.cnf` file:

```
[mysqld]
port=3306
datadir=/var/lib/mysql
socket=/var/lib/mysql/mysql.sock
# The file continues on...
```

Make sure the database is running before proceeding. Most Linux systems provide init scripts for starting and stopping services. These scripts are usually located in `/etc/init.d/`. For instance, in Gentoo you can check to see if the database is up by running the command `/etc/init.d/mysql status`. If the server is not running, using the command `start` instead of `status` will start the server.

```
root # /etc/init.d/mysql status
* Status: stopped
root # /etc/init.d/mysql start
* Starting mysql               [OK]
```

Once the database is running, you are ready to move on to finishing the MySQL setup.

MySQL on Windows

While it is possible to build MySQL from source on Windows, it is much easier to download the Windows binary from the MySQL site and install it. Detailed documentation can be found at `http://www.mysql.com/documentation/index.html`.

> Windows users may find it helpful to download the MySQL documentation in CHM or HLP help-file formats. They can be added to the Windows help system.

Make sure that you install the MySQL server on your `C:` drive (the default location, `C:\mysql`, is fine). Register MySQL as a service by opening a command shell and running the following command:

```
shell> C:\mysql\bin\mysqld -install
```

Alternately, if the MySQL icon appears in your taskbar, you can right-click on it and choose the option to register the service. After that, you should be able to use the Windows Service utility to manage MySQL.

Before proceeding, start MySQL. You can start the service from the MySQL taskbar icon, or type `NET START mysql` at the command prompt.

Finishing the MySQL Setup

Once MySQL is running, set the 'root' password. This 'root' user has total control over the database, but is not necessarily correlated with the root or administrator accounts on the operating system.

```
>mysqladmin -u root password mypassword
```

> In Linux, `mysqladmin` is usually in the `$PATH`. In Windows, you may have to open a command shell and go to the `C:\mysql\bin` directory.

Next, connect using the `mysql` client:

```
>mysql -u root -p mysql
```

In the command above, `-u root` indicates that you are connecting to the database as the root (administrative) user. `-p` provides an interactive password prompt, and `mysql` at the end indicates the database that we will use (`mysql` is the name of the administration database for MySQL). Once you have connected to the database, it is time to create the opencms database and the user accounts that OpenCms will use to connect to that database.

The MySQL command for creating a database is CREATE DATABASE [dbname]. So the command to create a database named opencms is:

```
mysql> CREATE DATABASE opencms;
```

Make sure you include the semicolon at the end of the line. Now, create the opencms user:

```
mysql> GRANT ALL PRIVILEGES ON opencms.* TO opencms@localhost
    -> IDENTIFIED BY 'mypassword';
```

This statement gives permission to add, delete, and modify tables in the opencms database to the user opencms@localhost, whose password is mypassword. If OpenCms is to be run on a different machine than MySQL, you will need to create a similar statement to give log-on permission to opencms@<OpenCmsHostname> (where <OpenCmsHostname> is the host name or IP of the host running OpenCms).

The database is now prepared for OpenCms. It's now time to configure the servlet engine.

Configuring the Tomcat Servlet Engine

OpenCms is a Web-based application. It runs as a servlet inside a servlet container. Sun Microsystems, the company behind Java, has published the servlet standard, and since OpenCms adheres to the Java servlet 2.3 standard (http://jcp.org/en/jsr/detail?id=053), it will run in any servlet container that fully implements the standard.

Before you can run any Java applications, you will need to install the **Java System Development Kit** (**JSDK**). OpenCms 5.0 is written to take advantage of the features of **JSDK 1.4**, and will not run with earlier versions. Sun also packages a *runtime-only* version of Java called the **Java Runtime Environment** (**JRE**). OpenCms requires the JSDK, and *will not run with just the JRE.*

> Windows and Linux do not include the JSDK by default. If Java is not already installed, you can obtain Sun's version for free from http://java.sun.com/. At the time of writing this, neither IBM's JDK nor Blackdown's JSDK had reached the 1.4 specification, and so neither will run OpenCms.

For this book, I will use the **Jakarta-Tomcat** servlet engine (usually called simply Tomcat), which is jointly developed by the Apache Software Foundation (makers of the Apache Web Server) and Sun Microsystems. Like MySQL, Tomcat is open source and is the main platform that OpenCms developers use. Tomcat source and binaries are available from http://jakarta.apache.org. The binary releases are almost always suitable for use, but you may download and compile the source code if you prefer. While there are releases for version 5, which implement the new 2.4 servlet specification, OpenCms was developed according to the 2.3 servlet specification. Therefore, it's best to use a 4.1.x release of Tomcat (4.1.30 is the current stable release).

To install Tomcat on either Windows or Linux, simply unzip the archive into the desired directory and set the CATALINA_HOME environment variable to point to that directory. For Windows, there is a Tomcat release that uses a graphical installer. If you choose to install it this way, do *not* check the box that automatically configures Tomcat as a service. Later in this chapter, I will explain how to configure Tomcat as a Windows service.

Linux Configuration

In Linux, Tomcat is generally installed into /opt/tomcat or /usr/local/tomcat. Assuming the former location, set the CATALINA_HOME variable by running the following command:

```
export CATALINA_HOME=/opt/tomcat
```

Also, make sure that the JAVA_HOME environment variable is set. You can check by running env|grep JAVA_HOME or echo $JAVA_HOME. If either of these does not return the path to the JDK, you will need to set this environment variable to point to the location of your JDK installation.

To start Tomcat, run $CATALINA_HOME/bin/startup.sh and to stop it, run $CATALINA_HOME/bin/shutdown.sh. To streamline things a bit, I usually create a small wrapper script that looks something like this (named tomcat.sh):

```
#!/bin/bash
###############################################################
# Simple script to start and stop Tomcat.
# This script should be named tomcat.sh, and be executable
###############################################################
export CATALINA_HOME=/opt/tomcat
export CATALINA_OPTS='-Dfile.encoding=ISO-8859-1'
# Usually this is already set. If not, set it.
# export JAVA_HOME=/opt/sun-jdk-1.4.2.02
case "$1" in
    start)
        $CATALINA_HOME/bin/startup.sh
        ;;
    stop)
        $CATALINA_HOME/bin/shutdown.sh
        ;;
    restart)
        $CATALINA_HOME/bin/shutdown.sh
        $CATALINA_HOME/bin/startup.sh
        ;;
    *)
        echo $"Usage: $0 {start|stop|restart}"
        ;;
esac
```

To start Tomcat with this script, you may just type `./tomcat.sh start`, and to stop it, use `./tomcat.sh stop`. This script will help you avoid one common mistake: it will keep you from accidentally typing `shutdown` (which shuts down Linux) instead of `shutdown.sh` (which shuts down Tomcat).

Windows Configuration

Whether you have installed with the graphical installer or by simply unzipping the archive into a directory, you will need to set two environment variables: `CATALINA_HOME` and `JAVA_HOME`. In Windows 2000, you can do this by right-clicking on My Computer and choosing Properties. Go to the Advanced tab. Select Environment variables and create two variables: `CATALINA_HOME` pointing to the Tomcat installation (e.g. `C:\Program Files\Apache Group\Tomcat 4.1`), and `JAVA_HOME` pointing to the J2SDK directory (e.g. `C:\j2se1.4.2`).

Because the Windows services do not use environment variables and OpenCms requires that extra options be passed into Tomcat, Tomcat must be installed from the command line rather than the graphical installer. Open up a command prompt, change the directory to Tomcat's `bin` directory with `cd %CATALINA_HOME%\bin`, and run the `tomcat -install` command as it is displayed below. Even though the following has been split for readability, it must be typed on *just one line* in order to run correctly:

```
>tomcat -install "Tomcat" %JAVA_HOME%\jre\bin\server\jvm.dll
-Djava.class.path=%CATALINA_HOME%\bin\bootstrap.jar;%JAVA_HOME%\lib\t
ools.jar
-Dcatalina.home=%CATALINA_HOME%
%CATALINA_OPTS%
-Dfile.encoding=ISO-8859-1
-Xrs -start org.apache.catalina.startup.Bootstrap -params start
-stop org.apache.catalina.startup.Bootstrap
-params stop -out %CATALINA_HOME%\logs\stdout.log
-err %CATALINA_HOME%\logs\stderr.log
```

After this has run, you should see a message saying something like:

```
The service was successfully installed.
```

If you ever need to uninstall the service, issue the `tomcat -uninstall Tomcat` command.

As with MySQL, Tomcat can be started and stopped either through the Windows Service utility or from the command line with `NET START Tomcat` and `NET STOP Tomcat`.

> Tomcat can act like a stand-alone web server. This is useful for development. Tomcat is sometimes used this way in production environments as well. However, Tomcat can also run cooperatively with another web server such as Apache or IIS.

Once Tomcat is installed, you may test it by opening your browser and typing in the server's IP address followed by port 8080 (for instance, `http://10.0.1.13:8080`). `http://localhost:8080` will automatically resolve to your local host, and if you are browsing from the machine on which you are installing OpenCms, using this URL is easier. For the remainder of this book, I will use the `localhost` notation for URLs directed to OpenCms.

Some machines, whether Linux or Windows, may have firewalls or other security measures that block access to port 8080. Consult your firewall documentation for information on configuring it. Alternatively, you may instead choose to configure Tomcat to listen on the standard HTTP port, port 80. On a production server, you should make sure that the application is available on port 80—either by configuring Tomcat, or by setting it up to work cooperatively with another Web server. This will ensure that your site is available to all web surfers—even those behind restrictive firewalls.

> To configure Tomcat to listen on the standard HTTP port, make sure you are not running another web server already, and then edit the `server.xml` file (under `$CATALINA_HOME/conf/` in Linux, `%CATALINA_HOME%\conf\` in Windows). Find the `Connector className=" org.apache.coyote.tomcat4.CoyoteConnector"` element and change `port="8080"` to `port="80"`. You will need to restart Tomcat before the change takes effect. Now, the URL no longer needs `:8080` at the end.

Configuring Encoding

There is one last step to configuring the environment before installing OpenCms. By default, OpenCms uses the **ISO 8859-1 character set** (sometimes referred to as the Latin-1 character set). To make sure that Tomcat uses this character set, you must pass it a special parameter: `-Dfile.encoding=ISO-8859-1`. In the Linux start script, I included a line that set this parameter as a value of `CATALINA_OPTS`. I also specified the parameter in the online command for adding Tomcat as a service on Windows. However, if you intend to start Tomcat with other tools, you can add the parameter to the `catalina.sh` (for Linux) or `catalina.bat` (for Windows).

OpenCms supports other character sets. Later in this chapter, I will cover configuring and using the UTF-8 character set, which supports multi-byte characters.

> The step of configuring character encoding is often overlooked, as it appears to be unimportant or unnecessary. However, *not* configuring encoding can result in strange, seemingly inexplicable errors.

After configuring encoding, restart Tomcat and make sure the default URL loads in your browser. Now that Tomcat and MySQL are configured, it's time to install the OpenCms **Web ARchive (WAR)** file.

Tuning the JVM

One of the easiest, and most common, ways to increase the performance of a Java application is to adjust the memory settings for the JVM. In Sun's version of the `java` command, this can be done by setting the `-Xmx` and `-Xms` flags.

Use the `CATALINA_OPTS` environment variable (which we used for setting encoding) to set initial and max heap sizes. The example below sets the encoding to ISO-8859-1 (the default for OpenCms), and then sets the maximum amount of RAM allocated to Tomcat to be 512 MB, and the initial amount to 256 MB. These settings would work well on a system with 1 Gigabyte RAM, though you could certainly experiment with more aggressive settings.

```
CATALINA_OPTS="-Dfile.encoding=ISO-8859-1 -Xmx512M -Xms256M"
```

These options will control how much memory the JVM attempts to use. The higher you can set these, the better. Just remember that the database will need plenty of memory too. If the applications cause the system to start swapping to disk, performance will actually diminish. It may take some experimenting to find the right balance, but the improvements can be quite noticeable.

Installing the OpenCms WAR File

As with most open-source projects, OpenCms is available in both source and binary releases. In Appendix A, I cover building OpenCms from source, but in this section, I will refer only to the binary build. Download the 5.0.1 release (`opencms_5.0.1.zip`) from `http://www.opencms.org/opencms/en/download/index.html`, the OpenCms downloads page.

OpenCms, like most Java servlets, is packaged in a WAR file. This file contains all the files necessary for running the application. In Tomcat, all WAR files go under the `webapps/` directory (in `$CATALINA_HOME/` on Linux and `%CATALINA_HOME%\` on Windows).

Once you have downloaded the `opencms_5.0.1.zip` file, unzip it to a temporary directory and copy the `opencms.war` file into Tomcat's `webapps` directory. While Tomcat will eventually automatically detect the new WAR file, it is best to manually restart Tomcat, which will force it to reload all web applications. Note that OpenCms requires that the WAR be unpacked into a directory (`$CATALINA_HOME/webapps/opencms`).

By default, Tomcat unpacks WARs automatically, but other servlet containers may require additional configuration to elicit this behavior.

Configuring OpenCms to Use UTF-8

UTF-8 (Unicode), which supports multi-byte character encoding, is also supported in OpenCms. To use UTF-8, you will have to change the `-Dfile.encoding=ISO-8859-1`, set earlier in the *Configuring Encoding* section, to `-Dfile.encoding=UTF-8`. If you are running Windows and have already installed Tomcat as a service, you will need to uninstall the service and rerun the install script with `UTF-8` in place of `ISO-8859-1`.

Also, you will need to edit the OpenCms properties file to set the correct encoding. Stop Tomcat and edit the `opencms.properties` file under `$CATALINA_HOME/webapps/opencms/WEB_INF/`. Find the line that reads:

```
defaultContentEncoding=ISO-8859-1
```

Change `ISO-8859-1` to `UTF-8` and save the file.

It is possible to use other character sets, but if you do so, you may also have to configure the encoding that your database uses. Consult your database documentation to find out.

Verify that Tomcat is using the correct character encoding (see the *Configuring Encoding* section), and then start Tomcat again.

Running the Install Wizard

Once the `opencms.war` file is in place and Tomcat is restarted, you are ready to run the installer.

> Regarding browsers, the OpenCms installation and workplace utilize advanced JavaScript. Because JavaScript implementations vary widely, OpenCms developers decided to target only the two most popular browser flavors: Internet Explorer and Mozilla (including Netscape and Firefox). Even between the two, there are some discrepancies in functionality. The OpenCms installation and workplace may or may not work with other browsers.

Open a browser and enter the following URL to the OpenCms installer:

```
http://localhost:8080/opencms/ocsetup
```

This will bring up the first screen of the OpenCms installation wizard. There are two installation modes: standard and advanced. Choosing the advanced mode will add three more screens of configurable details. Usually, the standard install is sufficient; however, for the sake of completeness, I'll go through the advanced setup.

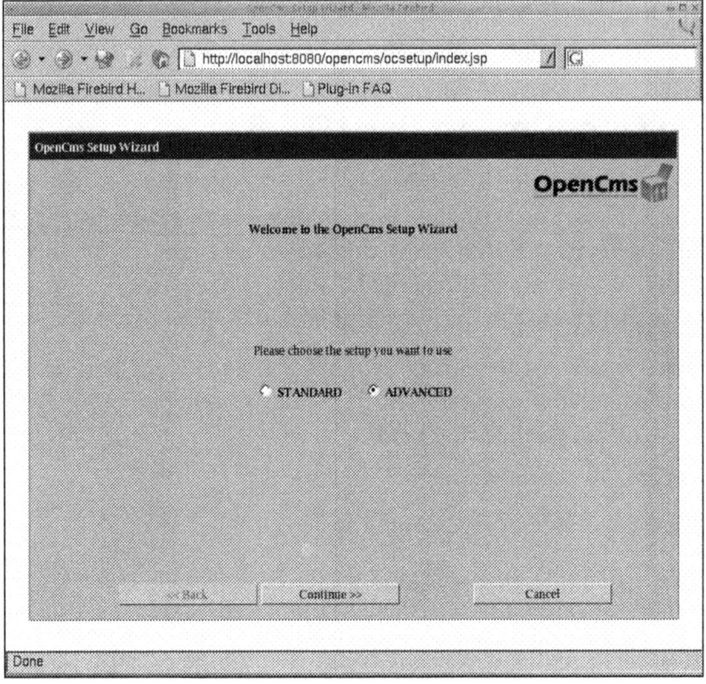

Click on Continue to proceed to the database setup screen:

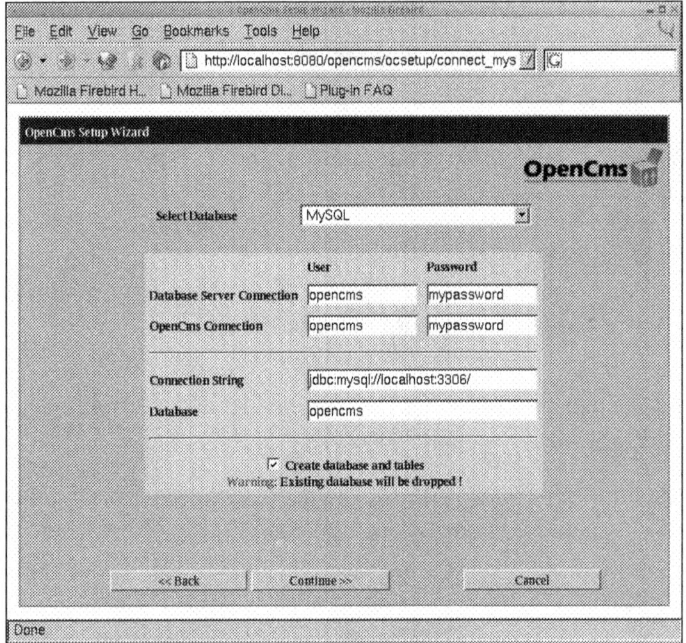

Set the User and Password fields for both Database Server Connection and OpenCms Connection to be the MySQL user created during MySQL setup. The rest of the fields should default to the correct values. Clicking on Continue will bring you to a page that warns that the existing `opencms` database will be dropped. Allowing the database to be dropped is fine as it contains nothing.

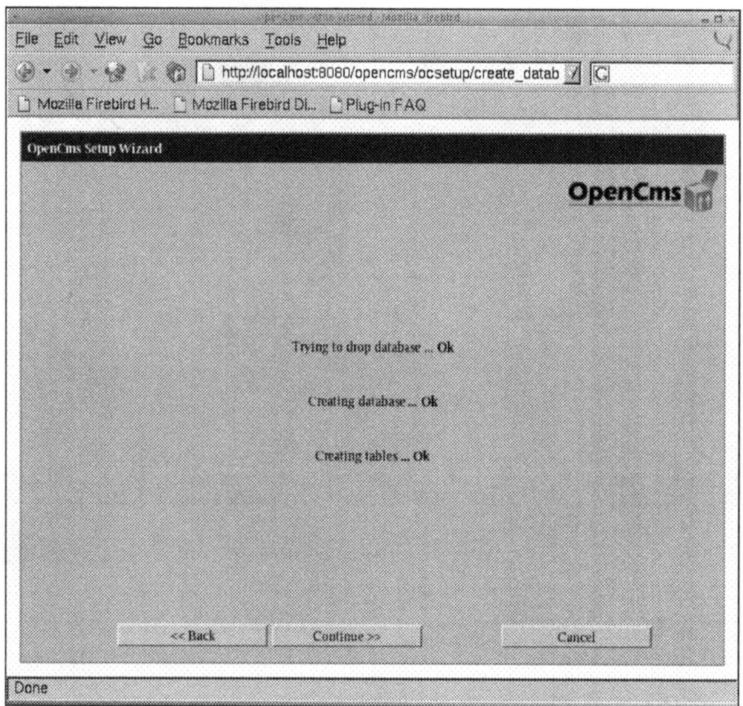

If everything on this screen says Ok, hit Continue. Failures during database installation usually indicate that the permissions for the MySQL user `opencms` were not set correctly. You can log in to the database and check the user by running a `SELECT` against the `mysql.user` table. Review the `GRANT` statements in the **Finishing MySQL Setup** section, and make sure that the user has the appropriate permissions.

The version-checking screen that follows will verify that all of the components are recognized. Since we are using the well-tested JDK 1.4/Tomcat/MySQL platform, things should check out here:

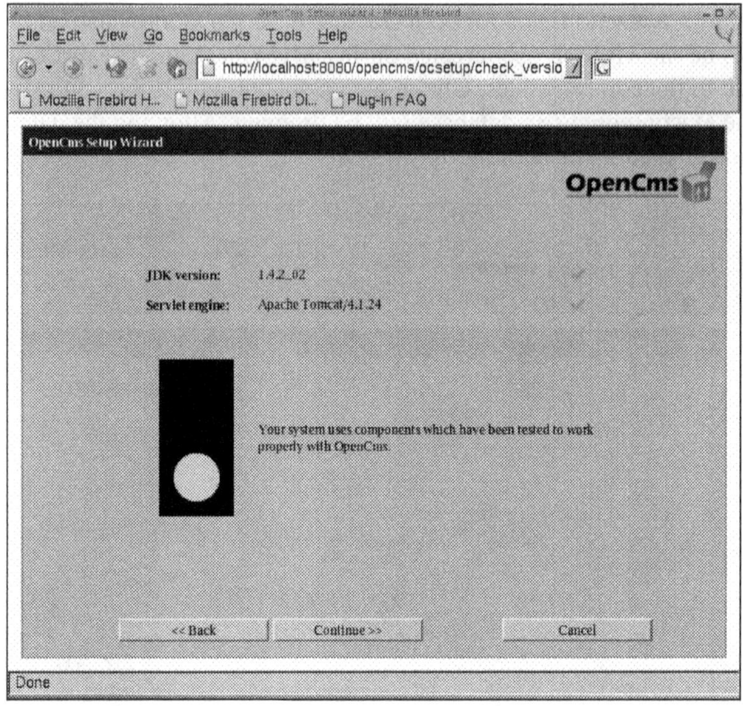

From this point, there are a few configuration screens that will show up only for the advanced setup mode. They provide an opportunity to tune parameters for caching, logging, and running. The first time you run the configuration, be cautious with changes to the advanced screens.

All of the parameters in these screens are written to the `opencms.properties` and `registry.xml` files, both of which are in `$CATALINA_HOME/webapps/opencms/WEB-INF/config/`. They can be changed after installation.

Advanced Setup Screens

If you are not running the advanced setup, which includes many options for configuring details of the system, you may prefer to skip to the *Basic Setup Screens* section.

Here is the first advanced screen:

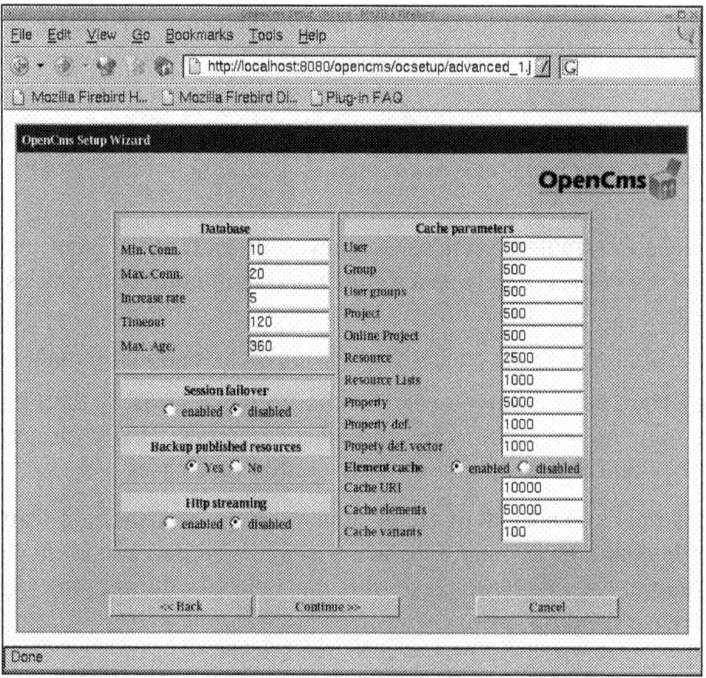

Of note here is the database configuration section. If you are strapped for resources, lowering the minimum and maximum connections can boost performance. Also, if you are on a slow or overloaded machine, upping the timeout is a good idea. Usually, the defaults work fine.

Here are the details of the fields:

- Min. Conn. and Max. Conn.: Control the minimum and maximum number of connections that OpenCms makes to the database. When the servlet is started, it will establish the minimum number of connections specified here.
- Increase Rate: Determines how many new connections will be created at a time. The default, 5, specifies that when all open connections are exhausted, five new ones will be created unless the maximum limit is reached. Requests will then wait for an open connection.
- Timeout: Determines how long OpenCms will wait for a connection to return results before it gives an error.
- Max. Age: Determines how long a connection will live before it is cleaned up.
- Session Failover: Determines whether or not OpenCms will attempt to reuse session data on a different connection if the first connection fails.

- Backup Published Resources: Determines whether or not backup copies are made of each document when it is published. You should always leave this enabled.
- Http Streaming: Determines whether the servlet should buffer data before sending it to the client. This is covered in greater detail in Chapter 8. Enable this for now.
- The Cache Parameters section: Contains settings for the OpenCms caches. The first ten entries merely specify the maximum number of entries for each data type.
- Element Cache: Used to cache XML Templates. It should remain enabled.
- Cache URI, Cache Elements, and Cache Variants: Used by the **FlexCache** to determine how it caches JSPs and other resources. This is discussed in Chapters 4 and 8. The default is sufficient for most cases.

OpenCms can statically export all of the documents in the repository, a feature that we will later cover in detail. By default, OpenCms is configured to export all pages. This is not always desirable. For this reason, I disable that behavior during setup. These default values are otherwise good for now.

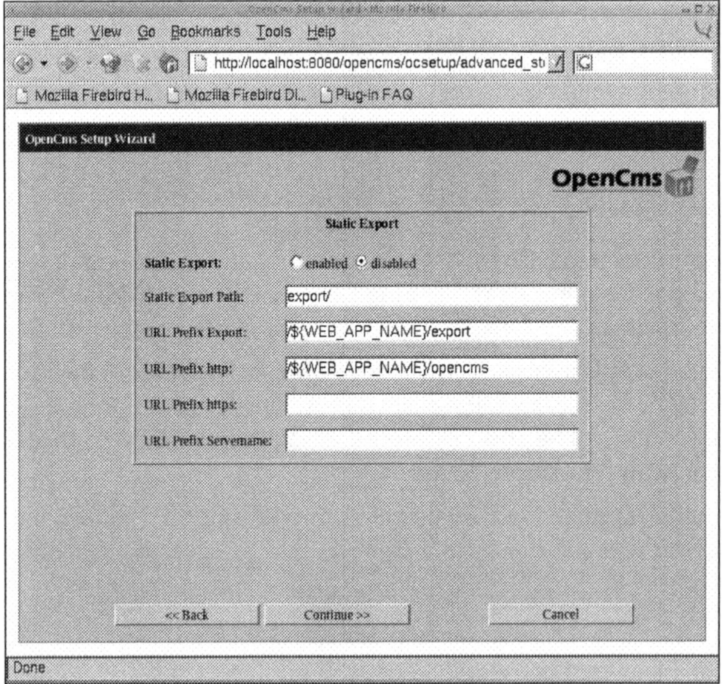

Each of the properties in the preceding screenshot will be discussed in detail in Chapter 8. As I said previously, it is possible to make the same change at any time by editing the `$CATALINA_HOME/webapps/opencms/WEB-INF/config/opencms.properties` file.

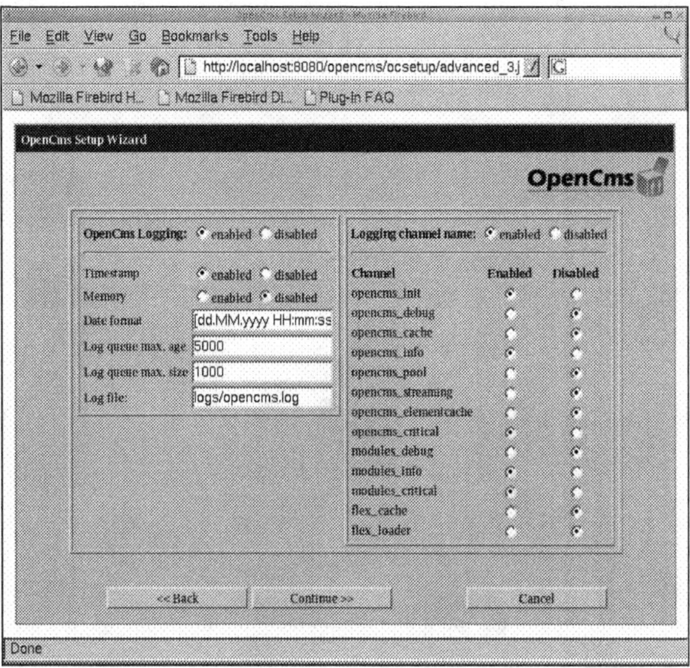

Logging can be a big performance killer on a production machine, but a lifesaver during development. To allow for optimum flexibility, OpenCms has a robust logging system. The defaults are sufficient for our needs. On a production server, consider turning off the *_info channels. The fields depicted in the screenshot are:

- OpenCms Logging determines whether logging will be used at all.
- If Timestamp is enabled, each log will be marked with date and time info.
- If Memory is enabled, each log entry will include information on memory use. This is useful in debugging problems with memory consumption.
- Date Format allows you to specify an alternative date format.
- Log Queue Max Age and Log Queue Max Size allow you to specify time and memory size constraints for log queuing and flushing.
- Log File identifies the location and name of the file to which log information will be written.
- Logging Channel Name determines whether the logger will determine how to log information based on log channels. If enabled, the logger will analyze the

channel of every log message and determine whether the message should be logged.

- The thirteen radio boxes identify the available logging channels for OpenCms. If enabled, the logger will write messages for that channel to the log file. If disabled, log messages for that channel will be silently discarded.

The final advanced configuration screen allows configuration of some miscellaneous details:

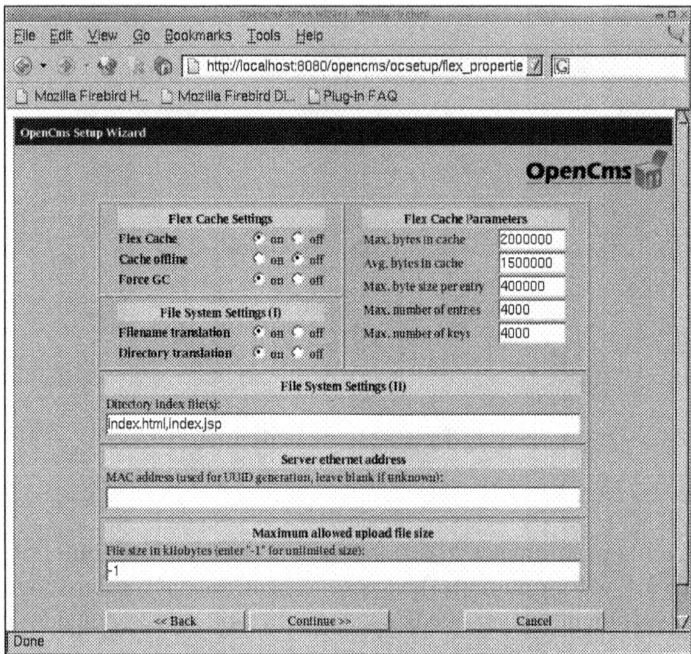

There is one slightly misleading parameter here. The final setting, Maximum allowed upload file size, is only the maximum file size OpenCms will attempt to store in the database. MySQL has a maximum file size, too, and it is only 2 MB by default.

- The first three parameters are for FlexCache, described in detail in Chapters 4 and 8. Flex Cache [so spelled here] should be enabled.
- The second parameter, Cache Offline, determines whether the offline project is cached.
- Force GC determines whether the Java garbage collector will be explicitly called on the FlexCache. After the cached objects are deleted from FlexCache, OpenCms will request that the VM run the garbage collector to delete those objects.

- The Filename translation and Directory Translation are used to determine how to handle file and folder names from previous versions of OpenCms. To be on the safe side, you should leave these enabled.
- The five FlexCache parameters, discussed in Chapters 4 and 8, determine how much space is given to the cache as a whole, and to the individual entries and variants in the cache.
- Directory Index File(s) determines what files OpenCms will try to find and use if a directory (rather than a file) is requested.
- The MAC Address field can be used to specify the MAC address of the system's NIC card. OpenCms will automatically determine this unless you set it here. Since MAC addresses are unique, OpenCms uses them to generate unique IDs.
- Finally, File Size determines the upper size limit on uploaded files.

This completes the advanced configuration; we now return to the regular setup screens.

Basic Setup Screens

On this screen, you are given the opportunity to import the workplace, as shown in the following screenshot. The workplace is the suite of content-management tools—something you definitely want.

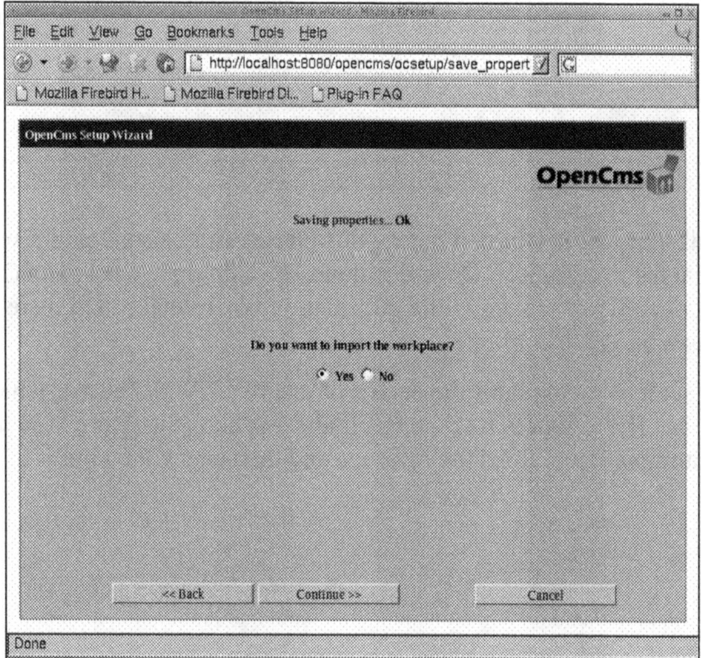

Click **Yes** and continue.

> On the standard installation, there is a second question on this screen: **Do you want to use directory translation?** Answering **Yes** ensures compatibility with old OpenCms databases and modules, but doesn't affect performance adversely.

The following screen loads the workplace:

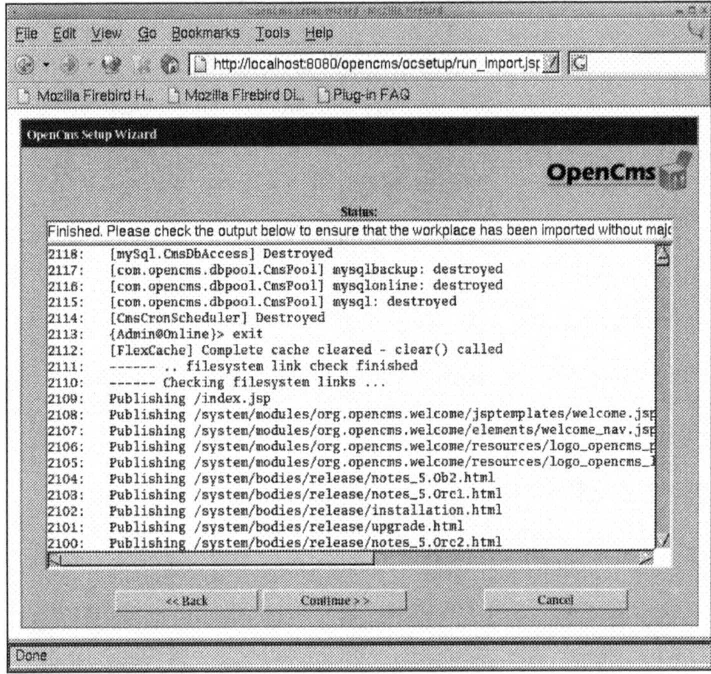

2118 individual steps are performed during this phase of the install, and it will take around five minutes to complete. Once it is done, the **Continue**, **Back**, and **Cancel** buttons will become active. Scroll around in the information box to make sure there aren't any errors. If things look good, continue.

The following screenshot explains the details of the WYSIWYG editor, which requires ActiveX (and thus IE) to function correctly. It also explains that there is an advanced sourcecode editor available. Read the message and then check the box.

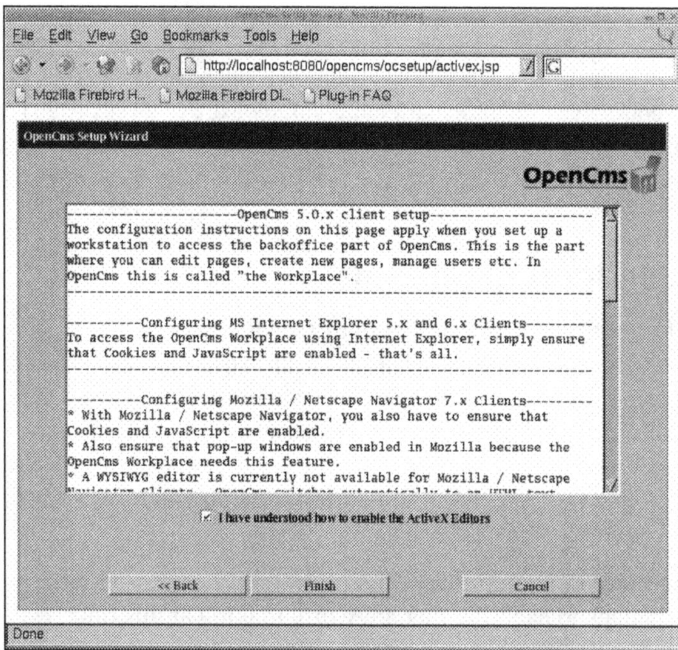

The setup is now complete. Congratulations! Clicking on the here link in the screenshot that follows loads the OpenCms workplace, which we'll discuss in the next chapter.

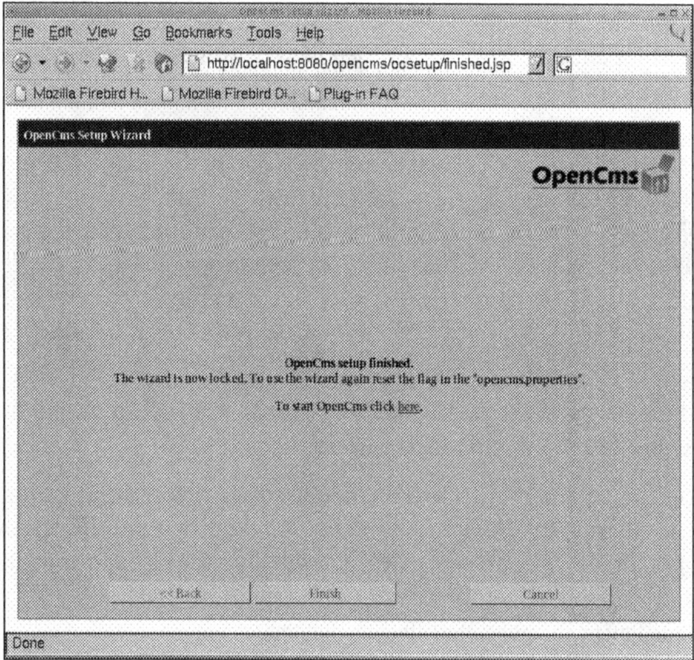

> If the installation fails for some reason and you have to re-run the wizard, you will need to edit the `$CATALINA_HOME/webapps/opencms/WEB-INF/config/opencms.properties` file and change the value of the `wizard.enabled` property to `true`. This unlocks the installation wizard. Otherwise, this property should always be set to `false`.

Manually Configuring Settings

OpenCms uses two configuration files, both of which are located in `$CATALINA_HOME/webapps/opencms/WEB-INF/config/`. The first file is called `opencms.properties`. It conforms to the Java standard for properties files. As a general rule of thumb, the directives in this file have to do with the core operations of the server, though there are a few parameters in this file that do not necessarily meet that criterion. The second file, `registry.xml`, is an XML file containing directives for the structure and operation of the content management system.

While OpenCms should function fine without any modifications to either of these files, there are a few changes to each file that are worth making at this time.

By default, when resources are published, OpenCms attempts to convert most of them (excluding JSP files) to static HTML files. This is called **static export**. While statically exporting documents enables them to be served faster, it also means that most dynamic elements will be replaced with static representations. Static exports can be very useful for large sites, high traffic, or underpowered servers, but to take full advantage of the dynamic nature of OpenCms, static export needs to be turned off. See Chapter 8 for a more thorough discussion of exporting.

> Static export only affects published resources. One of the greatest sources of confusion for the new user is that dynamic pages will function correctly in the offline project, but when they are published, they are no longer evaluated dynamically. In some cases, the result is that a static rendering of a dynamic page will be returned. In other cases, the user will just receive an error or a string of question marks (?????). Turning static export off fixes this problem.

If you followed the instructions in the advanced setup, you should have already turned off static exports. Otherwise, you will need to do so manually.

To turn off static export, open the `opencms.properties` file in a text editor. Find the `staticexport.enabled` property (it is about halfway through the file) and set it to `true`. This means that resources that are specifically tagged for static export (such as images) can still be exported. The next property after this should be `staticexport.default.export`. Set that to `dynamic`.

This setting will make sure that unless explicitly marked otherwise, files will be treated as dynamic, and not exported to static HTML. In Chapter 8, *Deploying an OpenCms Solution*, we will revisit the exporting issue in more detail.

Now open the `registry.xml` file. In order to take advantage of e-mail notifications in the workplace, you will need to configure a few parameters in this file. Set `<smtpserver/>` and `<smtpserver2/>` to point to your own mail servers. On Linux and UNIX machines that run sendmail, this value can usually be set to `localhost`. `<defaultmailsender/>`, `<mailto/>`, and `<mailfrom/>` all need to be set to valid e-mail addresses. In particular, `<mailto/>` should be set to the OpenCms administrator (which is probably you).

The relevant section should look something like this:

```
<smtpserver>localhost</smtpserver>
<smtpserver2>mail.mydomain.com</smtpserver>
<defaultmailsender>opencms@mydomain.com</defaultmailsender>
<checklink>
    <mailfrom>opencms@mydomain.com</mailfrom>
    <mailto>me@mydomain.com</mailto>
</checklink>
```

Also, if you are running a Linux server, you need to replace `<tempfileproject/>` with `<tempfileproject>3</tempfileproject>`—a bug in the installer fails to set this correctly.

Once you have completed this configuration, manually restart Tomcat to effect the new changes.

Configuring the Client

The OpenCms workplace provides a rich user interface (UI). Many of the features it employs, such as the file hierarchy and the navigation system, are achieved with very complex JavaScript that requires IE or Mozilla. Two notable features, the WYSIWYG content editor and the advanced sourcecode editor, require IE to function properly. This section explains the configuration of the browser clients.

Mozilla-Based Browsers

Mozilla, derived from the Netscape browser, is the core of several different web browsers, including the Netscape 7.x family, Mozilla, Firefox (formerly Firebird, originally Phoenix), and Galleon. OpenCms will function well with Mozilla-based browsers provided that they have JavaScript and cookies enabled, and do not block popup windows.

Since none of the Mozilla browsers support ActiveX or the built-in IE controls, the WYSIWYG editor and the advanced source control plug-in can't be used. OpenCms will default to a sourcecode editing text area for all editing.

Because of the inconvenience this causes, there has been discussion in the OpenCms developer community of changing to Java-applet based editing or another rich JavaScript-based editor. They may be put together in one or more OpenCms modules.

Internet Explorer

Internet Explorer requires that cookies and JavaScript be enabled. Some IE extensions, such as the Google Toolbar, block pop-up windows. If you run an IE extension that blocks pop-ups, you will need to disable that feature in order to use OpenCms. The WYSIWYG editing feature of OpenCms is enabled by default, and no configuration must be done to make it work.

Additionally, OpenCms can use an 'advanced' ActiveX control for sourcecode editing (for JSP and XML Template files). The advanced **LeEdit OCX Control** (available from AY Software: `http://www.aysoft.com/ledit.htm`) provides 'cut' and 'paste' buttons within the source code editing pane (even without the LeEdit control, *Ctrl+C*, *Ctrl+X*, and *Ctrl+V* work for cutting and pasting).

A trial version of the LeEdit source code editor is available for free, though it will pop up a 'Buy Me' window randomly. The full LeEdit control cost (at this time of writing) is $145 US for an individual license—a hefty price for simply adding cut-n-paste buttons. If you are interested in configuring the LeEdit source control, configuration information is available on the `opencms.com` site (it is also included on the ActiveX screen of the OpenCms installation wizard).

> Mac users will find that neither the WYSIWYG editor nor the LeEdit control work—not even on IE. Because both controls require ActiveX, a Windows-only technology, neither of them functions on a Mac platform. Additionally, OpenCms 5.0.0 is known not to work with the Mac Safari browser because of differing JavaScript models.

Installation Troubleshooting

Not all installations go flawlessly. Here, I've tried to identify the most common installation problems and have explained how to fix them. Additionally, the OpenCms website—particularly the developers' mailing-list archives—is a good resource for troubleshooting information.

Character-Set Issues

The most common sort of problem with OpenCms installations is that the character set of the Java VM and that of OpenCms do not match, which causes a number of different errors that all have messages that look something like this:

```
Java VM file encoding: Cp1252
OpenCms encoding: ISO-8859-1
```

In almost every case, the solution is to make sure that the `-Dfile.encoding=ISO-8859-1` flag is passed into the Java VM, either through the `CATALINA_OPTS` environment variable or by hardcoding the value into the `catalina.sh` (Linux/UNIX) or `catalina.bat` (Windows) files. If Tomcat is installed as a Windows Service, you will need to run the service uninstall/install routine I explained in the *Windows Configuration* section earlier.

It is also possible to change the OpenCms character set to match the system character set. To do this, edit the `defaultContentEncoding` property in the `opencms.properties` file under `CATALINA_HOME/webapps/opencms/WEB-INF/config/`, changing it to match the system character set (in the above example, it would be `defaultContentEncoding=Cp1252`). Be forewarned, though, that the system character set may not provide all of the necessary characters.

When configuring character sets, your best bets are the ISO-8859 sets and UTF-8.

Temp File Project ID Error

On Linux installations of OpenCms 5.0, it is not uncommon to see a message as follows:

```
com.opencms.core.CmsException: 0 Unknown exception. Detailed error:
Can not read projectId of tempfileproject for creating temporary file
for editing! java.lang.NumberFormatException: null.
```

This error is caused by a bug in the installer that doesn't always set the appropriate value for the Temp File project ID. To fix this, edit the following file:

```
$CATALINA_HOME/webapps/opencms/WEB_INF/config/registry.xml
```

Change the element `<tmpfileproject/>` to `<tmpfileproject>3</tmpfileproject>`. Once you've saved the change, restart Tomcat.

Restarting Tomcat versus Reloading OpenCms

Tomcat includes an application for reloading individual servlets without restarting Tomcat. However, it is unclear whether all of the OpenCms classes (particularly the `com.opencms.core.OpenCms` singleton) are garbage collected. Many users have reported on the opencms-dev list that simply reloading the OpenCms servlet causes strange errors. So, it is always best to restart Tomcat rather than reload the individual servlet.

Importing Workplace Screen Freezes

As I noted in the *Running the Install Wizard* section, when installing with a Mozilla-based browser, the installation wizard will sometimes appear to hang during the importing of the workplace. This is due to a bug in the client-side JavaScript. The installation continues to run on the server. It is best to wait five minutes (ample time for the workplace installation to finish) and then reload the page using the browser's refresh button. You should then see a message that the import is complete.

This bug has been fixed in OpenCms 5.0.1, but still exists in earlier versions.

MySQL User/Password Changes

If you change the username or password for the MySQL database user that OpenCms uses, you will need to edit the following file:

```
$CATALINA_HOME/webapps/opencms/WEB-INF/config/opencms.properties
```

Change the value for the `pool.mysql.user` and `pool.mysql.password` variables. Restart Tomcat after saving your changes.

Finding More Installation Help

For more help on installation issues, try the OpenCms developers' mailing list and archives available at `http://www.opencms.org/opencms/en/development/mailinglist.html`.

Summary

At this point, OpenCms is up and running inside the Tomcat Servlet container with a MySQL database. Configuration is complete. In the next chapter, we'll take a detailed look at the OpenCms Workplace, the primary tool for content management.

3

The OpenCms Workplace

The OpenCms Workplace is the primary interface for managing the contents of your OpenCms repository. It includes tools for editing, project management, workflow, publishing, and server administration. This chapter will start with a brief tour of the Workplace, and then will cover:

- Managing projects
- Using modules
- Setting and using permissions
- Editing and publishing documents
- Creating new pages
- Customizing the Workplace
- Working with the standard modules

A Tour of the OpenCms Workplace

The Workplace is the centre of OpenCms. Editors will use the Workplace to author their documents. Project managers will use it to create workflows, structure the site, and control publication of material. The vast majority of technical administration is done through the Workplace as well, and the system administrator will use the Workplace to manage the caches, check logs, and install new modules. All of these tasks are incorporated into one web-based interface.

The OpenCms developers have made a concerted effort to create an enterprise-class interface, and while it takes a while to get used to the Swiss-army-knife approach to interface design, experienced users appreciate its power and compactness. This tour is intended to help the new user understand the layout and navigation of the Workplace. While I will illustrate the components of the system, I'm leaving the details for the following sections.

To begin, point your browser to `http://localhost:8080/opencms/opencms/`, the OpenCms URL. This is the main OpenCms page. You should see the default index page:

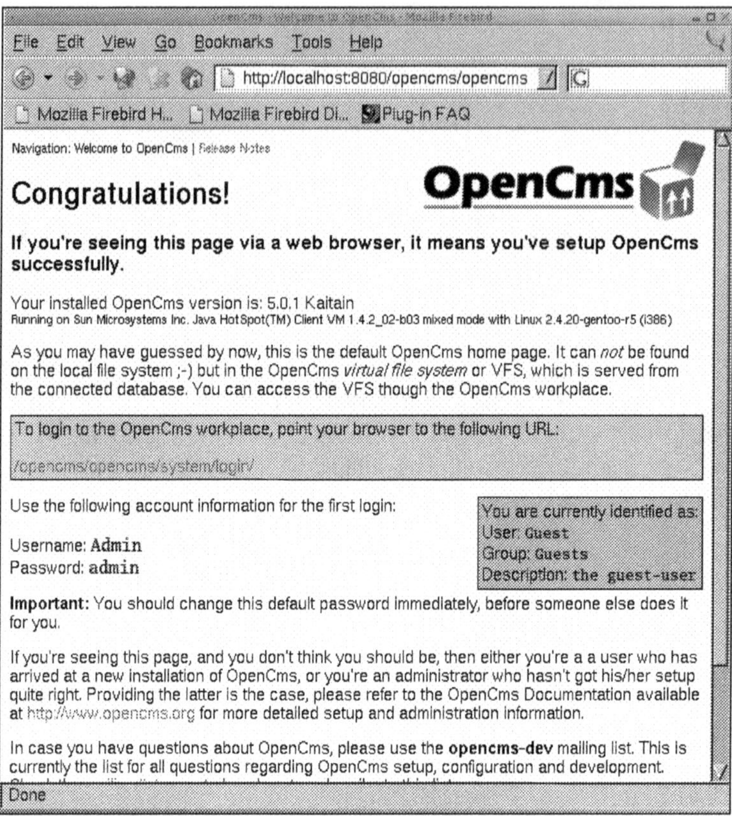

The link in the red box in the centre is the URL to the Workplace. If you click on it, a log-in window should pop up.

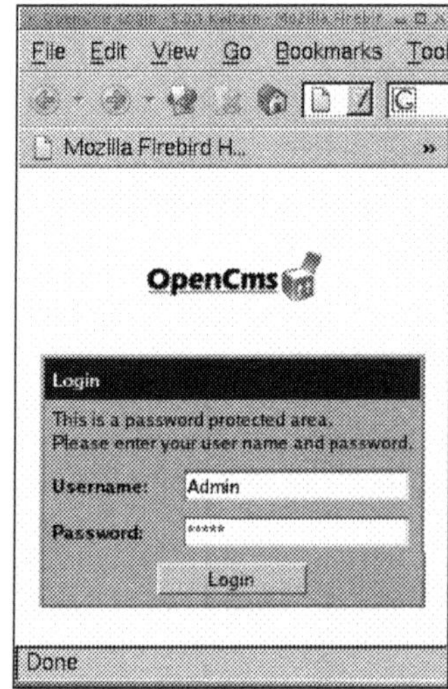

The default login is Admin and the default password is admin. We will be changing that shortly. After clicking on the login button, you should see a new window pop open. If not, make sure that pop-up windows are not being blocked by your browser. Depending on your browser, you may also see a dialog asking if you want to close the calling window. Click OK. Welcome to the Workplace.

> In the OpenCms Workplace, the normal browser navigation is hidden. This is because using the standard back and forward commands can cause unexpected results in OpenCms (as in many dynamic Web applications). When using the OpenCms Workplace, it is best to use the OpenCms navigation.

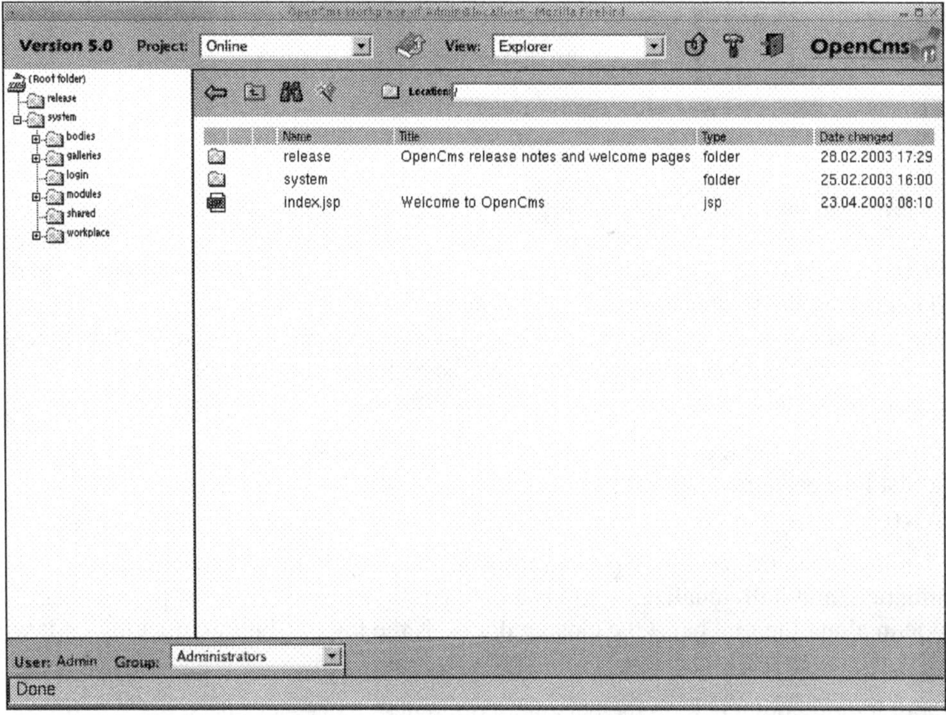

The Toolbar

Along the top of the workplace window is the **toolbar** (sometimes referred to as the header strip).

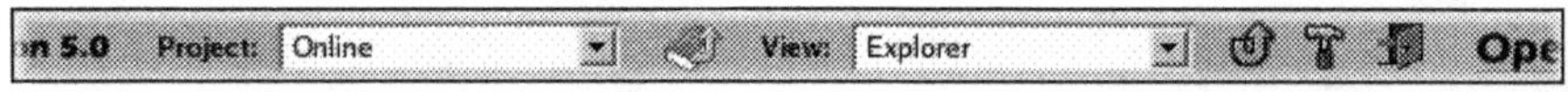

The Project drop-down list allows you to choose the project in which you will work. By default, there are two projects: Online and Offline. The Online project contains files currently published. No documents in the Online project can be edited. The Offline project contains all of the files in the repository. In a way, it is the master working copy of the repository. Other projects (we will create one in the following section) are essentially sub-projects of Offline. Later in this chapter, we will examine creating projects and assigning project managers to those projects.

The next button along the toolbar is the **publish** button. Clicking on this button will publish all of the resources in the given project. In the Offline project, this button publishes all of the documents in the repository. In the Online project, it is always marked inactive (gray), as in the image on the previous page, since the Online project is where things go when they are published. This may seem a bit confusing at the outset, but we will return to projects and publishing several more times during the course of this book.

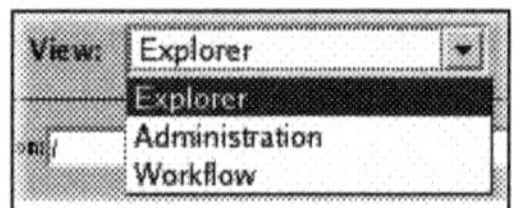

The View drop-down list contains three items: Explorer, Administration, and Workflow. The explorer view is the current view. Most editorial work is done inside the explorer. The administration view provides access to all of the technical management tools, and is used mainly by the system administrator. Finally, the workflow view provides a project manager with a task-based interface for handling projects, rather than individual pieces of content. For the time being, we will focus on the explorer view, but will return to administration and workflow views during this tutorial.

Continuing along the toolbar, we come to the green arrow—the **reload** icon. As the name suggests, it reloads the page. In fact, it works identically to the reload button in your browser.

The hammer icon brings up the **personal preferences** dialogue. Password, user information, and individualized settings are all configurable in personal preferences. The final icon along the tool bar—the closing door—is the **log out** button (clicking on it will bring you back to the log in screen).

Without logging out, click on the personal preferences icon—let's personalize a little:

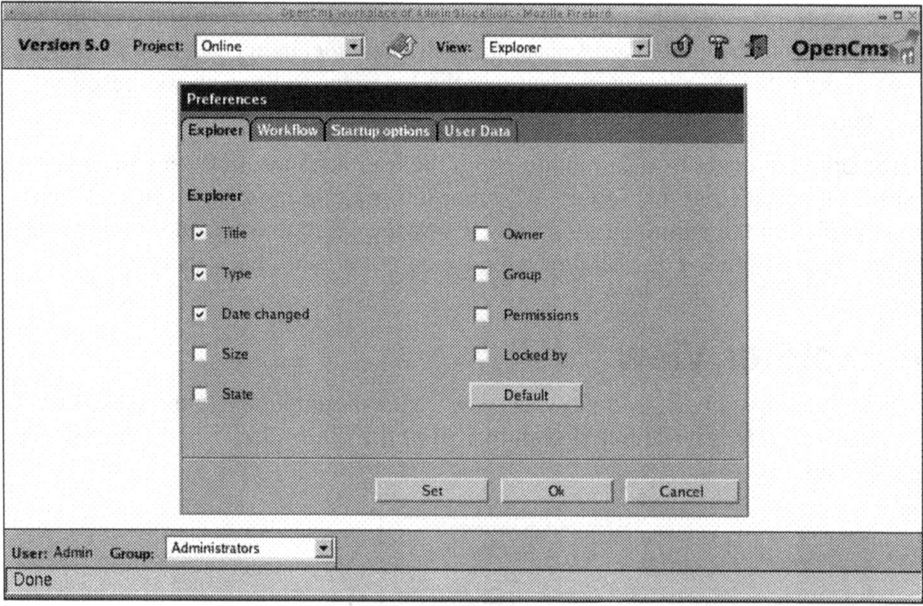

The first tab of the preferences dialogue pertains to what information is shown in the explorer view discussed earlier. Likewise, the Workflow tab allows you to set look-and-feel preferences for the workflow view. Checking a box will add a column for that piece of information to the explorer view. At some point, you may decide to tinker with these settings, but for our purposes, the defaults are fine.

The Startup options tab allows you to configure global options that will take effect when you log in. By default, the Workplace starts in the Online project. Since almost all tasks are done in other projects (for an administrator, often the Offline project), I find it more efficient to set the default project to Offline.

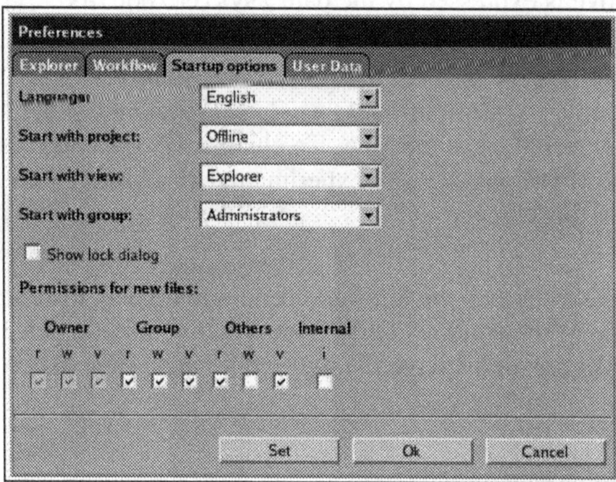

You may also set the default language for the Workplace. While this converts the locale of all of the navigation in the Workplace itself, it does *not* change the language of the contents of the CMS. For instance, changing the language to Spanish will result in Spanish pop-up menu text, but files written in English will not be translated.

The User Data tab contains information about the user account. In OpenCms 5.0, only the password can be set from this screen. All other information must be set by an administrator from the administration view. Click the Change Password button and enter passwords as prompted. You will now need to log out and log back in again.

The Explorer View

Once you have logged back into the Workplace, you should be back in the explorer view. On the left-hand side is a file tree that shows all of the file folders in the **Virtual File System (VFS)**:

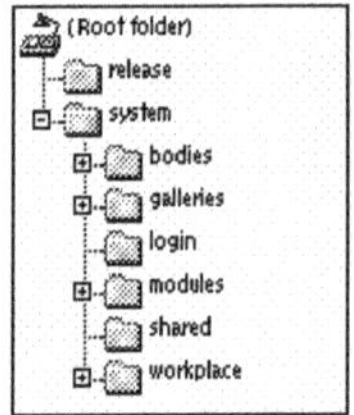

The VFS is a file-system-like storage mechanism that looks and acts like a normal file system, but stores information inside tables in the database. For that reason, you will not be able to find any set of files on your regular file system that corresponds to the files in the VFS. Because the VFS looks and acts like a file system, VFS paths are expressed like URL- or UNIX-style paths. The root folder is `/`, and subsequent folders are noted by a name followed (optionally) by a slash. For instance, the location of the `bodies` folder in the image on the above is expressed by the path `/system/bodies/`.

> During publishing, OpenCms can publish resources into the regular file system. These files are copies of those inside OpenCms. Editing these copies is not the same as editing the content of the VFS. To change the content of the VFS, you must use OpenCms or configure the experimental synchronization feature discussed later in this chapter.

Clicking on any of the folders in the left-hand pane will display the contents of that folder inside the center pane of the window. Only folders show up in the left-hand file tree; folders, files, and links are all displayed in the center frame (just like Windows Explorer).

The root folder is the base of the document repository. When you publish the Offline project, for instance, you are publishing everything inside the root folder. Items directly in the root folder are published to the root of the OpenCms URL. For instance, a file named `foo.jsp` under the root folder would be published to `http://localhost:8080/opencms/opencms/foo.jsp`. The `release` folder contains OpenCms release notes. `http://10.21.77.7:8080/opencms/opencms/release/` gives you access to the release notes.

The `system` folder has special significance. It contains items that are functionally important for OpenCms. Normal content is never placed inside the `system` folder, and each of the subfolders has a particular function.

- The `bodies` subfolder contains the body files of XML Template Page objects, which we will discuss in detail later. While it can be useful for debugging, it is rarely used for day-to-day tasks, even by developers.
- Various OpenCms tools can leverage shared resources (such as images or commonly-used fragments of HTML). These are grouped together into **galleries**. Each of the galleries is stored as a subfolder inside the `/system/galleries/` folder. While it is possible to maintain the galleries by working directly with these folders, there are tools in the Administrator view much better suited for the job.
- The `login` subdirectory contains all the files for managing user logins.
- The `modules` directory is the location in which new OpenCms modules are placed when installed. Modules are used to extend the basic function of OpenCms. Help text, for instance, is packaged in a module, as are functional add-ons such as calendar widgets, search engines, and guest books. Later in this chapter, we will dive into modules in more depth.
- The next subfolder, `shared`, contains a couple of templates that are shared by many resources. It is unlikely that you will ever have to work with the contents of this folder, and it may even go away in subsequent releases.
- Finally, the `workplace` folder contains all of the files—templates, images and content—that make up the very Workplace we are using. Developers can customize the Workplace itself (through the Workplace) by modifying these files. As you may have guessed, editing these files can be dangerous, and mistakes can lead to disaster. If, at some point, you decide to edit these files, do so on an installation that does not have important data on it.

The central pane of the explorer view displays a detailed look at the information in the VFS. At the top of the pane is the Explorer **button bar** (sometimes referred to as the button strip or the nav bar). It contains icons specifically related to exploring and editing content.

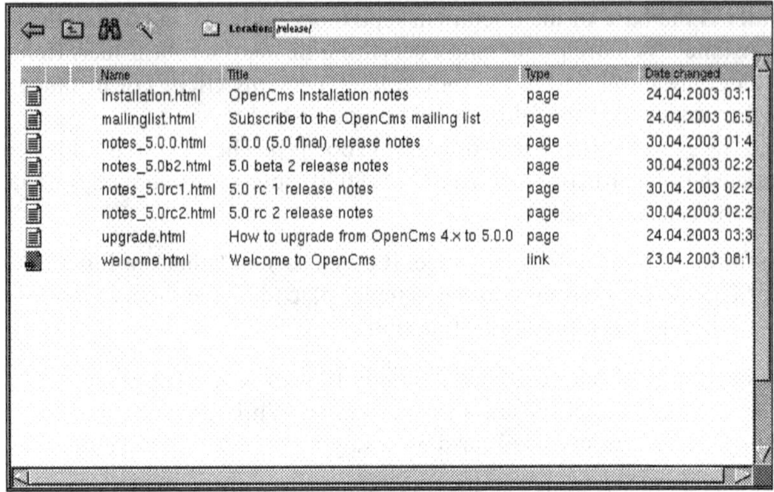

Just like in the Windows Explorer, the **blue back arrow** changes the location to the previously visited folder, the **folder with the up arrow** goes up one directory in the file hierarchy, and the **binoculars** icon opens a file-find dialogue. The **magic wand** icon is for creating a new file, and Location shows the directory whose contents are currently being displayed.

The file listing below the navigation bar shows the details of each file in the current directory. Like Windows, the icon at the beginning of each line indicates what type of data a file contains. Left-clicking on the icon will display a context menu of actions. For instance, clicking on the page icon next to `installation.html` opens a context menu like the one that follows:

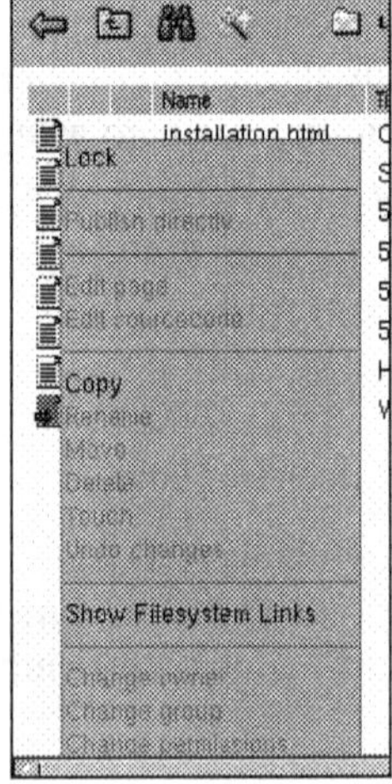

Note that most of the values are grayed out, indicating that they are not available. To enable these actions, you must first Lock the file (the first action on the list). Once the file is locked, you will have access to many of the previously inaccessible functions.

> OpenCms uses a left-click rather than a right-click to open context menus. Using a right-click will open the Browser's own context menu. While this change in default behavior can be confusing at the outset, it allows the end user to take advantage of the browser's context menu.

When you lock a file, an **unlocked** icon will appear between the file icon and the document name.

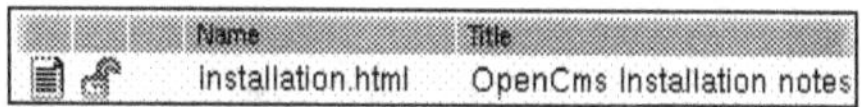

While this sounds confusing, it is meant to indicate that there is a lock on the file, but you can edit the file anyway (in other words, you own the lock). The file is unlocked for you, but locked for all others. Conversely, a file with a **closed lock** icon (🔒) means that someone else has the file locked, and you cannot edit it.

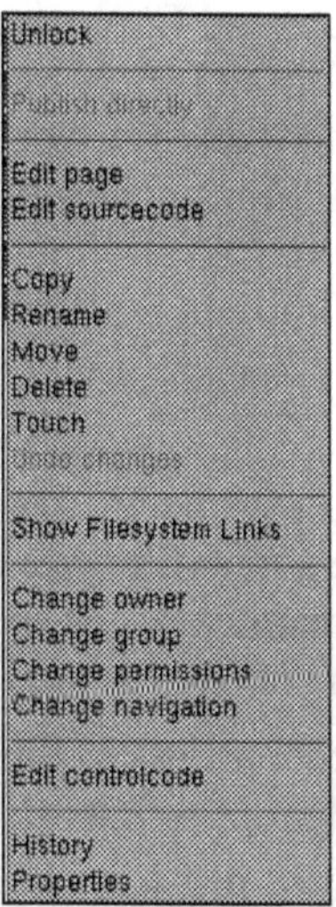

During the course of this book, the function of each of these menu items will be explored fully; for now, I will provide a brief summary of each:

- Lock/Unlock creates or removes, respectively, a lock on the file.
- Publish directly publishes just this file and any resources on which it depends (e.g. images or templates). This is a nice alternative to publishing everything

in the project. It becomes active when the file in the current project (Offline, in this case) differs from the version in the Online project.

- Edit page opens the page in the WYSIWYG editor on Windows/IE, and the sourcecode editor on other browsers. Not that this is only available for files of type Page.
- Edit sourcecode opens the page in the sourcecode editor. This allows you to edit HTML, XML, and JSP pages within OpenCms.
- Copy copies a file to another destination. Rename allows you to change the name of a file. Move relocates the file to a different directory.
- Delete removes the file. Note that it will still be visible with a strike-through mark, until it is published (which will remove it from both the Online and Offline projects).
- Touch changes the time stamp on the file, effectively marking the page to be re-published the next time a publish event occurs.
- Undo changes allows you to roll back to the previous published version of the file.
- Show Filesystem Links lists the files to which this file is linked.
- Change owner, Change group, and Change permissions allow you to change the UNIX-like permissions for the file. For every file, there is a single user that is the owner, a group, and then the "world." For each (owner, group, world), there is a set of permissions consisting of **read (r)**, **write (w)**, and **view (v)**. Using these tools, you can set fine-grained permissions on your files. There is one extra checkbox in the Change permissions window: **Internal (i)**. This is for pages that are used only in the Workplace, and should not be published.
- Change navigation allows you to change the way this file appears in navigation. When you create a new file, you may choose to include it in navigation, which is built dynamically for each directory. This option allows you to change the navigation settings created along with the file.
- Edit controlcode provides direct access to the XML format in which each file is stored. Occasionally, this feature is useful for troubleshooting.
- History shows all of the changes that have been made to a particular file, and allows you to roll back to any earlier version of the document in the repository.
- Properties contains data about the document. Title, keywords, and position in navigation are examples of properties.

Note that not all types of file will have all of these actions. Some, like plain documents, have only a few possible actions.

Creating and Editing Content

Thus far, we've examined how to navigate through the VFS using the explorer view. However, it is through the explorer view that we create and edit content, as well.

To start, let's create a working area in which we can store some test files. In the left-hand file-tree pane, click on the (Root folder) icon. This will take you to the document root. The central pane of the explorer should now show a couple of folders and the `index.jsp` file. Here, we will create a new folder.

Creating a Folder

Click on the magic wand icon to open a file-creation dialogue:

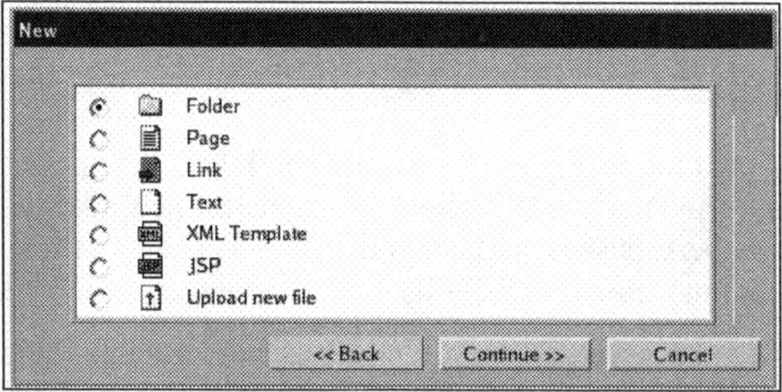

The first step in creating a new file is to declare the file type. Folder will create a new directory. This is what we want. However, before moving on, let me briefly explain the other choices on this menu:

- Page is an HTML document that can be edited in the WYSIWYG editor. We will create one of these soon.
- Link creates a pointer from this location to a document existing at another location. This is similar to a symbolic link in UNIX/Linux or a shortcut in Windows.
- Text (called **Plain** elsewhere in the Workplace) is a generic word for any piece of text-only content that should not be edited with the WYSIWYG editor. While it is usually used to store formatted text-only documents like README or installation texts, occasionally it may be used to store data for a program.
- XML Template and JSP files are both used to create dynamic content. XML Templates are an older technology developed for OpenCms. They are slowly being replaced by Java Server Pages. In later chapters of this book, we will cover development of dynamic content using these technologies.

- The last item on the list is Upload new file. This provides a method for taking an external source (including an image file) and loading it into the CMS, creating a new file in the VFS.

Since we are creating a folder, simply leave the Folder icon checked and click the Continue button.

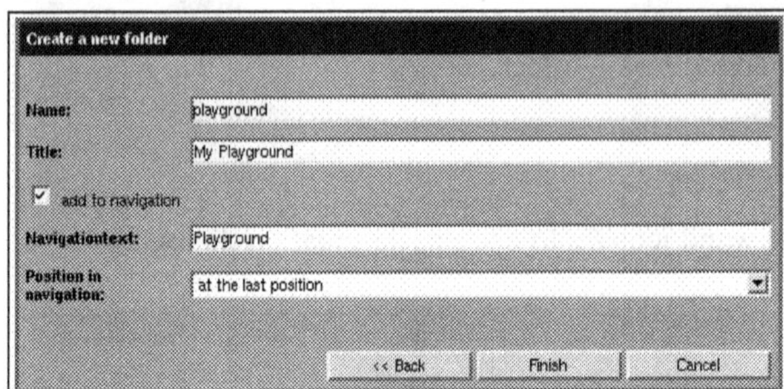

Since this is just an area for us to play around, let's call this area our playground. In the Create a new folder form, Name will become the name of the folder in the VFS. It should have only letters, numbers, dashes, and underscores. Title is a more human-friendly version of Name, and may contain spaces as well as letters and numbers.

The add to navigation checkbox allows you to decide whether this folder should be included in automatically generated navigation menus. Leave it checked. Note that if you uncheck it, the next two fields disappear, as they are no longer needed.

Navigation text is usually similar to Title, and is used when menus are dynamically generated. Since space in navigation bars may be limited, sometimes navigation text is a shorter version of the title. The Position in navigation drop-down box allows you to determine *where* in the navigation this item will appear. For now, we'll leave this at the default, too.

Clicking Finish will create the folder and immediately prompt you to create a new index page in that folder. It is good practice to always create an index page inside a new folder. It prevents visitors from getting errors or directory listings when trying to load the folder.

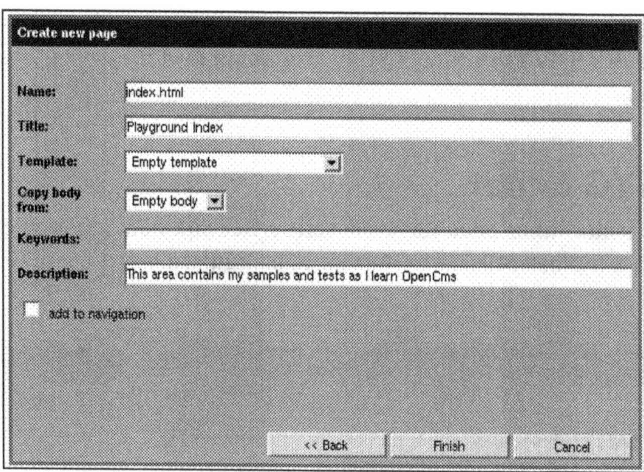

The Name should be set to `index.html` already. Leave that as is. As above, Title is a human-readable title for the page. Titles for pages appear much more frequently on published pages than titles of folders do, so make sure you add good titles to your pages. The Template setting determines *which* template is applied to the content of this page. For now, leave it set to Empty template. Later on, we will create templates that we can use instead of the default empty one.

The Copy body from dropdown allows us to create the basic page layout from predefined HTML snippets. However, since we haven't defined any yet, we'll leave it set to Empty body. The Keywords field can be used by search engines (such as the Lucene module discussed later in the book) to identify key information about this folder. Likewise, the Description field is used to provide a human-readable summary of the folder's contents.

We don't need to include the index in navigation since we have already included the folder in navigation, and both URLs will load the same content. So, uncheck the add to navigation box and hit Finish. You should now be back in the explorer view in the `/playground` folder. There should be a new line for the `index.html` file that looks like this:

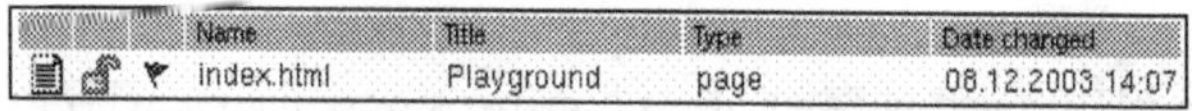

The first icon, as you will remember, indicates that the new file is a page. The lock icon indicates that you currently have the file locked—if the lock is open, you own it, and if it is closed, another user owns it. The little red flag indicates that this resource has not yet been published. That means this file does not exist (yet) in the Online project, and visitors to the site will not see (or have links to) this document.

If you click on the name of the file (here `index.html`), OpenCms will pop up a preview window and load the contents of `index.html`. In this case, we have not yet created content for this file, so the preview will be empty.

To edit the file, left-click on the page icon and choose Edit page from the menu. In IE, this will open the WYSIWYG editor. In all other supported browsers, it will load the sourcecode editor.

The WYSIWYG Editor

The WYSIWYG editor takes advantage of ActiveX components to create an HTML editor. It provides a toolbar of buttons similar to a standard word processor or HTML editing tool:

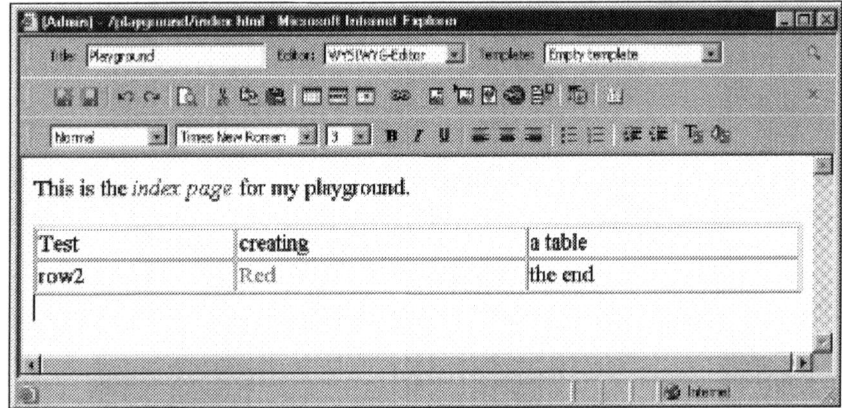

Most of the buttons are self-explanatory. However, the top row has some fields that are worth mentioning. The Editor drop-down box allows you to switch from the WYSIWYG editor to the sourcecode editor. The Template dropdown allows you to change the template applied to this content. If you are intending to preview this page, you might want to choose the other default template, the Welcome/Release notes template, as it has the basic HTML structure already defined. Note that the template data is *never* displayed inside the WYSIWYG window; only the editable content is displayed here. On the far right of the top row is the preview button (a magnifying glass icon). Clicking it will display a pop-up window with the contents of the file displayed within the template.

> The disk icon with the red X ( ) often confuses new users, who think it means 'do not save'. In fact, this is the 'save and exit' button. The plain red X on the far right is the 'Exit without saving' button.

The Sourcecode Editor

To open the sourcecode editor on IE, left-click on the page icon and choose Edit sourcecode from the menu, or load the WYSIWYG editor and choose the sourcecode editor from the Editor drop-down menu. In Mozilla-based browsers, right-clicking on the page icon and selecting Edit page or Edit sourcecode will load the sourcecode editor, since no WYSIWYG editor exists for non-IE clients.

The sourcecode editor is a stripped-down no-frills editor. In fact, the main content area of the text editor is generated with the `<textarea/>` HTML tag. While this editor is basic, it contains all of the tools necessary for developing text resources (both content, which we cover here, and executable scripts, which we will see later).

For HTML editing, there are a few tricks to learn. First of all, you will notice that the only thing created by default is a CDATA section: `<![CDATA[ ]]>`. OpenCms stores all its content inside XML documents. Since HTML contains many characters that an XML parser will try to interpret, the HTML content must be enclosed within an XML CDATA section, which warns the XML parser that the content within should be left alone. So, make sure that the first line of the document begins with the `<![CDATA[` demarcation, and that the document ends with the CDATA close demarcation: `]]>`.

Also, the template will provide the main HTML layout code such as the header, the menu, and the footer. This leaves you to concentrate only on the content. Here's a bit of code created in the sourcecode editor:

```
<![CDATA[
<p>This is a sample paragraph written in the sourcecode editor. </p>
<p>This is a second paragraph. It contains a <b>bold</b> word as well
as a word in <i>italics</></p>
<p>The end.</p>
]]>
```

Note that I've enclosed everything in a CDATA section and haven't defined the header or the body, but have simply created a few paragraph tags with some content. The rest of the structuring has been left to the template file. You can click the save-and-close icon (the disk with the red X) to exit the editor.

If you do not need to edit the resource again immediately, it is a good idea to unlock the resource. In fact, since we created the `/playground/` directory, we have all its content locked. To unlock it, we go back to the root folder, left-click on the folder icon next to the playground item, and choose Unlock. The open blue lock should disappear. If you look inside the `/playground/` folder, you will notice that the lock icon next to `index.html` has disappeared as well.

Publishing Your Changes

There are two ways to publish the changes we've made. One is to publish the entire project (the Offline project, in this case). This will copy all of the changes in the current project to the Online project. To do this, simply press the Publish icon in the main toolbar. If any resources are locked, you will be prompted to allow OpenCms to release all locks. Choosing Ok will automatically remove all of the locks and then continue the publishing process:

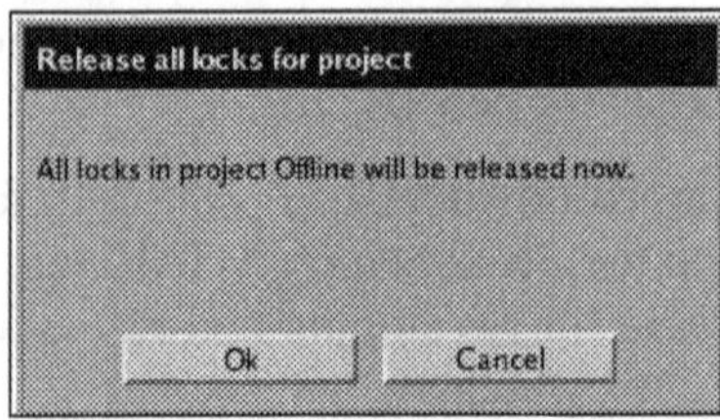

You may want to publish only a small set of changed files rather than the whole project. To do this, left-click on the icon next to the resource you wish to publish and select Publish directly. Note that this option will be marked inactive if you have a lock on the file or the file has not been changed since the last time it was published. A file must be unlocked before it can be published directly. Try publishing the `/playground/` directory directly. That will publish the folder as well as all of its contents. After asking you to confirm the publish request, it will display progress information as it publishes all the resources to the Online project.

During the course of a publish event (either Publish directly or a Publish of the complete project), OpenCms runs a number of tests on the content to make sure that all the resources upon which it relies are also published. For this reason, publishing only a few pages may still take a long time.

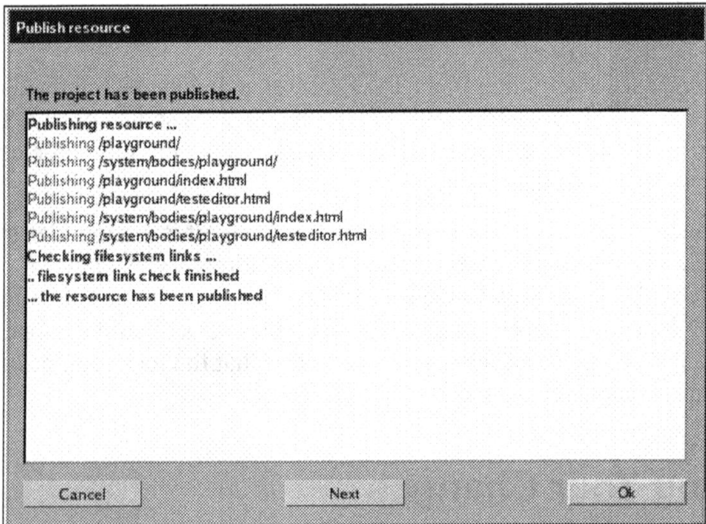

Once publishing is complete, a ... the resource has been published message is displayed and the Ok button becomes active. Click on Ok to return to the explorer view. At this point, you should be able to switch to the Online project and see `/playground/` and its contents.

Versioning

Now that the new resources are published, OpenCms will keep version information on these files. To view a file's history, left-click the file's icon and select History from the menu. Now, every change made to the file is recorded. If a mistake is made, we can open the history menu, select a version, and roll back to that version of the file.

To do this, go back to the Offline project and lock and edit the `/playground/index.html` file. Once you have changed a line or two and saved it, left-click on the page icon for `index.html` and choose History. You will see an entry for the last published version.

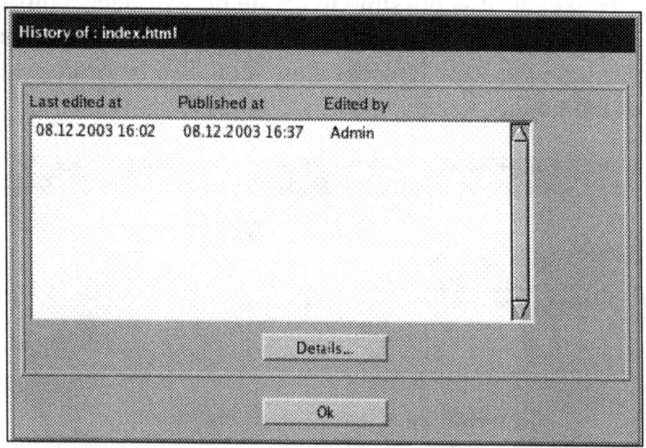

Select the first row and press the Details... button. This will bring up a dialogue with more information, including, at the bottom, a button that says Restore version. Clicking this will overwrite your current working version with the contents of the already published version.

> The Restore version button will only appear if you have locked the resource.

As you work with a file, making changes and then publishing, and then changing it again, OpenCms will build up a version history for that file. Using the history, you will be able to track the file's changes for every version since it was first published.

At this point, you should be fairly comfortable with using the explorer view for traversing the VFS and creating and modifying files. Next, we shall move on to the **administration view** to learn how to manage OpenCms.

Administration

The **administration view** contains the tools you will need to administer the OpenCms server. In this section, we will walk through each of the tools included in this view.

In the administration view, menus are laid out with icons (like Windows 3.1). Clicking on an icon may load either an administration screen or another set of icons. To navigate back from a child menu to its parent, use the blue arrow (⇦) in the navigation bar above the menu.

Project Management

The first icon () on the administration menu is for project management. By default, OpenCms includes two projects: the Offline project, which contains the current version of all of the files in the repository, and the Online project, which contains everything that has been published. However, it is possible to create new projects confined to a specific subset of the files in the Offline project. Click on the project management icon. Create a new project by clicking on the **New Project** icon. You will be prompted to define the fields and content of the new project:

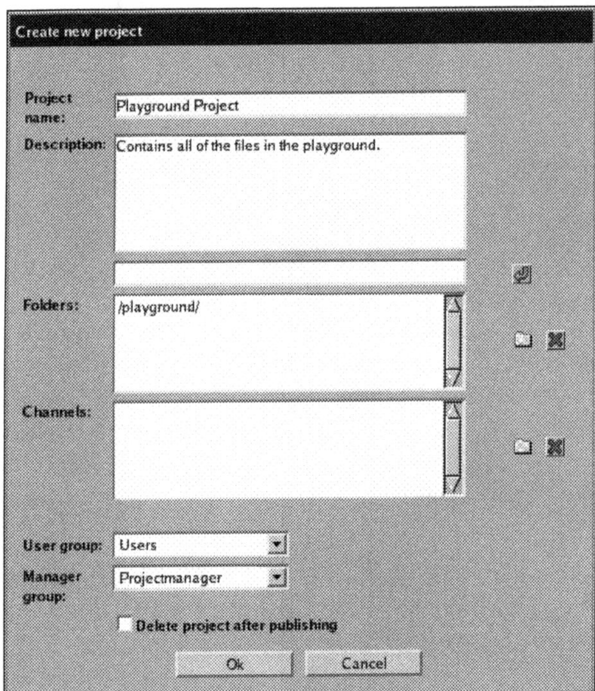

We will create a project that includes just our playground directory. Project name needs a human-readable name (spaces are allowed), and Description ought to contain some text that explains the purpose of the project.

Using the folder icon to the right of the Folders section, select the `/playground/` folder and add it to the list. In a little while, we will discuss channels; for now, leave the Channels section empty. The User group and Manager group drop-down lists allow you to specify *which* groups should be able to create and edit content (users) and *which* group should control and publish the project (managers). Since we have not yet defined any other groups, these can be left on their default values.

Finally, there is an option to Delete project after publishing. This works well for projects that only need to exist until their content is published once (for instance, a promotional offer). Leave this unchecked for now, though. Click Ok to create the project.

Once the project is created, choose Playground Project from the Project drop-down list on the toolbar, and then go to the explorer view.

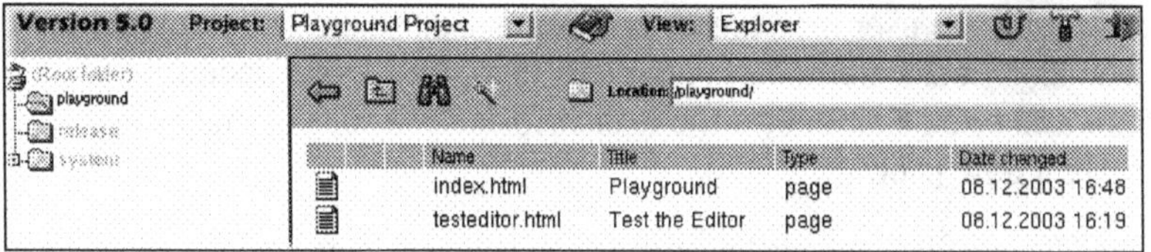

The Playground Project provides access to just the `/playground/` directory. Note that the file tree shows that only the `/playground/` directory is active in this project. Lock and edit the `/playground/index.html` file and save the changes. Doing this will give us something to track from project administration. Once you've done that, go back to the project management section in the administration view.

The Current projects screen shows a list of all of the projects along with their current status. If you modified the `/playground/index.html` file from the Playground Project and left the file locked, you will notice that there is a lock icon on the left of the project name.

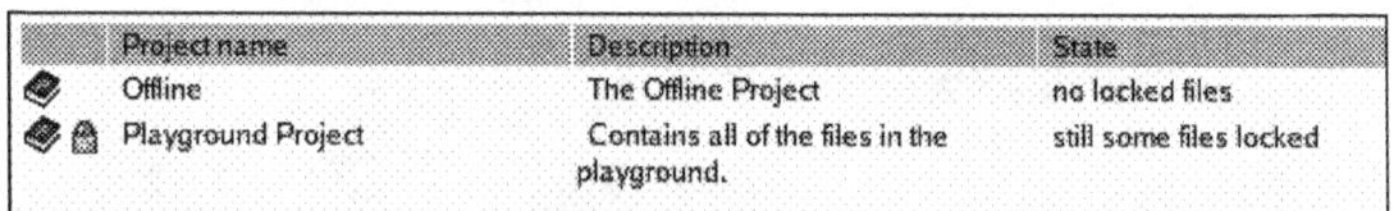

Clicking on the book icon brings up a context menu with only three items: Remove lock for unlocking all of the resources in the project, Publish for publishing the entire project, and Delete for removing the project (but not the files in the project). Remove the lock and then publish the project to push your changes to the Online project. Essentially, this does the same thing as pressing the publish button in the explorer view. Once the publishing is done, use the blue back arrow to return to the project management menu.

Project history lists each project and its current status. While it provides some useful information, there are no functions to be performed from this menu. You may notice that there are some projects here that do not show up any place else. These are special system projects that you will never work with explicitly.

The Manage history properties screen is for setting the parameters that determine how much history is stored. Unless space is really limited, I recommend never checking

Delete versions older than... and always checking Enable history. This will ensure that you have a good revision trail for your resources.

User Management

Up until now, we've done all of our work with only two users: Guest (the unprivileged user who can visit the published Online site) and Admin. Obviously, having only two accounts would be an inconvenience, to say the least, in a real-life situation. The **user management** section provides tools for creating and managing users and groups.

The first icon under the user management menu is Edit users. Click on this to add and edit users. The Edit users menu displays all of the current user accounts. You may select a user account and click Edit to edit the user information, or you may click the New button to create a new user.

Clicking the New button brings up a form for defining a new user:

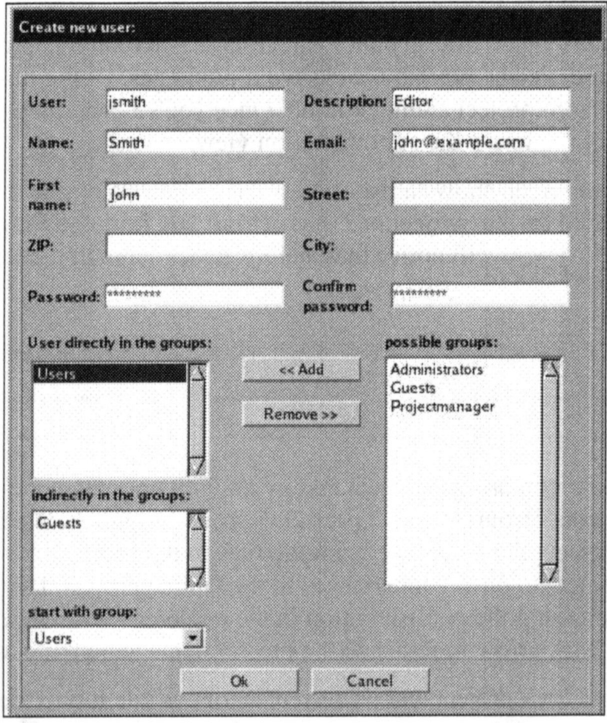

Unfortunately, the first two field names on this form are a bit ambiguous. User is the login name (jsmith, in the example above). Name is the user's surname. Many of the fields are optional, but it is a good idea to give the user a good Description and an Email address that the system can use to contact the user (we'll set this up in the next section).

Also, you will need to set a password for the new user by completing the Password and Confirm Password fields.

Since our user is an editor, he belongs in the Users group. Users have sufficient privileges to log in and edit content, but they cannot publish or administer the site. Groups can be arranged in a hierarchy, and the Users group happens to be a child group (with more privileges) to the group Guests. For that reason, adding users to the Users group automatically adds them to the Guests group as well. Members of the Guests group have permissions to view the published public site, but cannot login to the Workplace. To make sure that our new user can log in, we need to set the start with group dropdown to Users. Click Ok to create the user.

> If you belong to multiple groups, you may switch the currently active group at any time by choosing the desired group from the drop-down list at the bottom of the workplace window: User: Admin Group: Administrators

Once the user is created, you will return to the Edit users screen. Click Ok to return to the user management menu. The Edit groups menu is similar to Edit users. It allows you to create and edit groups. Click on the New button to create a new group:

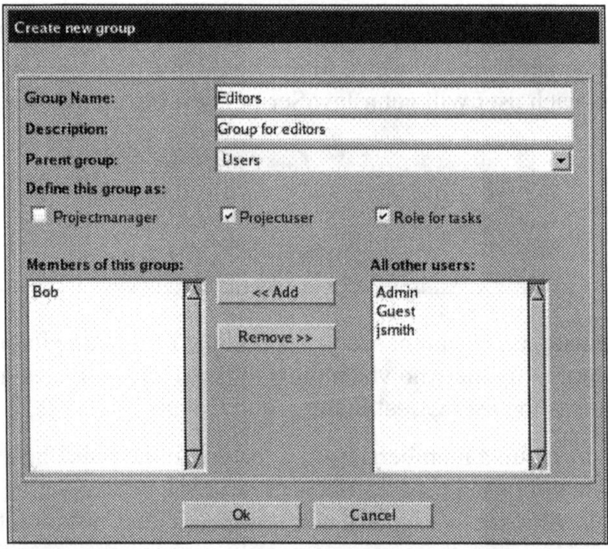

Set the Group Name and Description fields and choose a Parent group. Since all of the Editors will be Users, it makes sense to mark Users as the Parent group. In the section entitled Define this group as, you have three choices:

- Projectmanager gives this group permission to manage projects, including publishing and assigning tasks.

- Projectuser allows users in this group to log in to the Workplace and work on content.
- Role for tasks allows tasks to be assigned to this group as a whole. Since I may want to assign a task to all of my editors, I have checked that box.

Finally, the bottom frames allow you to select users to add immediately to the group. You may also add users to groups through the Edit users screens. Clicking Ok will create the group. Click Ok again to go back to the user management menu.

The last item in the user management menu is the Messages screen. This tool provides a means to send messages to all the users currently logged in to the system:

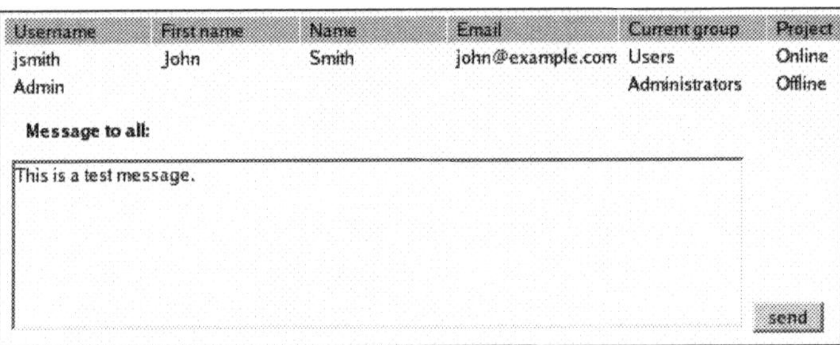

At the top, the Messages utility displays a list of all the users currently logged in to the system (Admin and jsmith on my system). Simply type in a message and click Send. A few moments latter, each user will get a JavaScript Alert popup message.

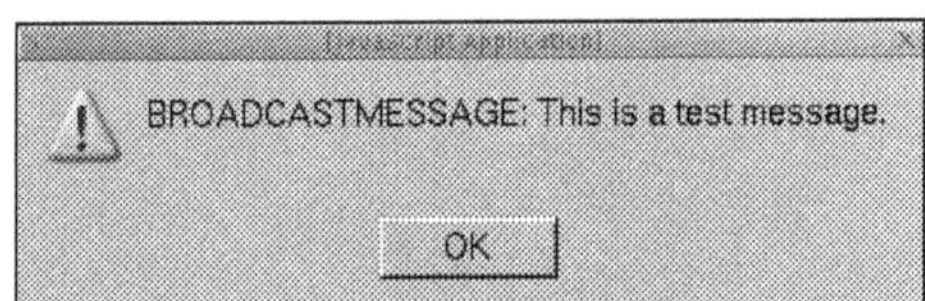

As you can see, the user management section is designed for managing users who log in and use the Workplace. Anyone who visits the published site and does not log in is automatically treated as the user Guest in the group Guest.

It may be desirable to set up a membership-like feature to the published website where users can visit certain published (but restricted) resources, but cannot log in to the Workplace. Unfortunately, the Workplace administration does not facilitate setting up this sort of behavior. However, there are two possibilities for obtaining this functionality, though each will take a little work:

- The first is to set up authentication at webserver level. If you are interested in this method, you will need to consult your webserver documentation.
- The second is to develop custom OpenCms tools to take advantage of the built-in **webuser** concept. OpenCms defines a webuser flag, which

demarcates a user as one who cannot log in to the Workplace, but can log in to the published site.

These concepts are discussed in more detail in Chapter 8.

Database Management

The **database management** tools facilitate exporting and importing the OpenCms database. This is useful for making backups as well as transferring data from one server to another.

The Export database screen allows you to selectively export resources within the database for import into another OpenCms instance:

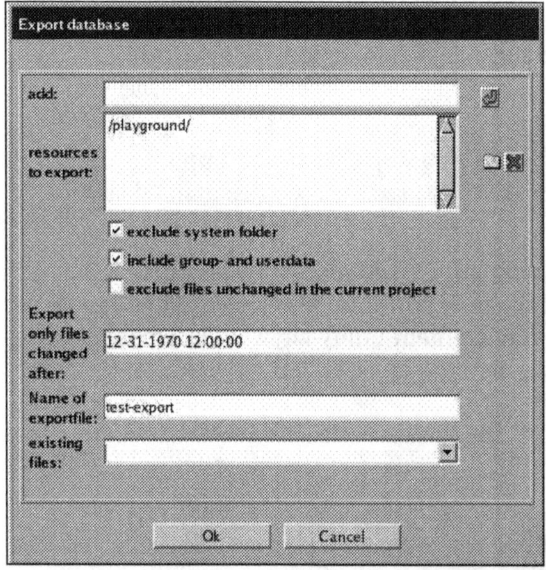

Using the file folder icon, choose resources to export. If you are making a full back-up of the system, you should uncheck the exclude system folder box, which will include the system information for this OpenCms instance. Checking include group- and userdata will ensure that importing into another OpenCms will include all of the correct users and groups.

The exclude files unchanged in the current project checkbox allows you to export only the differences between the current project and the Online project (obviously, this would have no effect if you are currently in the Online project). Alternately, you may specify a date with the Export only files changed after textbox. If this field is left empty, no date constraints are enforced.

> In some versions of OpenCms (including 5.0.1), the date-checking JavaScript always generates errors on Mozilla browsers and fails to perform proper format checks on IE browsers. Consequently, using a date constraint can cause unexpected behavior. If you do not need a date constraint, leave the Export only files changed after field blank.

Give the file a name (the `.zip` extension will be automatically appended) and click Ok. After a few minutes of dumping the data, the file will be exported to the directory `$CATALINA_HOME/webapps/opencms/WEB-INF/exports`.

To import an exported file, choose Import from the database management menu. If the ZIP file that you want to import is on the machine you are using, choose the Local computer setting, otherwise, you may put the file in the `$CATALINA_HOME/webapps/opencms/WEB-INF/exports` directory and choose Server. Select the correct file and click Ok to import it.

> OpenCms is very careful about what is imported, and will not create duplicate copies of existing users or groups. However, imported files will always overwrite existing files in the same location and will be marked as needing to be published.

The **Export module data** utility is for exporting specific modules. Since we have no modules, there is nothing to export from this screen. Modules are usually exported through the **Module management** utility anyway. Database exports and imports are discussed more thoroughly in Chapter 8.

Static Export

The **static export** option is only available in the Online project. It will render all of the pages in the Online folder (executing all necessary code and transforming the results to HTML) and write the contents to the file system of the underlying OS. Essentially, this turns the entire Online project into a static HTML site that can be served from another server. This process is discussed more completely in Chapter 8.

Clear Element Cache

OpenCms uses a number of caches to optimize frequently accessed items. The URI and element caches speed up the performance of XML templates by storing frequently rendered content in memory. To clear the items stored in the URI cache and the element cache, choose this item.

Resource Type Management

There are a number of schemes for determining *what* sort of content a file contains, for instance, Windows guesses at file type based on a three-letter extension and browsers use **Multipart Internet Message Encoding** (**MIME**) typing. OpenCms has several predefined file types, including Page (HTML in XML), Plain, JSP, Binary, Image, and XML template. Using file extensions, OpenCms maps all of its content into these file types.

The Resource type management screen provides a mechanism for explicitly associating an extension with a file type. Since OpenCms is missing a PNG (Portable Network Graphic) definition in the image type, we'll set one now:

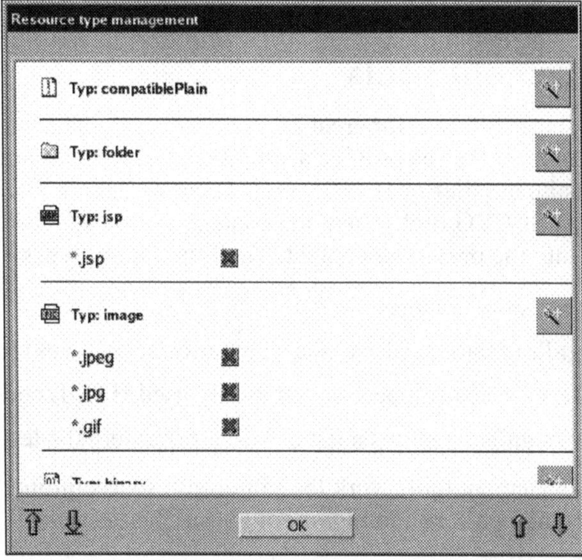

Locate the Typ: image section, using the blue up and down arrows to scroll, and click on the magic wand icon.

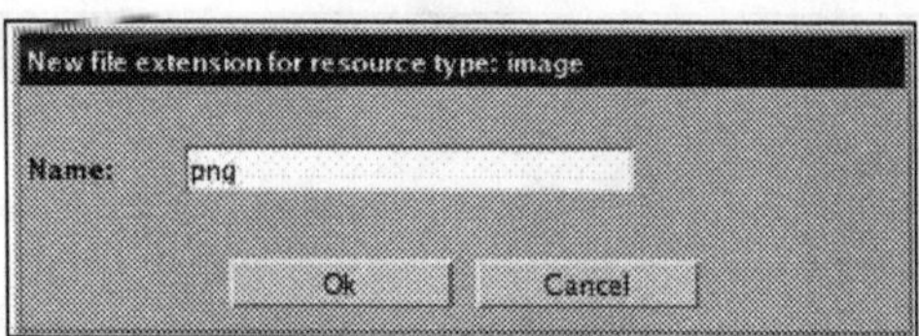

Set the name to png and click Ok. It will add *.png under the Typ: image section. To delete an extension, simply click on the red X next to the extension entry.

Properties Management

Not all information about a file is stored inside the file. OpenCms stores certain information, including the title, description, and navigation information, in a separate location in the database. This speeds retrieval of frequently accessed data and separates content itself from data about the content (usually called metadata). Every file type has a set of properties. By default, binary files only have three properties: Description, Keywords, and Title. Page files, which contain HTML content, have eight different properties, including content-encoding and NavPos (navigation position, used for building menus).

If you need to add a new property to a file type, you can use the **properties management** tool to do so. Its operation is identical to that of the resource type management tool.

Gallery Management Tools

The next four tools are all used for creating galleries, each management tool for a different kind of content. Galleries provide a simple mechanism for sharing commonly used content, such as image files or HTML snippets, among users. Each gallery can be accessed from the WYSIWYG tool, where the content editor can click on an item in the gallery and insert it into the present document. The four gallery types are:

- **Image gallery**: stores images
- **Download gallery**: stores files (such as binaries or archives) for download
- **HTML gallery**: stores snippets of commonly used HTML code
- **External links gallery**: stores a list of URLs for external sites

All of the gallery management tools work the same way; so to eliminate redundancy, I will only cover the **Image gallery management** tool in this section.

The first screen of the gallery management tool lists all the separate galleries. Since we have not yet created any, the list is empty. Create one by clicking on the magic wand icon.

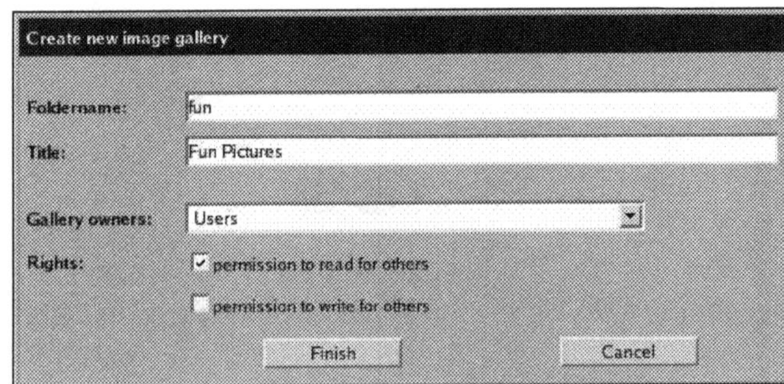

This is not much different than creating a new folder. The Foldername cannot have whitespace, but the Title may. Set the Gallery owners group to the group that will manage the gallery. Under the Rights section, you may specify whether users not in the Gallery owners group may read or write to the gallery. Click Finish to create the gallery.

Now, under the gallery management screen, you should see the fun folder. Click on the name to enter the gallery. It is no surprise that there are no images in this gallery yet. Click on the arrow pointing up ( ) to upload a new image from the file system of your local computer.

Use the Browse button to navigate your local file system until you find the image you want to upload into the gallery and click Continue. Add the Title and Description, and click Finish to load the image into the gallery.

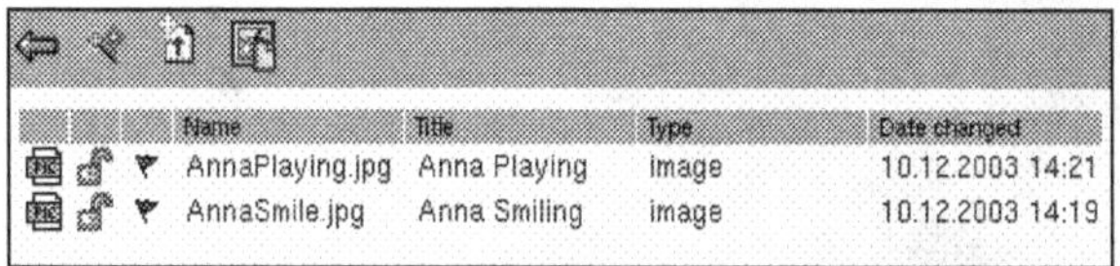

Now, images are listed in the gallery (I've added two images of my baby daughter). The fourth button along the toolbar, an icon of a picture with a page over it, opens a display of all the images in the gallery.

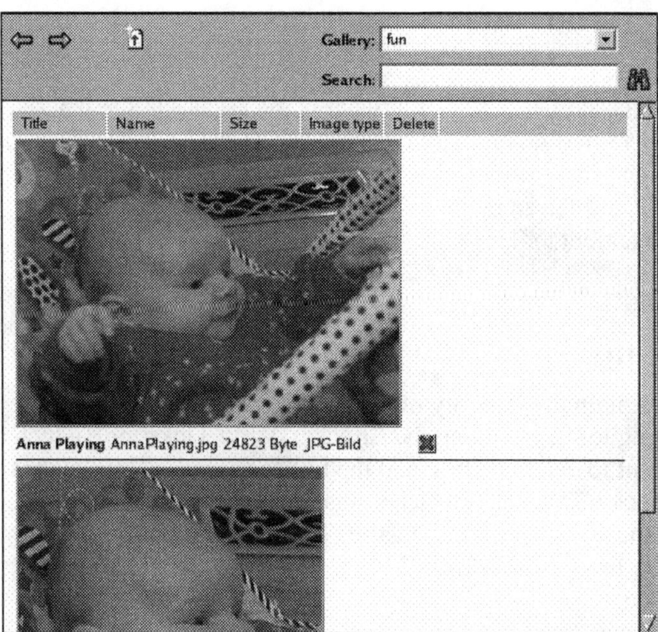

The other three gallery types work the same way: define a gallery and load content into it.

From the WYSIWYG editor, you may access the galleries with the gallery buttons (). Using cut-and-paste or drag-and-drop, you can select items from the galleries and include them in your page.

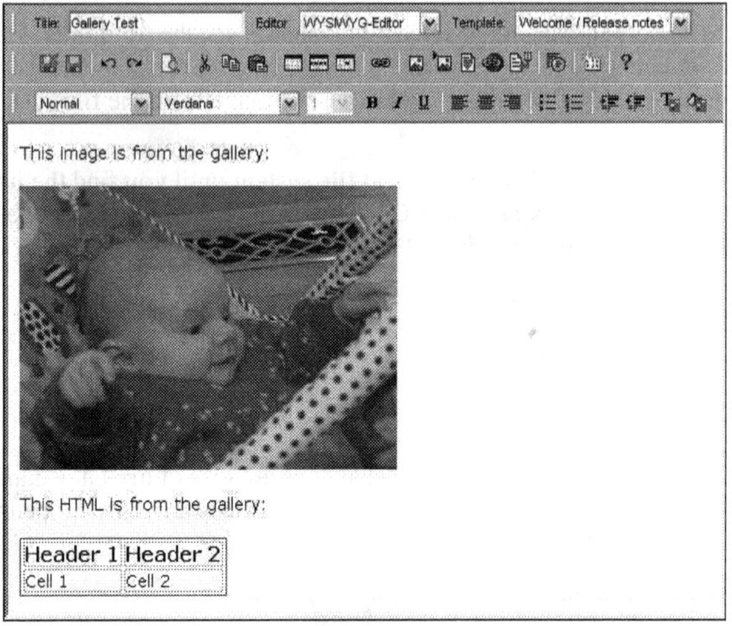

> All galleries are written to the VFS, where they are written to the `/system/galleries/` folder. It is possible to add and remove items in the gallery simply by manipulating those directories. The files work just like any other file under OpenCms. The preferred method for handling galleries, however, is via the gallery management tools.

Link Checking

In order to maintain the integrity of your resources, OpenCms provides a number of automatic checking tools, including the Check External Links tool, which checks link resources that point to external sites, and the two tools under Check Links. The first of those tools is Check HTML links, which scans through the HTML documents to make sure the links in the documents are all valid. The second tool, Check filesystem links, makes sure all file links are working.

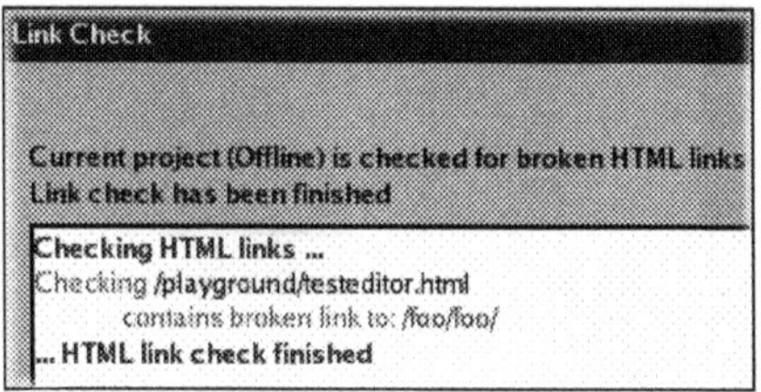

For example, if I create a bad link in a document and run the Check HTML links, it will show me an error message indicating where the broken link is.

It is useful to occasionally run these checks. However, OpenCms automatically runs a link check every time a publish event takes place, so most of these mistakes should be caught before they make it to your published site.

Module Management

The module management tool is for importing and exporting modules. OpenCms modules are portable collections of code and content, including JAR files, Java classes, JSP and XML template pages, and normal resources. Modules often extend the functionality of OpenCms. Loading and using modules will be covered in detail at the end of this chapter, and creating your own modules will be discussed at length in Chapter 6, *Creating an OpenCms Module*.

Synchronization Management

Synchronisation (so spelled here) is an advanced feature of OpenCms that allows developers to work on content outside the VFS, and synchronize it with the VFS. While this may be useful for developing JSPs or static content, it should be used with care, because it bypasses many of the safeguards of OpenCms.

From the synchronization management menu, you can configure one or more folders for synchronization.

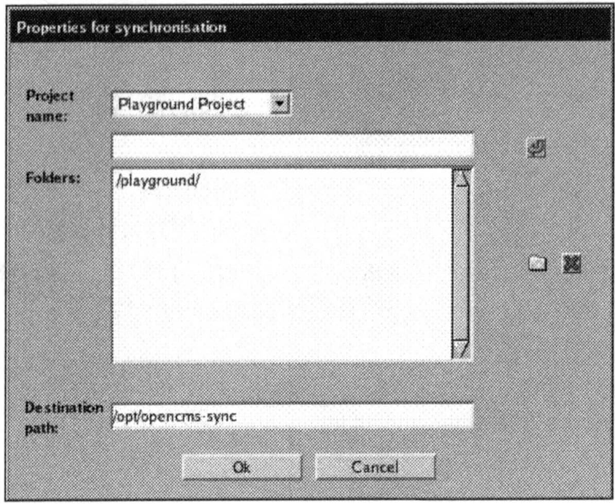

You may synchronize a project. For developers, Offline is probably the preferred project. In the preceding screenshot, I've chosen to synchronize just the Playground Project we created earlier in this chapter. Choose Folders with the yellow folder icon. The Destination path should be set to a valid path in the file system. For instance, on my Linux machine, I created a `/opt/opencms-sync/` directory before filling out this form (on Windows, you would use the entire path including the drive letter, e.g. `C:\opencms-sync`). Clicking Ok will not synchronize—it will only configure synchronization in the `$CATALINA_HOME/webapps/opencms/WEB-INF/config/registry.xml` file.

Once synchronization is configured, you will notice a new icon (a folder with arrows:) on the OpenCms toolbar. Clicking this icon will synchronize the VFS and the directory specified in the previous screenshot. At this point, the files in the Destination path (`/opt/opencms-sync`) reflect the files in the VFS (`/playground/` in our example). If you create a new file in the local disk copy and then click the synchronization icon in OpenCms, the new file will be imported into the VFS. Likewise, any other changes to existing files will be uploaded.

> You may have noticed that page files contain only an XML file, and not the HTML content. That is because the HTML content is stored in a separate file (the file listed in the `<TEMPLATE/>` tag). Synchronization is not really intended for editing page files, so it does not assist in editing them. If you really must synchronize HTML page files onto the local file system, you will need to synchronize one of the VFS subdirectories in `/system/bodies/`.

Again, synchronization management is a developer tool, and is not intended to become the primary interface for working with OpenCms. When used correctly, it can expedite development time; however, its abuse can lead to lost data and corruption of content.

Scheduled Tasks

Like Cron in UNIX/Linux or the Task Scheduler in Windows, OpenCms has a tool for running programs at a given time. Unlike its Windows and UNIX/Linux counterparts, the OpenCms **scheduled task** tool requires that the task be a Java class that implements the `I_CmsCronJob` interface. Scheduling a task will be covered in detail in Chapter 6, *Creating an OpenCms Module*.

Log File Viewer

OpenCms logs significant events to an `opencms.log` file located in `$CATALINA_HOME/webapps/opencms/WEB-INF/logs/`. The **Log File Viewer** provides access to the log file through the Workplace.

Channels

Channels can be used for categorizing content in a different way, e.g. topically. While channels can be created and managed through the **Channels** administration menu, the rest of OpenCms makes scant use of them, and much custom development is required to make them truly useful.

One of the popular modules, the News module, uses the channels concept to organize content, but it uses its own interface for managing channels.

In future releases of OpenCms, the functionality surrounding the concept of channels is likely to be expanded. For now, though, there is not much to do with them.

Flex Cache Administration

Earlier versions of OpenCms did not use JSP for page scripting, and relied entirely upon **XML templates** and custom Java classes for page rendering. In order to make JSPs work within the VFS, the OpenCms developers needed a way to efficiently store JSP pages on the file system where the JSP interpreter could find them. They developed the **Flex** package to accomplish this task. When a JSP is requested, Flex writes the VFS file into the real file system, storing it in `$CATALINA_HOME/webapps/opencms/WEB-INF/jsp/online` (or `offline` if the request is for a resource in one of the unpublished projects).

To expedite the process of rendering pages, the **FlexCache** stores the JSP and any elements included in the JSP, including plain text files and XML templates. Using a sophisticated algorithm, OpenCms manages the cache, keeping size down and providing JSP developers with a variety of cache control options. We'll cover practical use of the FlexCache in Chapter 4, *Customizing the Site*.

The Flex Cache Administration page provides tools to manually manage the cache. The complexity of the cache is mirrored in the multitude of functions available in the cache management screen. Before examining the tasks, I will explain how items are stored. Each cached element has a key, which identifies what resources in the VFS are being cached. Data is stored in variations. Each key may have multiple variations, where a variation indicates that the particular resource was loaded by another resource. This can be the case when two different JSP files both include a common third file.

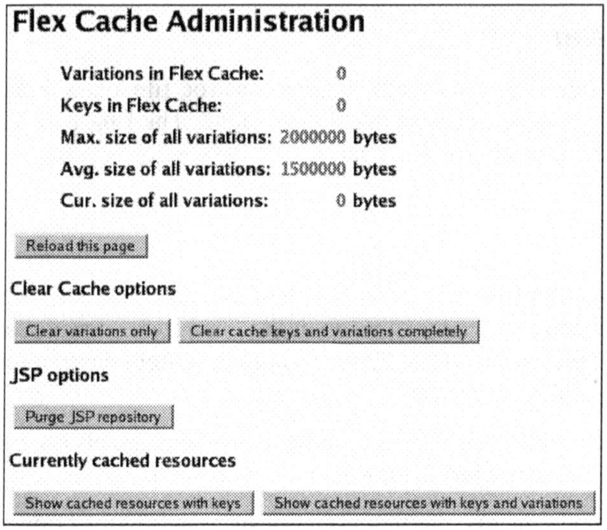

Flex Cache Administration

Variations in Flex Cache: 0
Keys in Flex Cache: 0
Max. size of all variations: 2000000 bytes
Avg. size of all variations: 1500000 bytes
Cur. size of all variations: 0 bytes

Reload this page

Clear Cache options

Clear variations only | Clear cache keys and variations completely

JSP options

Purge JSP repository

Currently cached resources

Show cached resources with keys | Show cached resources with keys and variations

- Clear variations only: Clears the data associated with each key, but leaves the keys in the cache. The key tells the location of the file in the VFS. The next time a resource is requested, OpenCms will reuse the key, assuming that the cache properties for that file have not changed. This gives you a slight performance boost as the cache is rebuilt. Most of the time, however, it is better to use the next option instead.
- Clear cache keys and variations completely: Clears everything from the cache. No information about resources in the VFS is saved.
- Purge JSP repository: Removes all cached JSP elements from `$CATALINA_HOME/webapps/opencms/WEB-INF/jsp/` (both the online and offline directories). The next time a JSP is requested, it will be copied from the VFS into the real file system again. This option is useful during development when JSP files are frequently changing and cached copies quickly become outdated.

- Show cached resources with keys and Show cached resources with keys and variations: Both display the items in the cache. If you click the latter button, it will list not only the keys, but also the variations of each cached object.

> By default, resources in the Offline project are not cached by the FlexCache. During development, you may want to enable caching for Offline. To do so, edit the `opencms.properties` file under `$CATALINA_HOME/webapps/opencms/WEB-INF/config/`, setting the flag `flex.cache.offline=true`. You will need to restart Tomcat after changing this file.
>
> The Flex Cache Administration tool will now allow you to specify *which* cache (Online or Offline) you want to clear.

The caching system in OpenCms is complex, and while many of these concepts seem foreign now, they will become clearer as we work with caching directives in Chapter 4, *Customizing the Site*.

At this point, we have gone through all of the tools in the administration view. From here, we move on to the workflow view.

Workflow

A fundamental aspect of good enterprise-level content management is the capability to handle workflow of resources as they make their way through the editorial process. The workflow view provides a task-based interface to the system. Already, we've created a project to manage a particular subset of our content. Through the workflow view, we will be able to assign editors tasks to complete within the project.

To enter the workflow view, select Workflow from the View drop-down box in the top toolbar.

Creating and Managing Tasks

Initially, the workflow task list is empty. We are going to create a task in the Playground project, so select Playground Project from the Project drop-down list in the toolbar. Once you've done this, click the red check-mark icon ( ) to create a new task.

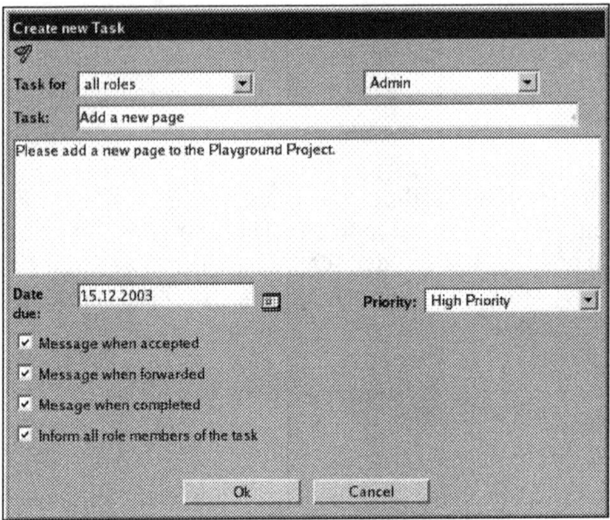

Choose the appropriate group from the Task for drop-down list. Since I want to assign it to Admin (me), and Admin is not in the traditional groups, I selected all roles from the list. The next drop-down box is for selecting the particular user. If you want to assign the task to everyone in the group selected in the Task for dropdown, simply leave it blank.

> In the workflow view, groups are often referred to as roles. The difference of terminology is meant to reflect *which* function the group is playing. This change in terminology can be confusing. Groups and roles are the same thing.

Use the Task textbox to give the task a title. The text area below is for providing a complete description. In a live scenario, the description should be fairly detailed. Use Due date to specify the date upon which the task must be completed. While the field defaults to the current date, the text field can be edited, or, by clicking the calendar icon, you can choose the date from a calendar widget.

> Versions of OpenCms prior to 5.0 did not correctly check this value. Consequently, neither the owner nor the editor was notified when the task was due. Current versions, however, correctly check the due date.

There are three values for Priority: high, medium (the default selection), and low. High and low priority items show special icons in the task viewer indicating their importance.

The next three checkboxes determine whether you, the task creator, will be notified when the task is accepted by the assignee, forwarded to another user, or completed.

The fourth item, Inform all role members of the task, determines whether the task will show up in the queue of other users in the same role as the assignee. Click Ok to create the task.

Once the task has been created, an e-mail will be sent to the assignee with some generic information about the new task. The following is an example message sent to the user Bob after I assigned him a new task:

```
From: bob@example.com
To: opencms@example.com
Subject: OpenCms task management: new task for Bob Editor (Bob) /
Editors

Automatic message from OpenCms task management:
A new task was created for you or your role.
Project: Playground Project
Task: Write an article
Task Initiatior:    (Admin)

http://example.com:8080/opencms/opencms/system/login/index.html?start
TaskId=34&startProjectId=13
```

> The link at the bottom of the message takes the user directly to the new task (though the user must first log in if they have not already done so).

The new task is added to the task viewer. By default, the task viewer only shows the new tasks for the currently logged-in user in the current project. To change the view, select different filters from the Filter drop-down list. Also, if you do not wish to constrain the results to the current project, check the For all Projects box.

After adding a few more sample tasks and applying All new tasks with the For all Projects box checked, here's what my task list looks like:

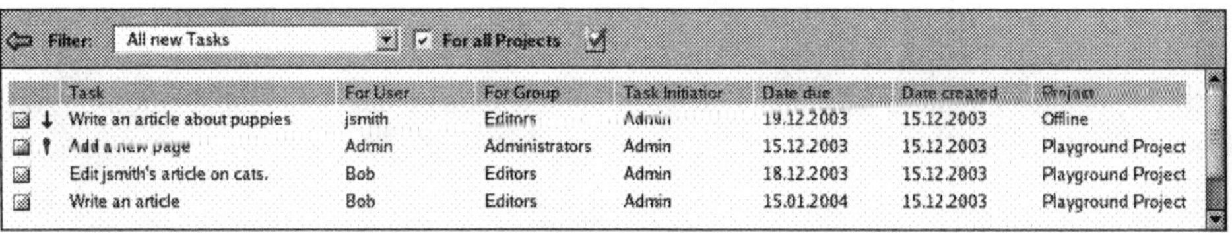

Note that low priority items have a blue down-arrow after the task icon, and high-priority items have a red exclamation point. To view the details of a task, click on the task name.

> There are four filter groups: **new tasks, active tasks, completed tasks,** and **tasks created by me**. The first group shows tasks that have not yet been accepted. The second group shows all tasks that are not marked as complete. The third group shows completed tasks. Finally, the fourth group shows tasks that I created. This last group is particularly useful for project managers, whose job it is to assign tasks.

For each group of tasks, you have the option of showing those assigned to you (the current user), your current role (group), or all tasks.

Clicking on the task name opens the task detail screen. The detail screen shows all of the important information about a task, with a summary at the top, and a documentation trail beneath.

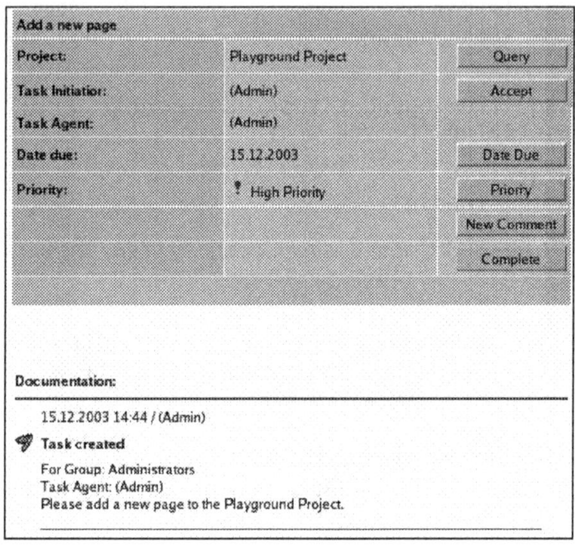

At the end of the Project line, there is a button labeled Query (if you are the assignee: Task Agent) or Message (if you are the Task Initiator). Clicking this button will open a text editor screen that you can use to create a message. If you are the initiator, the message will go to the agent. If you are the agent, the message will go to the initiator. While the message recipient will be notified of the new message by e-mail, the user will have to log into the system to actually read it. The message appears in the documentation section, and look like this:

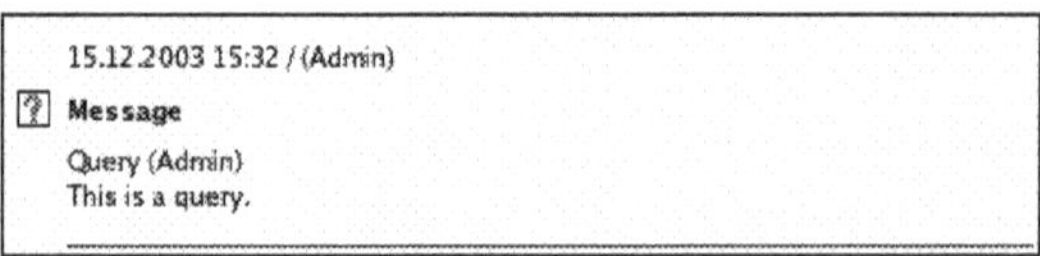

When assigned a new task, the agent must accept it before working on it. Click the Accept button to take the task. Once the task is accepted, this button will be replaced with a Forward button. Clicking this button will take you to a screen that allows you to assign the task to another role/user.

> Other users who are marked as neither the agent nor the initiator will see a Take button instead of an Accept or Forward button. By clicking that button, a user may become the agent on that ticket.

A task initiator can also change the Date Due and Priority of a task. While the buttons for making the change appear on both the agent's and initiator's screens, they are deactivated on the agent's screen.

New Comments opens a window very similar to the query/message screen. Comments are used to track the progress of a task—an editor may log progress on a task using the comments section.

15.12.2003 15:32 / (Admin)
Comment
This is a comment.

Until a task is accepted, the Complete button is deactivated. When the task is marked as accepted, OpenCms assumes that the user is working through the task, though it does no checking to see if the user is actually completing the task. Once the task is completed, click the Complete button. That will remove it from the active tasks list. Once the task is completed, all the buttons are deactivated except the Complete button, which is relabeled Recycle. Recycling a task reopens it for completion again. This is useful, for instance, when you have a task that has to be completed every week or month. Rather than create a new task each time, you may simply recycle the old task.

Workflow Management Strategies

The whole workflow system can seem daunting to the user new to the CMS concept. However, it can be a powerful tool in managing your content. Here are a few strategies for managing tasks using projects and workflow.

Use Projects to Manage Content Areas

Projects provide a way to cleanly divide the content into logical groups. It helps with access control by limiting an editor's permissions to only the resources in his or her projects. It helps with project management, as project managers have a well defined domain for which they are responsible. Over all, it is an effective way of organizing the content.

There are two strategies for defining projects. The first is to create a project for every major content area within the site. This setup takes the functional route in the division of content. A project manager may then be assigned multiple projects. The advantage to this system is that editors may be restricted to a small subset of the site. Also, projects may be moved from one project manager to another with a minimal amount of work.

The second method is to create one project per project manager, thereby reflecting organizational structure (as opposed to site structure). This structure makes the job of the project manager a little easier, as he or she must only keep track of one set of content and tasks. For editors that contribute to many different areas of content all under *one* project manager, this approach is easier. Like the project manager, they only have to track one project. There are two drawbacks to this configuration. If a content area is moved from one project manager to another, reconfiguring the projects is a little more tedious. Also, it is more difficult to restrict an editor's access to only one content area, as the project includes multiple content areas. This may be resolved with careful use of groups and file permissions, but that approach entails more maintenance.

Regardless of which route you choose, using projects will help manage content as your content repository grows.

Use Group Hierarchies for Inherited Permissions

One common catch in the editing process is that resources (files and folders) can only belong to one user and one group. If multiple editors in different groups need to access the same resources, you will need to go through a little more effort to make sure that all of the right people can access shared resources.

Consider a technical news site that has two groups of editors—one that handles hardware news and one that handles software news. Most of the time, these editors are dealing with different content, but both groups have to update the `headlines.html` file. The headlines file can only have one owner and one group, but hardware editors are in a different group than software editors. Since other users on the system should not be able to edit this file, simply opening the file up for write access to all would not work.

The answer to this problem lies in the structuring of groups. Groups can be organized in a hierarchy, where a child group inherits the permissions of its parent. If both the groups have the same parent, then changing the file's group to the parent will allow members of both child groups access to the file. As an example, consider this group structure:

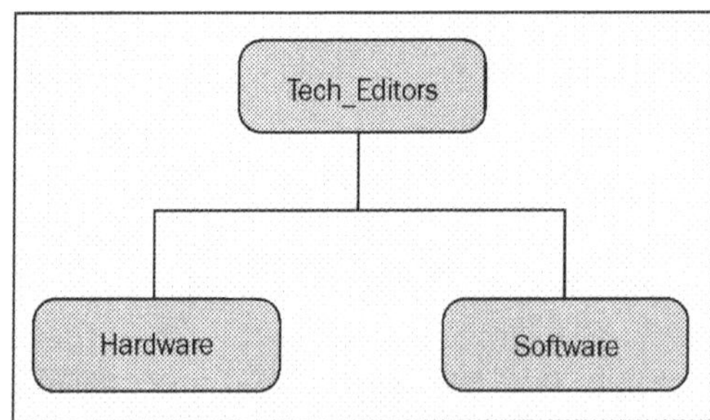

In this configuration, the parent group is Tech_Editors, with the Hardware and Software groups its children. Consequently, any file with write permissions set for Tech_Editors will be writable by members of either the Hardware or Software group.

Careful planning of group layouts can ease many of the access issues that arise in CMS management.

Track Work with Tasks

The workflow tools are designed to provide a functional approach to managing your content. Workflow provides a clear and intuitive way to track the state of the content that is being generated, edited, and maintained. Using the workflow tool can help you maximize the efficiency of the editorial process. I recommend assigning tasks for every step of the editorial and publishing process. For example, consider a project (we'll call it 'Project X') with only one article and a corresponding JSP. Here is an example of the tasks I (as the project manager) would create:

- Editor 1: Write the article in Project X.
- Developer 1: Create a JSP for Project X.
- Editor 2: Proof and edit the article.
- Editor 2: Proof the content on JSP.
- Project Manager: Approve article.
- Project Manager: Approve JSP.
- Project Manager: Publish Project.

I could trim down the number of tasks by requiring, for instance, Editor 1 to forward the article to Editor 2 once it was complete, and then have Editor 2 forward it to the Project Manager when it was ready for approval. Combining it thus reduces the number of tasks to track, but makes it a little harder to assess progress with just a glance at the tasks list.

One way to encourage users to use (and think in terms of) tasks is to set their default view to workflow instead of explorer.

Keeping a Trail

Simply using the assign-accept-forward-complete tracking of tasks can be a sufficient means of operating. However, in cases where there are numerous editors or editors and project managers are not in the same physical location, communication can break down and information can slip through the cracks. E-mail can go unnoticed or accidentally be deleted. Conversations, whether verbal or in chat/instant-messaging are apt to be forgotten. And these methods do not keep all of the information in a central location.

To avoid these problems, you may find it expedient to track the status of a task using the Query, Message, and Comment tools provided with the workflow tools.

If correspondence between the project manager and editor is handled through messages, and involved parties are diligent in making comments to record progress, then each task will have a self-contained paper trail. This can promote effective communication and prevent important information or requirements from slipping through.

We have toured each of the three views at length, and we are almost finished with our exploration of the Workplace. All that remains is a discussion of installing and configuring OpenCms modules.

Modules

No single program fits the need of every user. Given the complex nature of content management, developers of CMS systems in particular cannot adopt the one-size-fits-all perspective. In order to provide their users with the ability to fit OpenCms into their own environment, the OpenCms developers implemented a **module** architecture that can be used to extend OpenCms with new functionality and content.

OpenCms modules consist of a well defined set of directories and files stored in a ZIP archive. A module may contain **Java Archive (JAR)** files, **Java classes**, **JSP** scripts, **images**, **stylesheets**, and any type of content that OpenCms supports. Using the module management tool in the administration view, you can upload and install new modules, as well as create, edit, and export your own modules. In this section, we will cover obtaining and installing some of the common modules, including the **OpenCms help system**. Later on, in Chapter 6, *Creating an OpenCms Module*, I will explain the process of creating a new module from scratch and developing and deploying it.

Obtaining Official OpenCms Modules

The official OpenCms website hosts two repositories of modules. The first repository contains stable modules, primarily those released by Alkacon. For the most part, the material here is content (tutorials, reference), help text, and language localizations. Also, there is an official module sandbox. Modules in the sandbox are generally newer and undergo active development; however, they are usually stable enough for use. In addition, there is an unofficial module repository hosted on Alexander Langer's `al-arenal.de` site. To some extent, the modules here overlap with those in the sandbox. However, you will also find modules that, for one reason or another, were never submitted to the official site. Developers tend to post beta versions of their code to this site, so the versions in the unofficial repository may also be higher than their sandbox counterparts.

> Stable Repository:
> `http://www.opencms.org/opencms/en/download/modules/index.html`
>
> Sandbox: `http://www.opencms.org/opencms/en/download/sandbox.html`

Unofficial Module Repository: `http://opencms.al-arenal.de/`

The official **Concurrent Versioning System** (**CVS**) sourcecode repository has other Alkacon modules that are under development. In my experience, these tend to be the least stable of the publicly accessible modules, but developers may find them useful.

The Help System Modules

You may have already noticed that there is no help system built into OpenCms. Actually, the help system is implemented as a series of add-on modules. There is a basic online help module that provides the core functionality, and then there are localizations for a number of languages.

The help system is virtually a necessity, so we will be installing it in the next section. From the stable repository on the OpenCms site, download the basic module and any localizations that you want to install. Save them on your local workstation—we will upload them to the server from the browser. I am installing the following help modules:

- OpenCms 5.0 Workplace online help basic module
- OpenCms 5.0 Workplace online help English version

Importing OpenCms Modules

In the OpenCms Workplace, go to the administration view. Click on the module-management icon (). You may already see a few modules that were installed by default. Click the upload icon (the blue arrow pointing up) to begin the module import process. Choose local computer and click Continue. Select the file named `org.opencms.help_1.1.zip` (this is the base module, not the language localization. If you try to install the localization first, you will get an error message).

Click Continue to upload the file to the server. You should see an import screen that looks similar to the publishing dialogue. OpenCms will unpack the module and copy the files into the correct locations within the VFS. Once the import is finished, it will say `the module has been imported` and the Ok button will turn active. On clicking Ok, you should return to the module management tool, where the `org.opencms.help` module should now be listed in the modules list.

Click the upload icon again and repeat the same process for the `org.opencms.help.en_1.1.zip` module. Once you have finished that, you should also have the `org.opencms.help.en` module in your modules list. Unfortunately, there is no way to bulk import modules, so you will need to repeat the process for every language localization that you install.

> Modules are named by strict convention. A module name should always begin with the full Java package name for the module (e.g. `org.opencms.help`). The package name should be followed by an underscore, and then a version number of the form `MAJOR.minor` (`_1.1`). Finally, each module file must have the `.zip` extension.

If you reload your screen using the green arrow icon, or if you simply change view, you will notice a new icon—a cartoonish speech bubble with a question mark in it ()—appearing in your toolbar. Clicking on this icon will open a new window, displaying help information:

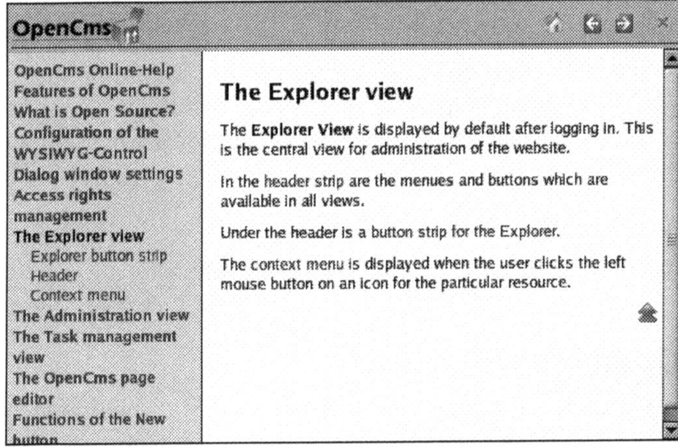

Close the online help browser by clicking the red X in the upper right-hand corner.

> If you install multiple language packs, OpenCms will determine which language to use based on the Language setting on the Startup options tab in the User preferences (to get there, click the hammer icon in the toolbar).

Congratulations. You've just installed your first OpenCms module.

Where Did All that Module Data Go?

Generally speaking, module data is written directly into the VFS (Java classes and JARs are also written into the real file system so that the servlet container can access them). Most of the data is placed in `/system/modules/` under the package name of the module (e.g. `org.opencms.help`).

Occasionally (as with the documentation modules discussed below), files or links are written outside the `/systems` directory; however, that is considered bad practice for anything that is not strictly content. Some modules also add classes and templates to the Workplace. Like just about everything in OpenCms, files from modules are treated just like content. You may add, lock, modify, publish, and delete module contents. You also may export a new version of the module to the file system in order to install it on other instances of OpenCms. In Chapter 6, *Creating an OpenCms Module*, I will cover this in more detail.

Online Documentation Modules

In addition to the help system, there are a few OpenCms documentation modules that come in handy. All of these are available from the stable repository on the official OpenCms website.

- The **Alkacon OpenCms 5.0 interactive documentation base module** is required by all other Alkacon documentation.
- The **Alkacon OpenCms 5.0 Howto: JSP template development** module contains reference material for developing JSP templates. We will create JSP templates at the beginning of the next chapter.
- The **Alkacon OpenCms 5.0 JSP basic documentation** and **Alkacon OpenCms 5.0 JSP scriptlet documentation** modules provide references, tutorials, and implementation information about using Java Server Pages in OpenCms.
- The **Alkacon OpenCms 5.0 JSP taglib documentation** module describes using the JSP taglibs as an alternative to scriptlets.
- The **Alkacon OpenCms 5.0 FlexCache documentation** module describes the cache directives used by the FlexCache mechanism.
- The **Alkacon OpenCms 5.0 Module mechanism documentation** module outlines the process of creating a new module in OpenCms.
- Additionally, there are a couple of modules that contain code examples. For those interested in translation and localization, the **Alkacon OpenCms 5.0 Howto: Translating the OpenCms Workplace** module explains how to translate the Workplace and help into another language.

When these modules are installed, they appear in the main repository. When you are logged in, `http://localhost:8080/opencms/opencms/`, the default home page, will have links to the tutorials along the top of the page.

Note that all of these modules are placed in a publicly accessible directory. It is probably wise to *not* install these on a production machine, or, if you do, to make sure they are not published to the Online project.

Other Modules

There are a lot of modules to choose from. Here is a little information on the most popular modules. All modules listed here are open source. Additionally, there are a few companies that provide proprietary modules. Some companies, including Alkacon, do custom development and OpenCms consulting. A list of these companies can be found at `http://www.opencms.org/opencms/en/support/solution_providers/index.html`.

- The **News** module, of which (by my count) there are currently six forks, provides news services to OpenCms. News implements its own version of channels, and includes additional tools in the administration view. The different forks each add different functionality, including scheduling, extra applets, and RSS support. The best place to locate information about the various versions of this module is the unofficial module site at `http://opencms.al-arenal.de/`.
- The **OpenCms Lucene Search** module, of which I am one of the maintainers, has also garnered a big following. It offers a search engine that operates within the VFS to intelligently index OpenCms resources. This module is managed as a SourceForge project, and its website is at `http://opencmslucene.sourceforge.net/`.
- The **Article Management** module provides a number of tools for managing articles in OpenCms, including article overviews and printer-friendly pages. It is available from `http://www.rueth.info/articlemanagement-documentation/`.

New modules are added all the time, though. Take a look at the various module repositories and find the ones that are right for you.

Summary

In this chapter, we toured the entire OpenCms Workplace, examining the explorer view for managing content, the administration view for managing OpenCms, and the workflow view for managing tasks. We wrapped up by looking at the OpenCms module system.

At this time, you should have a good idea of how to use and manage OpenCms. From here, we will begin looking at developing templates and JSP pages, controlling the cache, and using custom data sources.

4

Customizing the Site

We have already talked at length about using the system—creating and editing content, managing projects, and carrying out administrative tasks. Now, it is time to turn our attention to customizing the site. In this chapter, I will explain how to develop the look and feel of published content, adding dynamic elements and controlling resources. We will cover:

- Working with templates
- Using OpenCms JSP tag libraries
- Creating JSP scriptlets
- Managing **FlexCache** directives
- Configuring internationalization

Overview of Creating a Site

The goal of this chapter is to provide you with the tools necessary for developing a basic OpenCms site. These skills are necessary for developing the site:

- Configuring the backend for editors/writers
- Creating content
- Creating a basic module to hold templates and JSP files
- Creating templates (mainly JSP templates)
- Creating JSP scriptlets
- Publishing resources to the online project

In the previous chapter, we have already covered the first two—configuring the Workplace and creating content—as well as the publishing process noted at the end of the list. In this chapter, we will focus on development-related tasks: creating templates, JSP pages, and a basic site module.

By the end of this chapter, you should be equipped to handle general OpenCms development. We will begin by looking at templates and the site module.

Working with Templates and Tags

When a client requests a page, OpenCms retrieves the contents for the page, and then places the contents into a template that provides the look and feel, navigation, and surrounding structure for the content.

Since the 5.0 release, most templates are JSP pages, the preferred format. However, they may also be in the proprietary OpenCms XML template format. In fact, the 5.0 release requires that each JSP have an associated XML template—one which simply points to the JSP engine. This will change in subsequent versions of OpenCms, and XML templates will be phased out completely. Hence, we will focus primarily on JSP pages.

Before we can create our own templates, we need to designate a place to store them. We use a module for these purposes.

Creating a Site Module for Templates

In the last chapter, I talked about modules as a mechanism for extending OpenCms functionality. As we turn from use and administration to development, we are now focusing on extending OpenCms. For that reason, we need to add a module in which we will put our new templates and scripts. Modules can be complex, and we will cover the intricacies of the module mechanism in a later chapter. For now, however, we just need to create a bare-bones module for housing resources for our site.

To create a new module, go to the administration view and click on the Module Management icon. Click on the magic wand icon in the toolbar.

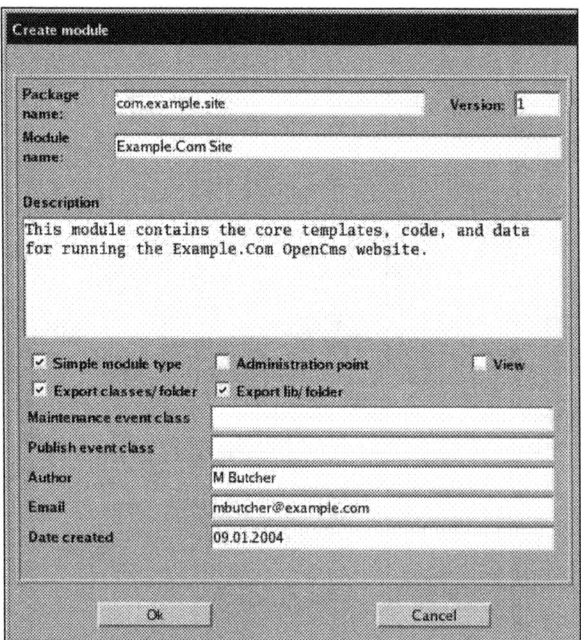

The first field, Package name, must be a Java-style package name. That means the first component must be a top-level domain (com, net, org, gov, or a country code). The second component should be the domain of your organization. From there, the name of the package should reflect the structure of the information in the package. Since the module we are creating is simply composed of functions that will be used to display the site, I've named the module Site. I find this convention very useful, but you are free to structure things however you see fit.

The Version field can be left alone. In the Module name field, type in a friendlier name for the package. Description should contain information about what kinds of files are in this module.

For now, leave all of the checkboxes set to their default, and don't put anything in the Maintenance event class or Publish event class lines. We will return to these in a subsequent chapter.

Set the Author and Email lines to your own name and e-mail address. Date created should be automatically generated. Click Ok to generate the module. When you return to the Module Management screen, you will see your new module.

Switch back to the explorer view. The new module is in the `/system/modules` directory. Four folders are automatically created under our `com.example.site` folder. Of these, we will be focusing on the `templates/` directory, as it is home to XML template files. Three more folders need to be created manually. Navigate to the `com.example.site` folder and create a folder named resources/, one named elements/, and one named jsptemplates/. By convention, JSP files are placed in the elements/ directory. Images, stylesheets and JavaScript files are placed in the resources/ directory, and JSP templates are placed in the jsptemplates/ directory.

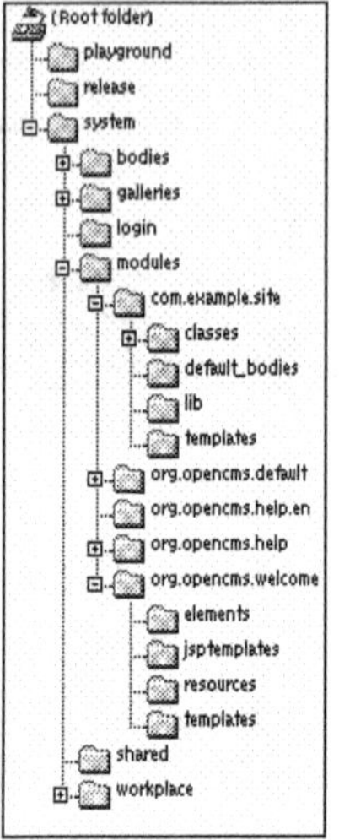

Once these extra directories have been created, we are prepared to move on and create some templates.

> Some directories, such as templates/, are explicitly referenced by OpenCms code. This is not the case for resources/, elements/, and jsptemplates/. Their naming and use, though, is a convention encouraged by the OpenCms development community, so while there is no requirement to create these directories or even to structure your module the way we are doing it here, you are encouraged to follow established convention.

Creating a New Template

Creating a template is a three-step process:

1. Create an XML Template file.
2. Create a JSP template.
3. Set content to use the new template.

As I mentioned before, every JSP template must have an accompanying XML template. In this case, the XML template simply relates a request for a template to the JSP template that should be used. For the most part, the XML template's functionality is a vestige of older versions of OpenCms, and the OpenCms developers have indicated that the requirement for using an XML template will disappear in the next major release of OpenCms.

To create an XML template, navigate into the `templates/` directory and click the magic wand icon. Choose XML Template from the list of file types and then click Continue.

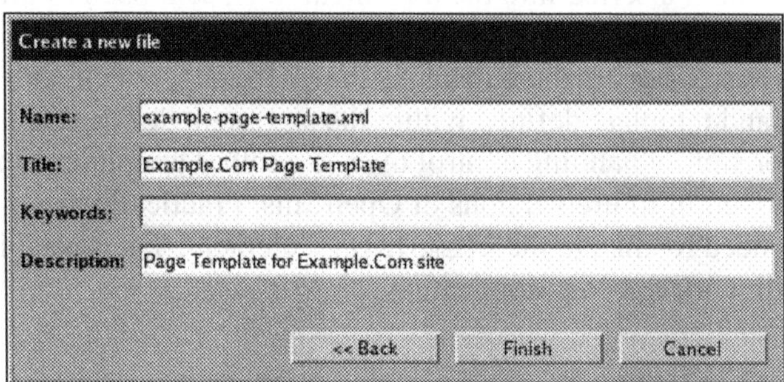

Name is the file name, and it cannot have spaces. Note that it should end with the `.xml` extension. Title is a human-readable name for the file. For XML templates, the title is very important. The template selection drop-down list used by the 'new page' Wizard, and the WYSIWYG and sourcecode editors use the titles of the XML template even if the XML template simply points to a JSP template. Keywords and Description provide fields for additional information. While neither of these fields is required, it is good practice to add at least a description. Clicking Finish will open up the sourcecode editor.

XML template files are written in well-formed XML. While they are not validated by a DTD or schema, making a mistake in the document structure will cause parsing errors.

```
<?xml version="1.0" encoding="ISO-8859-1"?>
<!--
  -- Template for example.com site. Loads a JSP template
  -->
<xmltemplate>
  <!-- For the WYSIWYG editor -->
  <stylesheet>/styles/myStyleSheet.css</stylesheet>
  <template>
    <element name="jsptemplate"/>
  </template>
  <elementdef name="jsptemplate">
    <class>com.opencms.flex.CmsJspTemplate</class>
    <template>
     <!-- Points to the JSP template -->
     ../jsptemplates/example-page-template.jsp
    </template>
  </elementdef>
</xmltemplate>
```

The example above instructs OpenCms to load and run `../jsptemplates/example-page-template.jsp` every time this template is executed. There are three elements within the `<xmltemplate/>` definition. The first, `<stylesheet/>`, is the path to the **Cascading Style Sheet** (**CSS**) that the WYSIWYG editor should use. This element is optional, and if you don't want the WYSIWYG editor to use a specific stylesheet, leave this element empty using the correct XML syntax: `<stylesheet/>`.

The `<template/>` element is used to create the resulting page. Everything inside the `<template/>` element is inserted into the document, then sent back to the client. When the XML template parser encounters the `<element/>` element, it finds the `<elementdef/>` whose `name` attribute matches the `<element/>` element's `name` and then executes the class and template defined within the `<elementdef/>`. All this may seem unduly complex for simply handing control over to another template—and it is. That is why it will be removed in future versions of OpenCms. Practically speaking, though, there is rarely any need to change the `<template/>` element. The way it is defined in the example above will work for your application.

> `<element/>` and `<elementdef/>` are coupled by the values of their respective `name` attributes. If you change the `name` of an `<element/>`, make sure you change the `name` of the associated `<elementdef/>`.

The `<elementdef/>` element defines what code is executed when the coupled `<element/>` is loaded. In the example above, it contains two elements. The first, `<class/>`, indicates that the associated class, `com.opencms.flex.CmsJspTemplate`, should be executed. This class is the JSP template rendering class, and it is probably the only class you will ever need to execute for JSP templates (unless you are planning on writing your own JSP handler).

The `<template/>` element is the most important. It defines which JSP template to load and execute. In the example above, we are referencing a template in the location `../jsptemplates/example-page-template.jsp`. There are two things about this path that are worth noting.

First, in this example the path is relative to the location of the XML template (not to that page which will call this template). The XML template is in `/system/modules/com.example.site/templates/example-page-template.xml`, and it is referencing a file in `/system/modules/com.example.site/jsptemplates/example-page-template.jsp`.

Second, the JSP template has the same name as the XML template file (but different extension and directory). While this is not mandatory, it is strongly encouraged, as it assists in the quick correlation between the two types of template files (remember: you will *always* have an XML template file for each JSP template).

> In a nutshell, the only two values that will change from template to template are the location of the stylesheet and the location of the JSP template. Also, remember to give a unique title to each XML template when you create it with the wizard, as the WYSIWYG editor uses this title (not the JSP template title) in the template list.

This is all there is to defining an XML template for JSPs. From here, we can move on to creating the `example-page-template.jsp` page.

The JSP Template

Now that the XML template is defined, we can define a corresponding JSP template. The JSP template will provide the layout for the contents of any associated pages. Like any 'regular' JSP, a JSP template may include JSP tags and scriptlets, and may also import other JSP files. In this section, we will create a simple JSP template that we will expand in subsequent sections.

JSP templates should go in the `jsptemplates/` directory of your module, and each should have the same name as its corresponding XML template (but with a `.jsp` instead of a `.xml` extension). In the `/system/modules/com.example.site/jsptemplates/` directory, create a new file with JSP as the type. Name it `example-page-template.jsp` and set the title and description properties. To edit the template, open the file in the sourcecode editor.

Here is an example of a very simple JSP template. It creates a basic HTML document and dumps the contents of the page into the body of the page.

```
<%@ page session="false" %>
<%@ taglib prefix="cms"
  uri="http://www.opencms.org/taglib/cms" %>
<!DOCTYPE html public "-//W3C//DTD HTML 4.01 Transitional//EN">
<html>
<head>
  <title><cms:property name="title" escapeHtml="true"/></title>
</head>
<body>
  <h1><cms:property name="title" escapeHtml="true"/></h1>
  <cms:include element="body"/>
</body>
</html>
```

The first tag instructs the JSP engine not to create a session object. While some applications will require session objects, this one will not, and we can speed things up by not tracking sessions. The second defines the JSP taglib for OpenCms. Any elements referenced with the `cms` prefix will use the OpenCms taglib described by the URI `http://www.opencms.org/taglib/cms`.

> A taglib is a library of special tags defined in Java for use inside a JSP. OpenCms defines a set of XML-like tags that can be used for extracting content from the VFS and displaying it inside pages. Almost every JSP template will need to import the OpenCms taglib.

Most of the template is simply HTML. Only the tags prefaced with cms are interpreted by the JSP engine. The rest are sent 'as-is' to the client. In this template, I've only used two taglib elements. The <cms:property/> tag was used twice: once to include the title of the page as the contents of the HTML <title/> element, and once to include the title of the page inside the <h1/> element. Let's take a closer look at that tag:

```
<cms:property name="title" escapeHtml="true"/>
```

The element name <cms:property/> specifies that the JSP interpreter should use the element property from the OpenCms taglib. The property element provides access to the properties of a document (see the discussion of properties in the previous chapter). The name attribute indicates that the property we want to access is named title. Finally, escapteHtml="true" instructs the JSP interpreter to escape any HTML tags that exist in that property. For instance, if the title of the page was 'Using the <pre/> tag', it would be converted to 'Using the >pre/< tag'. This prevents a case of accidentally interpreting the contents of a property as HTML.

> You can view all the properties for a file by locating the file in the explorer view, clicking on the file's icon, and selecting Properties from the popup menu.

The other tag is the <cms:include/> tag:

```
<cms:include element="body"/>
```

This tag takes the contents of a named element from the page's XML file and places it into the template. Each file in the VFS is stored inside a special XML file that describes the document. Page documents (remember, **page** is a specific type of document, different from plain, XML template, and JSP) actually have two separate XML files—one contains XML template control code, and the other contains the page's content. This <cms:include/> tag reads the XML file and puts the contents of the body element into the JSP template. Every page is automatically given an element with the name body—the WYSIWYG and sourcecode editors both edit the body section by default.

For example, in the previous chapter, we created /playground/index.html. Navigate to the /playground/ directory and left-click on the icon for index.html. Click on Edit Control Code (near the bottom of the popup menu) to view the XML data for the index.html file.

It should look something like this:

```
<?xml version="1.0" encoding="UTF-8"?>
<PAGE>
    <class>com.opencms.template.CmsXmlTemplate</class>
    <masterTemplate>/system/modules/com.example.site/templates
     /example-page-template.xml</masterTemplate>
    <ELEMENTDEF name="body">
        <CLASS>com.opencms.template.CmsXmlTemplate</CLASS>
        <TEMPLATE>/system/bodies/playground/index.html</TEMPLATE>
    </ELEMENTDEF>
</PAGE>
```

The `<ELEMENTDEF/>` element's `name` attribute is set to `body`. The `<elementdef/>` section contains two items: a `<class/>` that points to the code that reads page contents, and a `<template/>` that points to the location of the actual text of the body. The file referenced in the `<template/>` element is also an XML document that looks something like this:

```
<?xml version="1.0" encoding="UTF-8"?>
<XMLTEMPLATE>
    <TEMPLATE><![CDATA[
      <p>This is the <em>index page</em> for my playground.</p>
    ]]></TEMPLATE>
<edittemplate><![CDATA[
    <P>This is the <EM>index page</EM> for my playground.</P>
]]></edittemplate>
</XMLTEMPLATE>
```

Like the control-code template, this is a simple XML template document. It contains two sections: `<template/>` and `<edittemplate/>`, and each contains a `CDATA` section that, in turn, contains HTML.

> A `CDATA` section, XML markup that begins `<![CDATA[` and ends with `]]>`, demarcates content that should not be interpreted by the XML parser. In this case, it is used to prevent the XML parser from trying to interpret HTML tags.

You have probably noticed already that the two elements are almost identical. The contents of the `<edittemplate>` element are used by the editors (both the WYSIWYG and the sourcecode editor). Once content has been entered through an editor, OpenCms runs the results through JTidy (`http://jtidy.sourceforge.net`), an HTML syntax checker and pretty printer. The cleaned-up code is placed into the `<template>` element, which is then used to populate templates. You can see (in the example above) that the elements in `<edittemplate>` are in uppercase (as generated by the WYSIWYG tool). This is a violation of the HTML 4.01 specification, which states that HTML elements must be lowercase. The contents of the `<template/>` element, which have been run through JTidy, have been corrected to lower case.

In summary, when the JSP tag `<cms:include element="body"/>` is run, OpenCms opens the control-code XML file for the resource, finds the `<elementdef/>` whose `name` is body, and then executes the code in the <class> element on the file in the <template> element, which in turn returns the contents of the <template> element for the correct file in the /system/bodies/ directory. Fortunately, all we need to worry about is *where* to put the <cms:include/> tag in the JSP, as everything else is done automatically by OpenCms.

Now we're ready to test the templates by associating a page with the new template.

Associating a Page with the New Template

With the XML template and the JSP template created, we can assign a piece of content, a page, with the new template and test it out. Navigate to the /playground/ directory and open the index.html file in one of the editors. From the Template drop-down list in the top-right corner, select your new template. Save and close the document.

In the explorer view, click on the name of the file, and a preview of the document (rendered in the new template) will open in a new window. The code from the examples above produces a simple page that looks like this:

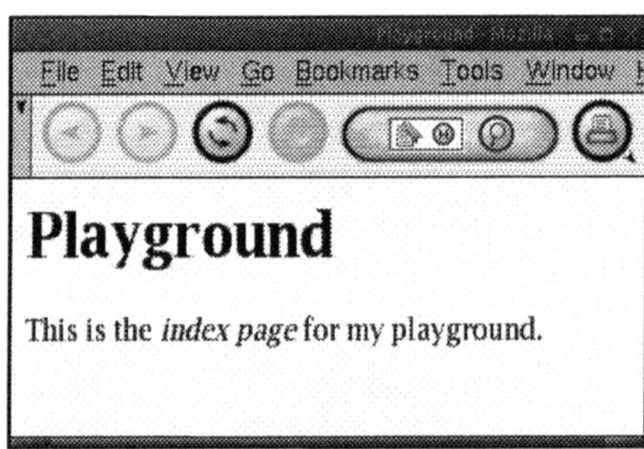

Here is the HTML output generated by the template engine:

```
<!DOCTYPE html public "-//W3C//DTD HTML 4.01 Transitional//EN">
<html>
<head>
  <title>Playground</title>
</head>
<body>
  <h1>Playground</h1>
  <p>This is the <em>index page</em> for my playground.</p>
</body>
</html>
```

Compare this to the JSP template, and you will see how the <cms:property> and <cms:include> elements were replaced with content from the /playground/index.html file. We have successfully created a new template. Now we will move on and talk about the taglib and JSP scriptlets in more detail.

JSP Tag Libraries and Scriptlets

Already we've examined a basic example of using JSP in OpenCms. This section will discuss JSP technology and the OpenCms tag libraries and APIs.

Essentially, there are two ways of writing JSP pages. The first is to leverage tag libraries to provide all of the functionality required in a page. In this case, a JSP page looks, for the most part, like an HTML page with some extra tags. Most of the page functionality is kept separate in Java classes, and the JSP deals simply with look-and-feel issues. Because this method of development strives to implement the **Model-View-Controller** (**MVC**) design pattern, Sun actively promotes this as the preferred way of developing JSPs. Also, since JSP taglibs look like HTML tags, HTML programmers can use them without needing to know anything about the complexities of Java code.

The second method of writing JSPs (and this method can be interlaced with the first) is to embed scriptlets—small bits of Java code—inside special JSP tags. At run time, these sections of code are compiled and executed like regular Java code. Scriptlets provide a way of embedding significant logic, with access to Java class libraries, inside JSPs. While scriptlets are considered a violation of the MVC pattern, they work particularly well within the OpenCms model of development. Scriptlets can be created and edited within the OpenCms VFS, and can be componentized and easily reused by multiple pages. Developing full-blown Java classes can be a little tedious in OpenCms, as each class must be imported into the VFS and the Tomcat process restarted in order to use the new classes. In contrast, scriptlets can be written quickly and debugged on the fly, without having to restart OpenCms. A word of warning: JSP scriptlets can become inefficient and difficult to work with when they are used for significantly complex programming, and this can cause huge headaches in larger projects. Typically, JSP scriptlets also take more time to load and execute. OpenCms, however, has mitigated this problem with the FlexCache, which we will discuss later in the chapter.

How should each be used, then? For purely pragmatic reasons, I would propose the following considerations for answering this question:

- Templates should use only tags (with the occasional exception of conditional logic, which should be kept to a minimum). If a template requires scriptlet functionality, the scriptlet should be created in a separate JSP (usually stored in the `elements/` directory of a module) and included, using `<cms:include/>`, into the template.
- Scriptlets should be used to encapsulate small portions of script-like (procedural) functionality. Since scriptlets will be included into other files, they should not be too context dependent. Scriptlets should not be used to encapsulate complex logic or descriptive code—such functionality should be moved to Java class files. When you start adding methods to JSPs, it is a good sign that you should migrate code to Java class files.

- Full-blown Java class files should be used for any significantly complex logic. Additionally, structured data that can be expressed as an object ought to be expressed as an object. For significantly complex and useful code, you may want to consider creating beans and taglibs that can be easily used in JSPs.

Breaking things up in this way should provide a good balance between clean structure and efficient development. It should also facilitate reuse of code between multiple pages, projects, and sites.

The rest of this section will be devoted to using the OpenCms tag library and scriptlet API. This will enable us to create templates and scriptlets, and will prepare us for creating complex modules, the topic of Chapter 6, *Creating an OpenCms Module*.

> If you set `flex.cache.offline` to `true` in `$CATALINA_HOME/webapps/opencms/WEB-INF/config/opencms.properties`, the results of your JSP pages will get cached. This greatly improves speed for the Offline project, but it can be very frustrating for debugging, as the JSP is not recompiled each time it is changed. You may want to set the directive to `false` while you develop JSPs.

JSP Tag Libraries

JSP tag libraries use XML-like (or HTML-like) element syntax for including dynamic functionality in a document. Core JSP tags use a special syntax, characterized by the use of the percent sign (%), to delimit core JSP elements from HTML elements. For example, the JSP page directive from the JSP template in the last section looked like this: `<%@ page session="false" %>`. A JSP expression, a Java statement that is converted to a string and automatically printed, also uses a percent sign. The following JSP expression, for example, prints out the date and time:

```
<p>Right now, it is <%= new java.util.Date() %></p>
```

Recent developments in JSP technology, especially in version 1.2, encourage moving from the original JSP percent-style tag format to an XML-compliant syntax. Core tags have been redefined to use XML namespaces, using the `jsp` prefix instead of the percent-style notation. Here's an example that rewrites both of the aforementioned tags in the new XML syntax:

```
<jsp:root xmlns:jsp="http://java.sun.com/JSP/Page" version="1.2">
  <jsp:directive.page session="false"/>
  <html>
  <head><title>Test XML Syntax</title></head>
  <body>
    <p>Right now it is:
      <jsp:expression>new java.util.Date()</jsp:expression>.
    </p>
  </body>
```

```
  </html>
</jsp:root>
```

The first element, `<jsp:root>`, declares the XML namespace for JSP, as well as the JSP version that is to be used. The `<%@ page %>` tag discussed above has been rewritten as `<jsp:directive.page/>`, and the `<%= %>` expression has been rewritten as the `<jsp:expression>` element. The example works perfectly in OpenCms 5.0, but this is not the case with all XML-style JSP tags.

In the *Flex Cache administration* section in the previous chapter, I pointed out that the FlexCache mechanism stores JSP pages on the real file system, as well as the VFS, so that those pages can be executed by the servlet engine. When these files are moved from the VFS to the local file system, OpenCms must replace VFS path information with absolute file-system paths. To accomplish this, OpenCms scans the JSP files, replacing paths in tags that it thinks need replacement. However, this scanning mechanism does not understand all of the JSP tags—in particular, it does not understand any of the XML-style JSP tags. It ignores any tag that it does not understand. The consequence is that XML-style tags that need path translation will be ignored. I will try to point out particular instances of this as we go through examples, and I will show examples of XML syntax when appropriate. But be careful: if you choose to use the XML-style JSP syntax, be wary of tags that reference file-system paths.

The OpenCms Tag Library

The OpenCms tag library is a built-in component of OpenCms. It provides access to the data managed by OpenCms and provides basic functions for presenting OpenCms data in a template. To begin this examination of the OpenCms tag library, we will return to the JSP template we created in the last section.

The JSP Template

Our original template simply printed the title and included the body of the requested page. This worked fine for our examples, but we can make the template much more versatile with a few extensions, making it useful for JSP pages, as well as pages.

To do this, we must break the template up into pieces that can be identified and selectively used by a JSP. In our first example, there was no way to address a particular part of the template. JSPs that utilize a template need to be able to identify where the top (head) of the template should go, and where the bottom (foot) should go. Here is our previous example partitioned into a header, body, and footer.

```
<%@ page session="false" %>
<%@ taglib prefix="cms"
  uri="http://www.opencms.org/taglib/cms" %>
<cms:template element="head">
  <html>
```

```
    <head>
      <title>
        <cms:property name="title" escapeHtml="true"/>
      </title>
    </head>
    <body>
      <h1>
        <cms:property name="title" escapeHtml="true"/>
      </h1>
</cms:template>
<cms:template element="body">
  <cms:include element="body"/>
</cms:template>
<cms:template element="foot">
  </body>
  </html>
</cms:template>
```

As you can see, there are three `<cms:template>` sections: `head`, `body`, and `foot`. Each of these sections can be called by name from a `<cms:include/>` tag. When processing pages, OpenCms reads through the template file in order, applying each template as it is encountered (that means if you defined `foot` before defining `head`, the `foot` would be printed before the `head`). None of the sections are added by default to a document of any other type besides page. You can specify additional template elements in their own `<cms:template>` sections. For instance, I could define a template element called `hello` that contained a short message.

```
<cms:template element="hello"><p><b>Hello!</b></p></cms:template>
```

While it would show up by default in any pages, it would be accessible to JSPs with a separate include. This mechanism allows you to conditionally apply template elements in JSPs that are automatically applied to page documents.

Before moving on to creating JSP documents, I wanted to illustrate the differences between the old-style JSP syntax and the new XML style. Here is the same template written in the XML syntax:

```
<?xml version="1.0"?>
<jsp:root
  xmlns:jsp="http://www.sun.com/JSP/Page"
  version="1.2"
  xmlns:cms="http://www.opencms.org/taglib/cms">
<jsp:directive.page session="false" />
<cms:template element="head">
  <![CDATA[
  <html>
  <head>
  <title>
  ]]>
  <cms:property name="title" escapeHtml="true"/>
  <![CDATA[
  </title>
  </head>
  <body>
    <h1>
```

```
    ]]>
    <cms:property name="title" escapeHtml="true"/>
    <![CDATA[</h1>]]>
  </cms:template>
  <cms:template element="body">
    <cms:include element="body"/>
  </cms:template>
  <cms:template element="foot">
    <![CDATA[
    </body>
    </html>
    ]]>
  </cms:template>
  </jsp:root>
```

Using XML syntax changes the behavior of the JSP parser—the parser now expects that the document is well-formed XML. That means that the overlapping construct `<jsp:tag1><tag2></jsp:tag1></tag2>` is illegal, and will cause exceptions. Since the template defines the `head` and the `foot` in separate areas of the document, each inside a `<cms:template>` element (a syntactical error similar to the example I just gave), it is necessary to encapsulate the offending HTML in `<![CDATA[ ]]>` sections. Escaping all the HTML in CDATA sections is unwieldy and certainly makes the templates harder to read. For that reason, you may prefer to use the older style (with the `%` notation) for the main templates even if you use the XML style for the rest of your templates. Both styles work fine, and you are free to choose that which suits your needs and preferences.

Creating a JSP Document

Now that our JSP template is complete, we can create a JSP document that utilizes that template. Create the document `/playgound/cms-info.jsp`. Make sure you give it a title and description.

Unlike page documents, JSPs do not require templates. In fact, there is not even a template chooser drop-down list such as the one in the page editors. Hence, to associate a template with our new JSP, we need to edit the file's properties. Before opening the new file in the editor, click on the file's icon and choose **properties** from the popup menu. Notice that there is no template property in the select box. Click **New** to add a new property. Select **template** from the select box, and in the text field labeled **Enter property value**, type the path to the JSP template (e.g. `/system/modules/com.example.site/jsptemplates/example-page-template.jsp`). When you click **Ok**, you should see the new **template** property and the full path to the template in the select box. Click **Ok** again to exit the property dialogue, and then open the file in the sourcecode editor.

We will start by creating the basic framework for the page.

```
<%@ page session="false" %>
<%@ taglib prefix="cms"
  uri="http://www.opencms.org/taglib/cms" %>
```

```
<cms:include property="template" element="head"/>
<!-- Body goes here. -->
<cms:include property="template" element="foot"/>
```

The page begins with the typical JSP declarations in which we import the `cms` taglib. Since we have a template property defined, we can selectively access the elements in that template. The `<cms:include/>` tags import the `head` and `foot` elements (respectively) from the template, including their contents at the beginning and end of the document. I have left the `<!-- Body goes here. -->` comment to indicate where we will place the content of the JSP.

Next, we will include some information about this file. The `<cms:property/>` tag gives us access to any of the properties associated with the file. For instance, we can access the `template` property that we just set.

```
<p>This file uses the template <cms:property name="template"/></p>
```

In fact, we are not strictly limited to the file at hand. Here's how we could grab the title property from the `index.html` page in the same directory:

```
<cms:property file="index.html" name="title"/>
```

Since we are referring to the `index.html` file anyway, we might as well provide a link to it. Any time you create a link to a file in OpenCms, you must make sure that it is mapped correctly to the VFS. Rather than try to translate things when creating the link, use `<cms:link/>`.

The `<cms:link/>` element is simple in and of itself. It has no attributes, and contains only the filename it will expand. For example, `<cms:link>index.html</cms:link>` generates the full path of the `index.html` file. In old-style JSP, a hyperlink with a corrected path would look like this:

```
<p>
Go to <a href="<cms:link>index.html</cms:link>">
<cms:property file="index.html" name="title"/></a>
</p>
```

However, in the XML syntax, things get a bit trickier, as nested XML elements are not allowed. The same example would have to be rewritten as follows:

```
<p>Go to <![CDATA[ <a href="]]>
    <cms:link>index.html</cms:link><![CDATA[">]]>
    <cms:property file="index.html" name="title"/>
    <![CDATA[</a>]]>
</p>
```

The ugly CDATA sections have returned! The best temporary workaround is, alas, to create the link in a scriptlet. Alternatively, a simple module could provide a taglib that generates a hyperlink with the VFS link correction done implicitly. The dire situation of XML syntax will probably be rectified when the JSP 2.0 specification becomes widely adopted, as the 2.0 version includes support for including attribute information with **Expression Language (EL)** accessors.

Another useful JSP element is the `<cms:user/>` tag. The `<cms:user/>` tag provides access to information about the current user.

```
<h2>User Info</h2>
<p>The current user is <cms:user property="name"/>.</p>
<p>The current group is <cms:user property="group"/>.</p>
```

The `property` attribute determines which user information will be returned by the `<cms:user/>` tag. The available properties are:

- `name`
- `group` (or `currentgroup`)
- `defaultgroup`
- `firstname`
- `lastname`
- `email`
- `street`
- `zip`
- `city`
- `description`
- `otherstuff`

The `otherstuff` value is not particularly useful. It is actually an unformatted dump of the contents of the `java.util.Hashtable` that stores extra user information.

The last tag that we will cover in the OpenCms taglib is the `<cms:info/>` tag, which returns information about OpenCms, the Java VM, and the underlying operating system. Syntactically, it is almost identical to `<cms:user/>`. Here is an example that prints out the vital information about the platform:

```
<h2>System Info:</h2>
<p>The requested URL is <cms:info property="opencms.url"/></p>
<p>Currently, you are running OpenCms
  <cms:info property="opencms.version"/> with the
  <cms:info property="java.vm.vendor"/>
  <cms:info property="java.vm.name"/> version
  <cms:info property="java.vm.version"/> on
  <cms:info property="os.name"/>,
  <cms:info property="os.version"/>
  (<cms:info property="os.arch"/>).</p>
```

On my system, it prints out something like the following:

```
The requested URL is
http://127.0.0.1:8080/opencms/opencms/playground/cms-info.jsp
Currently, you are running OpenCms 5.0.1 Kaitain with the Sun
Microsystems Inc. Java HotSpot(TM) Client VM version 1.4.2_02-b03 on
Linux, 2.4.20-gentoo-r5 (i386).
```

In addition to information about the platform, `<cms:info/>` provides a wealth of information about paths and URIs, and can be very useful for constructing links.

At this point, we have walked through the basics of the OpenCms taglib. In your JSP development, you may find it useful to install the **OpenCms JSP Taglib Documentation** Alkacon documentation module. For more information, see the section on modules in the last chapter. To close this section, here is the final result of the JSP I created in this section:

```
<%@ page session="false" %>
<%@ taglib prefix="cms" uri="http://www.opencms.org/taglib/cms" %>
<cms:include property="template" element="head"/>
<h2>Property Info:</h2>
<p>This file uses the template <cms:property name="template"/></p>
<p>Go to <a href="<cms:link>index.html</cms:link>">
  <cms:property file="index.html" name="title"/></a>
</p>
<h2>User Info</h2>
<p>The current user is <cms:user property="name"/>.</p>
<p>The current group is <cms:user property="group"/>.</p>
<p>Otherstuff is <cms:user property="otherstuff"/>.</p>
<h2>System Info:</h2>
<p>The requested URL is <cms:info property="opencms.url"/></p>
<p>Currently, you are running OpenCms
  <cms:info property="opencms.version"/> with the
  <cms:info property="java.vm.vendor"/>
  <cms:info property="java.vm.name"/> version
  <cms:info property="java.vm.version"/> on
  <cms:info property="os.name"/>, <cms:info property="os.version"/>
  (<cms:info property="os.arch"/>).</p>
<cms:include property="template" element="foot"/>
```

JSP Scriptlets

Instead of the HTML-like structure of JSP taglibs, scriptlets are written in Java. In some ways, it is similar to a server-side scripting language like PHP or ASP. But it isn't just a scripting language based on Java. It is, in fact, Java code. When it is first run, it is actually compiled into a servlet.

While scriptlets are made up of Java code, you do not have to be a Java guru to be able to write them. Since scriptlets don't define objects and rarely create methods, the actual process of writing a scriptlet bears more similarity to writing JavaScript than writing Java objects. If you are altogether new to Java and JSP, you may find it useful to read up on Java before writing scriptlets. While there are plenty of good technical books on the subject, you may find the best starting point to be the tutorials at `http://java.sun.com/developer/onlineTraining/index.html`.

In this part, we'll look at using scriptlets to deal with more complex UI issues (like creating menus), as well as adding functional elements to templates and JSP documents.

Basic Scriptlets

Like taglibs, scriptlets are embedded into pages with special tags. The same two styles—original and XML—are applicable to scriptlets. Here is an example of the original JSP syntax for scriptlets:

```
<%@ page session="false" import="java.util.Date" %>
<%
/*
 * This gets the date.
 */
 Date today = new Date();
%>
<html>
<head>
  <title>Test JSP Scriptlet</title>
</head>
<body>
<p>Right now it is <%= today %>.</p>
</body>
</html>
```

The page element is slightly different than in previous examples. Here, it includes an attribute named `import`. This attribute works like the standard `import` line in a Java class file. It makes the class `java.util.Date` accessible to the scriptlet as `Date`. (Like regular Java, you can still reference a non-imported class by supplying the full class name.) The first JSP section, which begins with <% and ends with %>, creates a new `Date` variable, `today`. A few lines down, the <%= `today` %> line writes the value of the variable `today` into the document. Essentially, using <%= `today` %> is the same as writing <% `out.println(today.toString());` %>. The equals sign (=) instructs the JSP interpreter to convert the object to a `String` and print it. Most of the action in JSP scriptlets occurs within <% and %> tags.

For reference, here is the example above rewritten in the XML syntax.

```
<jsp:root xmlns:jsp="http://java.sun.com/JSP/Page" version="1.2">
<jsp:directive.page session="false" import="java.util.Date" />
<jsp:scriptlet>
<![CDATA[
 /*
  * This gets the date.
  */
  Date today = new Date();
]]>
</jsp:scriptlet>
<html>
<head>
  <title>Test JSP Scriptlet</title>
</head>
<body>
<p>Right now it is <jsp:expression>today</jsp:expression>.</p>
</body>
</html>
</jsp:root>
```

Note that the <% %> section has been replaced with <jsp:scriptlet><![CDATA[ ]]></jsp:scriptlet> and the <%= %> has been replaced with a <jsp:expression/> element. The use of a <![CDATA[ ]]> section is not strictly necessary in this case, but it is good practice. Scripts that make use of common operators, such as > (greater-than), < (less-than), -- (decrement), and ! (not) will require the CDATA section.

The CmsJspActionElement Object

OpenCms provides an **Application Programming Interface (API)** for accessing OpenCms Java objects from JSP applications. All of the functions available through the JSP taglib are also available through the JSP API. In addition, there are objects that facilitate creating navigation, interacting with the OpenCms servlet, and accessing lower-level OpenCms objects.

The main class for developing OpenCms scriptlets is `com.opencms.flx.jsp.CmsJspActionElement`. To use it, import it into the page and execute its `init()` method.

```
<%@ page session="false"
  import="com.opencms.flex.jsp.CmsJspActionElement" %>
<%
CmsJspActionElement cms = new CmsJspActionElement();
cms.init( pageContext, request, response );
String requestURL = cms.info( "opencms.url" );
String title = cms.property( "title" );
String user = cms.user( "name" );
%>
<html>
<head>
  <title>Test JSP Scriptlet</title>
</head>
<body>
<p>You are logged in as <%= user %></p>
<p>The current page is <%= title %>
with the URL <%= requestURL %>.</p>
</body>
</html>
```

The page tag imports the `CmsJspActionElement` class. The scriptlet begins by creating a new `CmsJspActionElement`, named `cms`, and then it executes the `init()` method. The variables `pageContext` (an instance of `javax.servlet.jsp.PageContext`), `request` (`javax.servlet.http.HttpServletRequest` or a subclass), and `response` (`javax.servlet.http.HttpServletResponse` or a subclass) that are passed into `init()` are variables that the JSP engine always makes accessible to scriptlets.

Once `cms` is initialized, we use the `info()`, `property()`, and `user()` methods just like we did in the taglib examples before. The information returned from those three methods (`String` objects in all cases) is stored in the `requestURL`, `title`, and `users` variables respectively. In the following HTML segment, all three are printed. The resulting HTML looks like this:

```
<html>
<head>
  <title>Test JSP Scriptlet</title>
</head>
<body>
<p>You are logged in as Admin</p>
<p>The current page is Example of a Scriptlet
with the URL
http://127.0.0.1:8080/opencms/opencms/playground/scriptlet.jsp.
</p>
</body>
</html>
```

OpenCms Navigation

So far, all we've done is re-implement something we could do already with the taglib. Now we will turn our attention to solving a problem that every website creator must deal with: site navigation. A component that offers navigation could be used by a number of different resources—especially templates. So, we will create our navigation scriptlet, `example-navigation.jsp`, in `/system/modules/com.example.site/elements/`, where it can be easily accessed by templates and other JSPs.

```
<%@ page session="false"
  import="java.util.Iterator,
          java.util.ArrayList,
          com.opencms.flex.jsp.CmsJspNavBuilder,
          com.opencms.flex.jsp.CmsJspNavElement,
          com.opencms.flex.jsp.CmsJspActionElement"
%>
<%
/*
 * Provides basic site navigation.
 */
// Instead of using the default constructor and init(), we
// can use this constructor:
CmsJspActionElement cms =
  new CmsJspActionElement( pageContext, request, response );

// Get navigation info
CmsJspNavBuilder navigation = cms.getNavigation();
ArrayList navItems = navigation.getNavigationForFolder();
Iterator i = navItems.iterator();

// Loop through all of the items in the ArrayList and print the
// menu.
while( i.hasNext() ) {
  CmsJspNavElement navElement = ( CmsJspNavElement )i.next();
  String link = cms.link( navElement.getResourceName() );
  String title = navElement.getTitle();
  out.println("<a href=\"" + link + "\">" + title + "</a><br/>");
}
%>
```

This piece of code gets the navigation for the current page—it builds the menu from the other pages in the same folder. The `import` attribute in the page tag is significantly longer. Note that the classes are separated by commas. The line break between imported classes is cosmetic, but the comma is required. In addition to the `CmsJspActionElement` and the two familiar `java.util` classes, we are also importing the `CmsJspNavBuilder` and `CmsJspNavElement` classes. The `CmsJspNavBuilder` class collects and orders all of the navigation elements, while the `CmsJspNavElement` class contains information about each navigational element.

Next, we create and initialize a new `CmsJspActionElement` (named `cms`, as before). Note that I use a different constructor in this example. This constructor takes the `pageContext`, `request`, and `response` parameters, and initializes the object—there is no need to run the `init()` method.

Now that we have a handle on the `cms` object, we can get the `CmsJspNavBuilder` object (`navigation`) by calling `cms.getNavigation()`. From the `CmsJspNavBuilder` instance, we can get a specific set of navigational information. There are a number of `getNavigation*` methods in `CmsJspNavBuilder`, returning different views into the navigational hierarchy. We just want information on the navigable items in the current folder, and we can obtain an `ArrayList` of those items with `navigation,getNavigationForFolder()`.

The `Iterator` is used to loop through the `ArrayList`, retrieving each `CmsJspNavElement` from the list. We use the `cms.link()` method (similar to the `<cms:link/>` tag) to create a link to the resource represented in the `CmsJspNavElement`. The `navElement.getTitle()` method retrieves the `title` property for the resources described in the `CmsJspNavElement`. The final line in the `while` loop prints an HTML hyperlink tag to `out`, which is the output stream of the servlet.

> A `CmsJspNavElement` is only created for resources that are navigable. A resource is navigable if it has the two properties NavPos and NavText in its properties list. You can change navigation order by clicking on the file's icon in the explorer view and choosing **Change navigation** from the popup menu. Alternately, you can edit the NavPos and NavText properties directly by choosing **properties** from the popup menu.

To use this new element, we must include it into another file. We will add it to the template we created in `/system/modules/com.example.site/jsptemplates/example-page-template.jsp`. Use the `<cms:include/>` tag to include the JSP in the template. Here's the slightly revised JSP template file:

```
<%@ page session="false" %>
<%@ taglib prefix="cms"
  uri="http://www.opencms.org/taglib/cms" %>
<cms:template element="head">
  <html>
```

```
<head>
  <title>
    <cms:property name="title" escapeHtml="true"/>
  </title>
</head>
<body>
  <div name="menu" style="float:left;border:1px solid gray;">
    <cms:include file="../elements/example-navigation.jsp"/>
  </div>
  <h1>
    <cms:property name="title" escapeHtml="true"/>
  </h1>
</cms:template>
<cms:template element="body">
  <cms:include element="body"/>
</cms:template>
<cms:template element="foot">
  </body>
  </html>
</cms:template>
```

The only change is the inclusion of the `<div>` element, which contains the line

```
<cms:include file="../elements/example-navigation.jsp"/>
```

Using the `file` attribute of `<cms:include/>`, we import the entire contents of the `../elements/example-navigation.jsp` file. Remember, paths in templates are relative to the location of the template itself, not the file that uses the template.

If you view the `/playground/index.html` page in the browser, it shows the navigational menu in the right-hand column (note that I used the CSS formatting `float:left` and `border: 1px solid gray` to give the menu its placement and border. That is not done automatically by OpenCms).

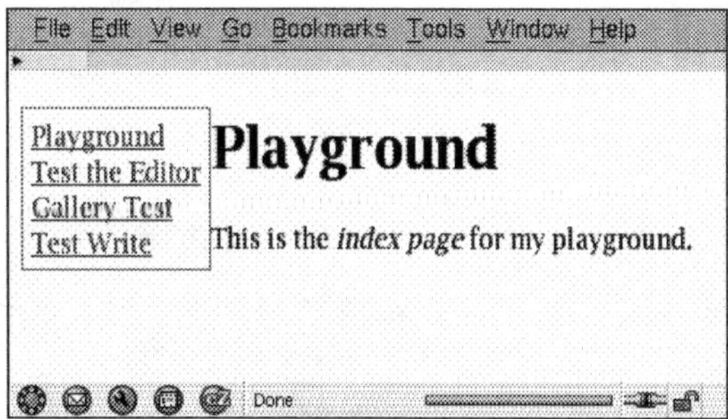

This example has only provided a basic implementation of navigation. The `CmsJspNavBuilder` is capable of building much more complex navigational structures, including depth-sensitive navigational trees.

> Just as you can import the OpenCms Java classes in a scriptlet, you can also import them into your own Java classes.

> You can, for instance, create a custom Java class to generate your own navigation, importing the OpenCms navigation objects as follows:
>
> `import com.opencms.flex.jsp.CmsJspNavBuilder;`
>
> `import com.opencms.flex.jsp.CmsJspNavElement;`

Getting the Contents of Other Files

Using the `CmsJspActionElement`, it is also possible to get the contents of other files on the system. Using this mechanism, a JSP can retrieve information from other documents, perhaps an XML or Comma-Separated Values (CSV) file, and display it as a resource. To illustrate this, we can take a simple CSV file and display its contents as a table.

To begin, we'll create a simple CSV file in the `/playground/` folder. It is not a regular piece of content. It needs to be plain text, so create it as a Plain document, not a Page document. Here are the contents of my CSV file, `/playground/simple-list.csv`.

```
NAME,TITLE,EMAIL
Matt Butcher,Boss,mbutcher@example.com
Babs Jensen,LDAP Expert,bjensen@example.com
John Doe,Everyman,jdoe@example.com
```

As with many CSV files, the first row is a comma-separated list of headers, and each additional line is a comma-separated list of values.

The next thing to do is create a scriptlet that can read the file and split the values out, printing them in a nice HTML table. Since this scriptlet might be useful for other applications, it would be a good idea to make it flexible enough for reuse and place it in the `elements/` directory of our module. Here is the CSV parser scriptlet, located in `/system/modules/com.example.site/elements/csv-parser.jsp`.

```
<%@ page import="com.opencms.flex.jsp.CmsJspActionElement" %>
<%
/*
 * Parses a CSV file and prints it in a table.
 * PARAMS:
 * csv_file: The name of the csv_file.
 */
CmsJspActionElement cms =
  new CmsJspActionElement( pageContext, request, response );
String csvFile = request.getParameter( "csv_file" );
String csvContents = cms.getContent( csvFile );
if( csvContents == null ||
    csvContents.length() == 0 ||
    csvContents.equals( "??? null ???" ) {
  out.println( "<h2>CSV file has no contents!</h2>" );
} else {
  // Split rows
  String [] rows = csvContents.split( "\n" );

  if( rows.length > 1 ) {
```

```
        // These will hold data from the CSV.
        String [] headers, items;
        int i, j; // Counters
        out.println( "<table class=\"csv-table\"><tr>" );
        // Assume first row is header info.
        headers = rows[0].split( "," );
        for( i = 0; i < headers.length; ++i ) {
          out.println( "<th>"+headers[i]+"</th>" );
        }
        out.println( "</tr>" );
        for( i = 1; i < rows.length; ++i ) {
          out.print( "<tr>" );
          items = rows[i].split( "," );
          for( j = 0; j < items.length; ++j ) {
            out.println( "<td>" + items[j] + "</td>" );
          }
          out.print( "</tr>" );
        }
        out.println( "</table>" );
      } else out.print( "No data" );
    }
    %>
```

Unlike previous examples, this scriptlet needs a parameter to function correctly. The parameter, which can be passed in either through the invoking JSP or through HTTP GET and POST variables, provides the filename (including path) to the CSV file. The scriptlet accesses parameters with the `request.getParameter()` method.

After retrieving the name of the file, the script uses the `getContent()` method of `CmsJspActionElement` to dump the contents of the file into a `String`. While you might expect `getContent()` to throw an exception if the file doesn't exist, it actually returns a `String` with the value ??? `null` ???. Since there is no method in `CmsJspActionElement` for checking if a file exists, we are stuck checking whether the file returned the ??? `null` ??? string (there *are* methods for checking for the existence of a file, but they are buried in the OpenCms API, well out of the scope of our example).

Once we have the file, the remainder of the script is run-of-the-mill code. Instead of using an industrial-strength CSV parser, such as the open source `com.Ostermiller.util.CSVParser` from `http://ostermiller.org/`, this script simply uses `String.split()` once to split the rows by `\n` characters, then again to split the comma-delimited list of values in each row. Since most CSV files (including the test file above) use the first row to store header information, the header line is read separately and written in a <th> (table header) element instead of a <td> element.

The scriptlet is complete. Now we need to create a JSP document to provide layout and tell the CSV parser which file to process. We will create a file in `/playground/` called `csv-info.jsp`. Since it is a JSP file, the `template` property needs to be set manually (see the *Creating a JSP Document* section for instructions on setting properties on files).

```
<%@ page session="false" %>
<%@ taglib prefix="cms" uri="http://www.opencms.org/taglib/cms" %>
<cms:include property="template" element="head"/>
```

```
<style>
/*
 * Make the table look pretty
 */
table.csv-table {
  border: 1px solid gray;
}
table.csv-table th {
  border: 1px dashed gray;
}
table.csv-table td {
  border: 1px solid gray;
  padding-left: 5px;
  padding-right: 5px;
}
</style>
<cms:include file="/system/modules/com.example.site/elements/csv-
parser.jsp">
  <cms:param
    name="csv_file">/playground/simple-list.csv</cms:param>
</cms:include>
<cms:include property="template" element="foot"/>
```

By now, most of the stuff in this JSP is familiar. There is a stylesheet to display borders around the table elements, but other than that, the only unique part is the small segment of code that I highlighted. It imports the `csv-parser.jsp` file with a `<cms:include />` tag. Note that while the other `<cms:include/>` tags are importing pieces of the template using the `property` attribute, this one imports the entire CSV parser JSP with the `file` attribute. Inside the `<cms:include/>` tag is the `<cms:param/>` tag. `<cms:param/>` provides a named parameter to the CSV parser. The name is specified by the `name` attribute, and the value is located between `<cms:param>` and `</cms:param>`.

> Use the `<cms:param/>` tag and `request.getParameter()` wisely. Values passed with `<cms:param/>` are put into the same parameter list as GET and POST variables. A coding mistake could leave the door open for hackers to send subversive GET or POST data to a JSP.

The example here is safe as long as the implementing JSP has the `<cms:param/>` tag specified. However, `csv-parser.jsp` has no way of determining whether the value of `csv_file` came from a JSP or a remote browser. If another JSP is implemented that loads `csv-parser.jsp`, but does not pass it a param (or relies upon GET or POST data), the script could be subverted. Consequently, data received by `getParameter()` should be treated as untrusted.

One alternative approach to passing information between JSPs is to use properties. This approach is demonstrated in the *Advanced Scriptlet Programming* section later. Another approach is to pass information in the JSP session object. See Sun's official tutorial for more information on using the session object: `http://java.sun.com/developer/onlineTraining/JSPIntro/contents.html#JSPIntro9`.

> If the `<cms:param>` is set, it always overrides the GET or POST data. In the example above, should someone attempt to send GET or POST data with the `csv_file` parameter, it would be ignored (or, rather, overwritten by the `<cms:param>`).

The output of `/playground/csv-info.jsp` looks something like this:

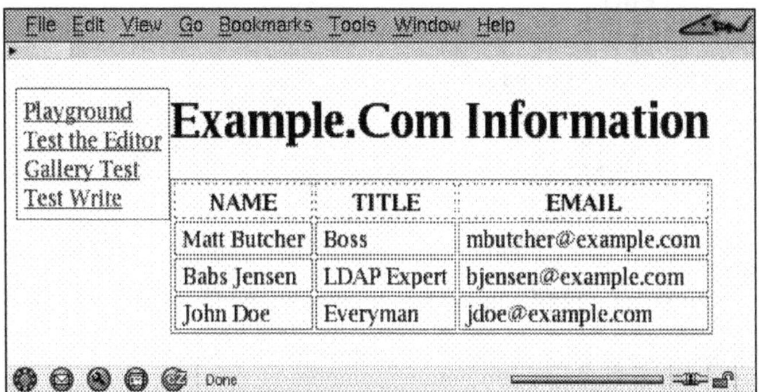

At this point, we've walked through the basics of the JSP scriptlet API provided by OpenCms. Alkacon Software, the company behind OpenCms, provides a documentation module with reference material and Javadocs for the `CmsJspActionElement`, `CmsJspNavBuilder`, and `CmsJspNavElement` classes. That module, along with all of the Alkacon documentation, is available for download from `http://www.opencms.org/opencms/en/download/modules/index.html`.

Advanced Scriptlet Programming

Most scriptlet programming can remain comfortably close to the surface, utilizing just the APIs discussed above. However, sometimes it is practical, or even necessary, to work with lower-level OpenCms objects. The risk in working with lower-level APIs is that they are more prone to change from one release to the next, but using these APIs may be the only way to get the desired functionality. While the intricacies of the OpenCms code are beyond the scope of this book, this section should get you pointed in the right direction for working with the core OpenCms libraries.

If you are planning on doing any serious development at this level, you will need the OpenCms Javadoc API documentation. Currently, it is only provided in the sourcecode release of OpenCms. See Appendix A for information about obtaining the code and building the Javadocs.

OpenCms uses a master object, `com.opencms.file.CmsObject`, to handle just about all requests. With 278 public methods, the `CmsObject` provides functionality for all core

CMS tasks and objects. Getting a handle on the `CmsObject` is the key to any significant manipulation of OpenCms. Fortunately, the OpenCms developers have made it possible to get the `CmsObject` from an instance of a `CmsJspActionElement`. The following simple script uses the `CmsObject` to print out a list of all of the items in a directory, regardless of their navigation properties. As usual, this script, named `dir-listing.jsp`, is in the `/system/modules/com.example.site/elements/` folder.

```
<%@ page session="false"
  import="com.opencms.flex.jsp.CmsJspActionElement,
          com.opencms.file.CmsObject,
          com.opencms.file.CmsFile,
          java.util.Iterator"
%>
<table class="dir-list">
  <tr><th>File Name</th><th>Size</th></tr>
<%
/*
 * Print list of files in the directory.
 * PROPERTY:
 * param_fetch_dir: Directory to examine.
 */
CmsJspActionElement cms = new CmsJspActionElement( pageContext,
                                                   request,
                                                   response );
String dir = cms.property( "param_fetch_dir" );
if( dir != null && !"".equals( dir )) {
  CmsObject cmso = cms.getCmsObject();
  Iterator i = cmso.getFilesInFolder( dir ).iterator();
  int lines = 0;
  String filename, fileURL, unit;
  int filelength;
  CmsFile file;
  while( i.hasNext() ) {
    if( lines % 2 == 0 ) out.println( "<tr class=\"color1\">" );
    else out.println( "<tr class=\"color2\">" );
    ++lines;
    file = ( CmsFile )i.next();
    filename =  file.getName();
    fileURL = cms.link( file.getAbsolutePath() );
    filelength = file.getLength();

    // print sizes in a more human-readable fashion
    unit = "Kb";
    if( filelength < 1024 ) unit = "bytes";
    else filelength /= 1024;
    out.println( "<td><a href=\""+fileURL+"\">" + filename +
                 "</a></td><td>" );
    out.println( filelength );
    out.println( unit + "</td></tr>" );
  }
} else out.println( "No directory" );
%>
</table>
```

In this example, we import two classes from the `com.opencms.file` package. The first, `CmsObject`, we've already discussed. The second, `CmsFile`, describes a file in the VFS. After creating a `CmsJspActionElement` instance, the script gets a `property` from the JSP. This property specifies which directory the scriptlet should read.

In the CSV parsing example, we passed parameters through the `<cms:param/>` tag, and the scriptlet fetched the param with the `request.getParameter()` method. If the data received can be treated as trusted, then that method of parameter passing is OK. (If I were to put the code we just saw into production on an externally visible site, I would add some regular expressions to make sure the file is a valid CSV file, and I would probably restrict the directories it could read). The preceding script, however, is printing a list of files, some of which are hidden from normal navigation. I wouldn't want a malicious user to be able to take advantage of a coding flaw and peek in any directory in the VFS. So, to increase security, this script uses properties instead of parameters. When we look at the invoking JSP in a short while, I will explain how to set this property.

After checking that the property is set, the script gets the `CmsObject` and executes the `getFilesInFolder()`, which returns a `java.util.Vector`, and then calls the `iterator()` method on the `Vector` object. Now, we have an `Iterator` full of `CmsFile` objects, each describing a file in the directory. The `while` loop iterates through the `CmsFile` objects, printing a table of file names and sizes.

```
fileURL = cms.link( file.getAbsolutePath() );
```

To create the full path for hyperlinking the file name to the file, this line of code retrieves the absolute path in the VFS file. It then uses the `cms.link()` method to get the adjusted path (relative to the web root, rather than the VFS root).

The invoking JSP, `/playground/show-dir.jsp`, displays the contents of the `/playground/` directory.

```
<%@ page session="false" %>
<%@ taglib prefix="cms" uri="http://www.opencms.org/taglib/cms" %>
<html>
<head>
  <title>Print Directory Contents</title>
  <style>
    table.dir-list {
      border: 1px solid gray;
    }
    tr {
      background-color: #ccc;
    }
    tr.color1 {
      background-color: white;
    }
```

```
      tr.color2 {
        background-color: #efefef;
      }
    </style>
  </head>
  <body>
    <cms:include
      file="/system/modules/com.example.site/elements/dir-
      listing.jsp"/>
  </body>
  </html>
```

The JSP contains nothing remarkable. It simply includes the `dir-listing.jsp` file. However, we still need to set a property, param_fetch_dir, to tell `dir-listing.jsp` which directory to read. Go to the properties dialogue (from the explorer view, click on the icon for `show-dir.jsp` and click properties from the popup menu). In the properties dialogue, press the Define properties button and create a new property called `param_fetch_dir` and click Add new.

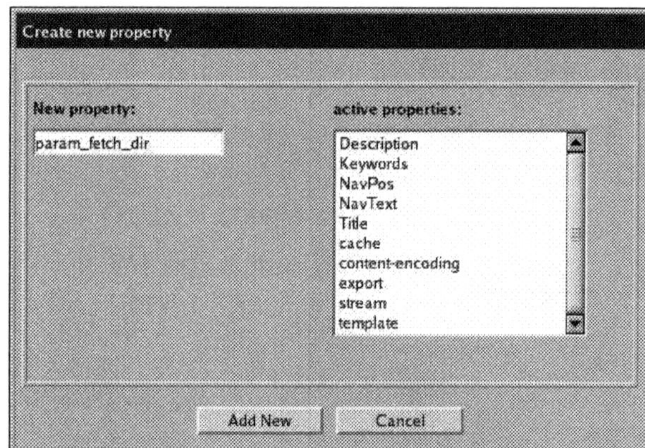

You should then return to the properties dialogue. Click New, select the param_fetch_dir property and give it the value /playground/. Once you click Ok, the property will be saved. There are a few drawbacks to using properties this way. First, maintaining properties can be tedious, as they must be managed through the property dialogue. Second, once a property is defined, it stays around. By defining param_fetch_dir for `show-dir.jsp`, we created a property name that is available to all JSPs. If you look at the Property management screen in the administration view, you will see param_fetch_dir listed under the JSP properties. In many cases, this is but a minor annoyance, but if you anticipate developing a large number of JSPs that utilize properties, be aware that the properties list can grow to be quite large.

When you load the show-dir.jsp page, it should look something like this:

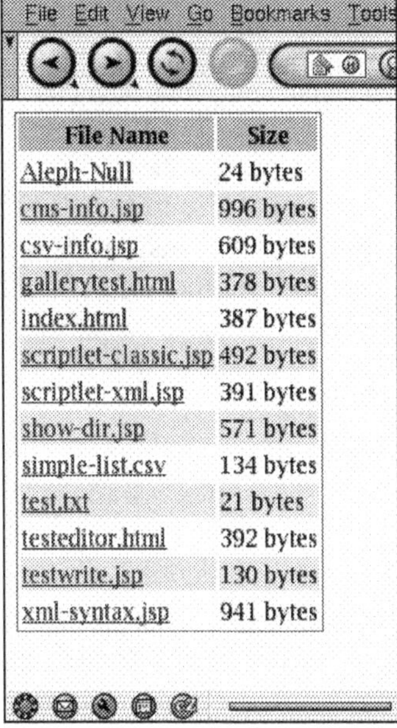

This exercise illustrates only one example of how to use the CmsObject to access information about the contents of the CMS. With access to the CmsObject, you can perform complex and low-level tasks in OpenCms.

> When one JSP, dir-listing.jsp in the example above, is included into another, show-dir.jsp, the included JSP has access to the properties of the page into which it was included. That is why the dir-listing.jsp file could access the properties of show-dir.jsp. Likewise, the JSP template file (and all of the files it includes) can access the properties of the file to which it is applied.

A Few Things to Watch Out For

Whether using the taglib or writing scriptlets, there are a few things that can cause confusion and surprise to developers new to the platform.

The File System

The VFS, in spite of its name, does not behave exactly like a real file system. Furthermore, neither the servlet engine nor the JSP interpreter is aware of the existence of the VFS. When using JSP tags, be wary of the <jsp:include/> and <jsp:directive.include/> tags (and the <c:import/> tag from the Java Standard Tag

Libraries (JSTL), if you use them). These tags do not handle the VFS/real-FS split very well, and can have some unpredictable results. According to OpenCms developers, judicious use of the `<%@ import %>` tag will work for some files, but the caveats for this tag are many, so I do not recommend it. The best way to handle inclusions is (as we have done already) to use the `<cms:include/>` tag, or the API equivalent, `CmsJspActionElement.include()`.

The built-in Java IO classes are also not aware of the VFS, and it is not possible, for example, to open a `FileReader` on a location inside of OpenCms. There should not be a need for this, as the `CmsObject` provides methods for VFS file access.

Redirecting and Forwarding

OpenCms provides a custom subclass of `HttpServlet`, and some of the behaviors of the subclass do not match what the JSP interpreter assumes. This is the case with forwarding (`<jsp:forward/>`), which simply does not work in OpenCms. In the OpenCms documentation, the recommendation is that developers attempt to use the provided taglib for handling the problem. Redirecting, however, is straightforward, and can be done in a scriptlet by executing `response.sendRedirect(location)`.

Java Synchronization

Java provides a mechanism called **synchronization**, which allows multiple threads to safely access the same object.

> The term synchronization is also used in OpenCms to describe the process of maintaining multiple copies of a resource (see the previous chapter). However, Java's use of the term synchronization refers to a code-level technology for allowing multiple threads to access the same object or objects. This one term is used to describe two very different things.

Many of the tasks performed by a CMS are sensitive to synchronization concerns—for example, to prevent overwriting or race conditions. Synchronization has always been slow in Java, and the more `Vectors` and `Hashtables` (both of which are synchronized) get created, the slower the system gets. Many times, the synchronization is justified. However, in some cases, you may need read-only access to some information (such as a directory listing) that is not particularly sensitive to immediate changes. In that case, you may find it more efficient to copy data from a synchronized class to a non-synchronized one (for instance, from a `Vector` to an `ArrayList`).

Be careful, however. Synchronization is a tricky issue, and in many cases it makes more sense to suffer slower performance rather than sacrifice data integrity.

Dynamic Content and Publishing

Development is usually done with a user that has administration privileges, and tests are often performed (as we've done so far) on the Offline project. Security settings for a visitor to the site, though, are markedly different from those of an internal administrator, and code that works during development may fail for security reasons when a visitor tries to execute it. Likewise, publishing files from the Offline project to the Online project can change expected behavior if some or all of the content is exported. When JSP pages are exported statically (not the default behavior), they will be rendered once into static HTML, and will loose all of their dynamic functionality. Likewise, hardcoded links that do not use `<cms:link/>` or `CmsJspActionElement.link()` can break or point to non-existent documents.

Obviously, the solution to this problem is to be aware of the problem, and test a lot. If you are writing scriptlets with `CmsObject`, be particularly wary of changing user info, file contents, and permissions. The Javadoc information usually includes security information, which can help avoid these problems before they crop up.

If you are doing static exports of content, make sure you test out the template code. When content is rendered as static HTML, the JSP template is rendered once, as well. In my early exposure to OpenCms, I discovered this when I included a call to `java.util.Date` in my main template. Two days after publishing my files as static resources, I realized with horror (or acute embarrassment) that the date hadn't changed since I published the project. If you are not sure about how publishing is configured on your server, look at `$CATALINA_HOME/webapps/opencms/WEB-INF/config/opencms.properties`. Chapter 8 details many of these properties, and all of them are well documented in the properties file itself.

Structuring Code and Content

OpenCms is designed to be flexible, allowing organizations to fit OpenCms to their own needs, instead of vice versa. Because of this, JSPs can get scattered around the VFS and valuable (and reusable) functionality can be lost in a labyrinth of content folders. A well designed development process, though, should not allow this to happen.

The OpenCms module structure provides an ideal mechanism for structuring code in a way that promotes reuse and organization. That is why we created a module before writing the first JSP. By structuring things wisely from the beginning, we avoided a JSP diaspora.

As a general rule, move as much JSP code, particularly that which performs useful functions, into a module. Using a site module as a 'catch all' usually works well, and if you find that a large number of scripts bear a functional similarity (e.g. a set of blogging scripts), you may decide to create a new module specifically for that set of tasks (`com.example.blog`, for instance).

As an added advantage, modules are designed to be versioned and moved, and they can vastly improve the development-to-production process. The site can be designed and developed in a module on a development server, and then exported. Then, it can be imported into the testing and production environments. Since content exists separately (outside of the module), there is no risk of losing valuable content or migrating development content into production. The built-in versioning makes it very easy to quickly ascertain the state of each server.

Other JSPs—those that just include scriptlets—should remain under the root in the main part of the file system. As in the preceding CSV example, it is good to use a simple JSP in the main file system (`/playground/csv-info.jsp`) that includes more complex elements from a module (`/system/modules/com.example.site/elements/csv-parser.jsp`). This has cosmetic and security advantages (you don't want URLs that point to the `/system` directory). It also addresses the content/functional component dichotomy by putting a content-like JSP with the rest of the content, but keeping the logic in a centralized (and developer-friendly) location.

The FlexCache

When a JSP file is executed, it is first scanned by OpenCms. All files that point to the VFS are adjusted and then resources are copied to the real file system (into `online` or `offline` under `$CATALINA_HOME/webapps/opencms/WEB-INF/jsp/`). The JSP engine then parses the files into Java sourcecode, which it compiles into servlet class files. The FlexCache mechanism caches the results of dynamic elements (e.g. navigation) to expedite subsequent requests for the same content. FlexCache uses a **Least Recently Used** (**LRU**) policy, which maintains the most requested items in the cache while bumping out items that are not requested very often. The result is that the cache doesn't get bloated with rarely requested information, and it can make an intelligent tradeoff between size and performance.

JSPs are cached individually. That is, if a JSP includes two other JSPs, all three will be cached separately. This means that one component of a page can be cached while the rest are not. Once again, it pays to keep functional elements partitioned into distinct files. In OpenCms, FlexCache primarily operates on JSP files, though future releases may make use of it for other content types as well. There is one exception to this statement, though. Other files that are included by JSPs, such as XML templates or plain text files, may also be cached in the FlexCache.

Tuning the FlexCache

In the previous chapter, we looked at the administration screen for FlexCache administration. From there, you can manage the various caches kept by FlexCache.

Additionally, the important caching parameters are tunable and can be configured in `$CATALINA_HOME/webapps/opencms/WEB-INF/config/opencms.properties`. Here is a list of the properties, along with their defaults and descriptions:

- `flex.cache.enabled` (type: boolean, default: `true`): Determines whether or not the FlexCache is used by OpenCms. Usually, you will want the FlexCache enabled.
- `flex.cache.offline` (type: boolean, default: `false`): Determines whether the FlexCache will be used to cache JSPs in the Offline project (and all of its sub-projects). When you are developing JSP pages, you probably would not want the pages cached. However, if development is complete and Offline is being used mainly for the editorial process, turning FlexCache on for Offline will speed things up for content editors. (Remember that all other projects are subprojects of the Offline project, so this effectively employs the cache for all projects except for Online.)
- `flex.cache.maxCacheBytes` (type: int, default: `2000000`): The upper limit, in bytes, that the cache can grow to. LRU pruning is used to keep the cache size down.
- `flex.cache.avgCacheBytes` (type: int, default: `150000`): Determines the threshold (in bytes) for the FlexCache to invoke LRU pruning. If the cache is bigger than `avgCacheBytes` when the FlexCache garbage collector runs, the least recently used items will be pruned from the cache. However, if the cache is smaller than `avgCacheBytes`, the cache will be left alone.
- `flex.cache.maxEntryBytes` (type: int, default: `40000`): The upper size limit, in bytes, of an object that will be allowed in the cache. Large objects are not cached.
- `flex.cache.maxEntries` (type: int, default: `4000`): The maximum number of entries that will be cached. Because of variations, there may be more entries than keys, so there is a separate parameter for specifying the upper limit of keys in the cache.

> Both byte size and entry size constraints are enforced for the cache. FlexCache uses an either/or determination—if either max byte size or max entries (or, for that matter, max keys) is reached, then the FlexCache garbage collector is run.

- `flex.cache.maxKeys` (type: int, default: `4000`): The maximum number of keys that will be stored in the cache.

- `flex.cache.forceGC` (type: boolean, default: `true`): If this is `true`, running the FlexCache garbage collector will also run the Java garbage collector, `System.gc()`. This can free up objects that were just released by the FlexCache, and thus improve performance.

When examining the cache size settings, consider the tasks that OpenCms will perform. On an individual developer's workstation, where the Online project is rarely used, it may make sense to shrink caches to free up resources. On a heavily loaded production box, it is often wise to increase cache sizes proportional to available memory.

When settings are changed in the `opencms.properties` file, you will need to restart the servlet engine so that OpenCms will pick up the changes.

FlexCache JSP Directives

The FlexCache will not cache anything by default. You will need to explicitly tag specific JSP pages that can be or ought to be cached. In OpenCms, this can be done with the `cache` property for each file.

If one JSP includes another JSP, FlexCache uses the `cache` property of each to determine whether it is cached. Hence, in the instance above, one may be cached while the other is not.

To set the cache property for a JSP, go to the explorer view and navigate to the file. Left-click on the file's icon and select Properties from the popup menu. Press New and select the cache property from the select list. Type your value in the textbox and click Ok.

There are ten different cache directives, which can be roughly categorized into four groups: absolute directives, user directives, time-sensitive directives, and URL directives. Multiple cache directives can be attached to a particular file by separating multiple parameters with commas.

The following table states each of the directives, divided by category. I will also walk through each category in detail.

Type	**Value**	**Additional Parameters**	**Example**
Absolute Directives	`always` (or `true`)		`cache: always`
	`never` (or `false`)		`cache: never`
User Directives	`user`		`cache: user`
	`groups`	List of group names (optional)	`cache: groups=(groupA,groupB)`

Time-Sensitive Directives	`timeout`	Time in minutes	`cache: timeout=30`
URL Directives	`uri`		`cache: uri`
	`params`	List of parameters (optional)	`cache: params=(id,name)`
	`no-params`	List of parameters (optional)	`cache: no-params=(page)`
	`schemes`	List of protocol schemes	`cache: schemes=(http,https)`
	`ports`	List of TCP/IP ports	`cache=(80,8080,443)`

Absolute Directives

There are two absolute directives: `always` and `never`. The `always` directive indicates that the element can always be cached. The `true` directive is a synonym for `always`. Conversely, the `never` directive (with the alias `false`) prevents an element from ever being cached. The default is `never`.

If the content will remain the same for all users who will access it, and the content rarely changes, then `always` is a good choice. For instance, the `csv-info.jsp` CSV file viewer we developed above would be a good candidate for the `always` directive; that page will rarely (if ever) change. Remember, that will not affect the caching of `csv-parser.jsp`, which will retain its own caching directive.

User Directives

User directives consider the user's configuration when caching objects. There are two such directives. The first is `user`. When `cache` is set to `user`, JSPs are cached separately for each user. This is an example of caching variations. Only one key is generated for each JSP, but variations are stored for each user.

The second directive that is based upon a user's configuration is the `groups` directive. Used without a parameter, the `groups` directive makes a separate variation for each group. Every user belongs to one or more groups, one of which is set as the default group. FlexCache uses the default group to decide *which* cached copy the user will see.

The `groups` directive can also take a list of group names. When this is specified, cache variations will only be generated for those groups, and no other group variations will be cached. A group list looks like: `groups=(administrators,developers,editors)`.

Time-Sensitive Directives

Some information can be cached for certain periods of time, but must be periodically updated. For instance, if a JSP displays the day of the month, it makes sense to serve a cached copy most of the time, checking only periodically for updates. The cache `timeout` directive provides this facility.

The `timeout` directive requires an integer indicating how many minutes to cache the JSP before updating it. For example, `timeout=60` would require the object to be updated every hour. The object is not updated when the timeout time is reached. Rather, it remains untouched till the next time it's requested, and then FlexCache refreshes and re-caches the object.

URL Directives

There are five URL directives: `uri`, `params`, `no-params`, `schemes`, and `ports`. Each of these performs caching based on a different part of the client's request.

Specifying the `uri` directive will cause the FlexCache to generate different variations depending on the path portion of the URL. This is particularly useful for components that behave differently depending on what the path of the request was. Consider the simple navigational element we constructed at the beginning of the scriptlets section. The navigation was constructed relative to the location of the requested page. While the same page always generates the same navigation info, moving to a page in a different folder would change the navigation. Setting the `cache` property to `uri` would cache different variations for the navigation menu.

The `params` directive caches variations based on the parameter string passed to the page (`http://www.example.com/opencms/opencms/show_item?id=437`). It takes an optional list of parameter names, e.g. `params=(id,name)`. If a list is specified, FlexCache caches a variation for each value of each combination of params. If no list is specified, FlexCache creates variations for all params.

Conversely, the `no-params` directive will prevent any request with a parameter from being cached. If the JSP does not have any parameters, it will be cached, but if parameters exist, the JSP will be rejected from the FlexCache. Like `params`, `no-params` takes a list of parameter names. If such a list is specified, only the requests containing the specified params will be denied by FlexCache. In other words, the list identifies *which* params should not be cached.

The `schemes` directive causes FlexCache to create variations depending on the protocol portion of the URL (e.g. `http://` or `https://`). If a list of schemes is provided, only requests from those schemes will be cached. For instance, to prevent pages requested over `https://` (HTTP encrypted over SSL) from being cached, specify `schemes=(http)`.

Finally, the ports directive causes a new variation to be generated for each port. Standard HTTP servers listen on port 80 by default. However, complex configurations may necessitate using multiple ports. A server administrator may decide, for instance, to have the web server listen on one port for internal editors and another port for public use. In this case, the ports directive would create different variations depending on the destination port in the URL. You may specify a list of ports whose requests FlexCache will allow to be cached. For instance, given the directive ports=(8080) and a server listening on 80 (standard) and 8080, the JSP resulting from the request http://www.example.com:8080/opencms/opencms/show_item.jsp will be cached, while the results of http://www.example.com/opencms/opencms/show_item.jsp (which comes over port 80) will not.

Controlling the Cache with URL Parameters

For users with administrator privileges, OpenCms will process a special set of cache commands received in parameters. This provides a quick and dirty way of testing the cache. For instance, if caching is turned on for the Offline project, and you want to view a page as rendered from the cache, and then compare it to a non-cached version, you could do this by using two URLs.

Cached version (assuming that this page is already cached):
http://www.example.com/opencms/opencms/get_item.jsp

Non-cached version:
http://www.example.com/opencms/opencms/get_item.jsp?_flex=nocache

The _flex=nocache parameter instructs OpenCms to not use the cached copy, though the cached copy will remain untouched in the FlexCache. There are a couple other values that the _flex parameter will take:

- clearcache: Clears all keys and variations for the requested URL and its included elements from the cache.
- clearvariations: Clears just the variations of the requested URL and its included elements, but keeps the keys.
- purge: Clears everything from the cache (not just the resources connected to the current URL).
- recompile: Recompiles the requested JSPs (including includes) and then replaces the currently cached version with the recompiled version.
- nocache: Ignores the cache.

Additionally, you can specify the project by specifying _flex=online or _flex=offline. For example, loading the following URL: http://www.example.com/opencms/opencms/get_item.jsp?_flex=purge&_flex=offline will purge only the Offline project.

Using FlexCache

FlexCache is a powerful mechanism for boosting the performance of OpenCms. However, unless files are tagged with the `cache` property, they will be excluded from the FlexCache. While it is often difficult at development time to determine the optimal level of caching for a given JSP, it is worth the effort to set the `cache` property before the resources are deployed to the Online project (or the production server). During development and testing, be aggressive with the cache settings—use `cache:always` and `cache:timeout` where possible. Caching elements for the home page and other often-requested documents is particularly helpful.

Internationalization

In Chapter 2, we looked at configuring character set encoding (ISO-8859-1 and UTF-8) for OpenCms. In Chapter 3, we looked at loading and using multiple languages for the Workplace. In this section, we will examine methods of creating multi-language sites using OpenCms.

While the OpenCms Workplace was designed to accommodate multiple languages, there is no formal structure to assist in developing multi-language websites. While it is possible to create multiple bodies (e.g. one for each language) in a particular page document, the properties can only be in one language. Consequently, it is usually easiest to create a separate document for each language.

The most widely deployed method of structuring multi-language sites with OpenCms is to create separate directories, one for each language, in the root directory. For instance, to host both German and English versions of my site, I would create two root-level directories: `/de/` and `/en/`. Inside these, I would place language-specific content. Ideally, each section would contain the same structure and the only difference would be the language in which the documents were written.

Modules

Modules may require support for different languages. The de facto standard for handling this in OpenCms is to create a core module (`com.example.mymodule`) and then locate the language-specific content in a second module (`com.example.mymodule.en`). The help and tutorial modules, provided by the creators of OpenCms, use this approach. Each language module, then, has its own content, and any JSP files in the `com.example.mymodule` refer to the language-specific modules for HTML pages. This approach works well if you have a lot of content in the module, or if you are developing modules for the OpenCms Workplace.

If there is not enough content to justify multiple modules, OpenCms facilitates the use of java.util.ResourceBundles for storing internationalized content. Java's support for internationalization is detailed and sophisticated, and if you are developing multi-language modules, I suggest reading about Java's internationalization (i18n) features. A good place to start is in the internationalization section of the J2SDK documentation, where you will find introductory material as well as a full-fledged tutorial (http://java.sun.com/j2se/corejava/intl/index.jsp). In this section, I will provide a simple example of using ResourceBundles to fetch language-specific information.

To begin, we need to create language-specific folders. Since we are using the /playground folder for everything right now, we might as well create our two language folders inside /playground. A production implementation would more likely put these folders in the root folder. I will create one folder for English (/playground/en/) and one for German (/playground/de/).

There are a number of ways to store information about which language a resource should be rendered into, but we'll take advantage of one of the more unique features of OpenCms, property searching, and assign each folder a property called locale, which we will set, respectively, to en and de. The locale property does not exist, so you will have to create one. See *Advanced Scriptlet Programming* earlier, for more information on creating a property.

> Java uses the ISO-639 language codes and ISO-3166 country codes. To maintain compatibility with Java, you should use these codes for the locale settings. You can access either of these standards, including the list of language and country codes, at http://www.iso.org/.

The com.opencms.file.CmsObject class supports property searching. Using property searching, an application can search through not only the properties for the current resource, but also for the file's parent folders (not, however, those of siblings). It will search up the file tree until it either finds the requested property or runs out of files to search. By taking advantage of this behavior, we will not have to tag every resource with a locale. Simply placing content in the right directories will be sufficient.

Creating ResourceBundles

Now that the directory structure is created, we will create the language resources. While it is possible to extend ResourceBundles with custom classes, we will just use the built-in java.util.PropertyResourceBundle handler, which takes its data from a Java properties file. Each language needs its own properties file, so in the /system/modules/com.example.site/classes/com/example/site/ folder, create two files: labels_en.properties and labels_de.properties.

> Java property files are accessed like class files, and must be placed in the same place that a module's Java classes belong. For that reason, the two properties files must go in the `classes/com/example/site/` subdirectory of the module.

Here is my `labels_en.properties` file:

```
# Sample resources file for English language
greeting=Good Day.
```

And my `labels_de.properties` file looks as follows:

```
# Sample resources file for German language
greeting=Guten Tag.
```

Each file defines greeting in its particular language. Note that the `PropertyResourceBundle` class assumes that the file names are created with the syntax we have used above (e.g. `[basename]_[lang].properties`). The full syntax of `ResourceBundle` names is available in the `ResourceBundle` Javadoc.

`PropertyResourceBundles` are read by the Java class loader. Consequently, like regular classes, they need to be published before they can be used. If you have not yet published your module, you will have to go to the `/system/modules/` folder, unlock the `com.example.site` folder, and then publish it (with the Publish Directly from the popup menu, or the Publish icon in explorer).

> Unpublished `PropertyResourceBundle` files cannot be used from OpenCms. You must publish the properties file before OpenCms can use them. Once published, the files are written to the real file system where the Java class loader can find them.

JSPs and ResourceBundles

Once the `.properties` files have been published, we can create a JSP file to utilize the resource bundle. Create the JSP `/system/modules/com.example.site/elements/greeting.jsp`. It will contain the following script for getting locale-sensitive strings:

```
<%@ page session="false"
import="java.util.ResourceBundle,
        java.util.PropertyResourceBundle,
        java.util.Locale,
        com.opencms.flex.jsp.CmsJspActionElement,
        com.opencms.file.CmsObject" %>
<%
  CmsJspActionElement cms =
    new CmsJspActionElement( pageContext, request, response );
  CmsObject cmso = cms.getCmsObject();
  String resource = cms.info( "opencms.request.uri" );
```

```
    Locale myLocale = Locale.ENGLISH; // default
    // true tells readProperty to look in parent properties.
    String language = cmso.readProperty( resource,
                                         "locale",
                                         true );
    if( language != null && !"".equals( language ))
      myLocale = new Locale( language );
    String bundle = "com.example.site.labels";
    ResourceBundle labels =
      PropertyResourceBundle.getBundle( bundle, myLocale );
    out.println( labels.getString( "greeting" ));
%>
```

This scriptlet displays a locale-specific message.

- First, as usual, we create a `CmsJspActionElement`. The `CmsJspActionElement` has a `property()` method, but this version of the method does not allow the recursive property checking that we want in order to fetch the folder's `locale` property. For that purpose, we need a `CmsObject`.
- With `CmsObject`, we call `cms.info("opencms.request.uri")` to retrieve the relative path to the resource in OpenCms. We need this to tell `CmsObject` which file's properties it should search.
- Java's `Locale` object describes the locale info (language, country, and variant settings). It also contains some predefined constants. `Locale.ENGLISH`, which we are setting to our default `Locale`, defines a `Locale` object with the language set to `en`.
- Next, we use the `readProperty()` method of `CmsObject` to get the value of the property named `locale` (a property we set for both the `/playground/de/` and `/playground/en/` directories). The `true` flag indicates that if `readProperty` does not find the desired property in the `resource`'s properties, it should look in the properties of each parent folder until it finds the property or hits the top of the hierarchy. If the `locale` property, stored in `language`, is found and is not an empty `String`, then a `Locale` object is created using the value of `language`.
- Next, a new `ResourceBundle` is created from the `PropertyResourceBundle.getBundle()` factory, which takes the base name of the bundle, in Java package notation, and the `Locale`, and creates a new `ResourceBundle` identified as `labels`. The `getBundle()` method will automatically append the locale information as well as the `.properties` extension.
- Finally, properties can be fetched by name with the `getString()` method of the `ResourceBundle`. The final line prints the value of the `greetings` property from the appropriate properties file.

To employ the JSP, we create `index.jsp` files in each language directory; both should look something like the following:

```
<%@ page session="false" %>
<%@ taglib prefix="cms" uri="http://www.opencms.org/taglib/cms" %>
<html>
 <head>
  <title>
   <cms:include
file="/system/modules/com.example.site/elements/greeting.jsp"/>
  </title>
 </head>
 <body>
  <h1>
   <cms:include
file="/system/modules/com.example.site/elements/greeting.jsp"/>
  </h1>
 </body>
</html>
```

When included, the `greetings.jsp` scriptlet will include the greetings property for the correct language. The body says Guten Tag when `http://127.0.0.1:8080/opencms/opencms/playground/de/index.jsp` is called. For `http://127.0.0.1:8080/opencms/opencms/playground/en/index.jsp`, it says Good Day.

The example presented here is fairly simple, but the concepts can be easily expanded to provide your modules with fairly sophisticated internationalization techniques for your JSPs. With this method, even templates can be used in a way that readily facilitates multi-language content.

Summary

In this chapter we have explored the basic methods of customizing OpenCms. We have created a basic module for containing custom code, and implemented custom templates within that module. Using the OpenCms tag libraries and scriptlet API, we have added useful functional elements to templates and documents.

We have looked at FlexCache and discovered how to control the way a JSP is cached. Finally, we looked into internationalization in OpenCms, as it pertains to JSPs as well as content. You should now be equipped with the basic tools to customize your OpenCms installation and create unique templates and applications for your site.

5

The OpenCms System Architecture

In this chapter, we will examine the structure of OpenCms, looking at the mechanisms that drive the content management system. Where appropriate, I will include Java code samples; however, the majority of the material in this chapter should be useful even if you are not a Java coder. In this chapter, I will cover:

- Resource types
- Content definitions
- The Virtual File System (VFS)
- The class structure of OpenCms

Resource Types

By now, you are familiar with the built-in resource types in OpenCms: Page, Plain, Binary, Image, JSP, and XML template. These provide generic types that are often sufficient for running CMS applications. However, it is often desirable to have more specific definitions of content. In OpenCms, there are two ways of defining custom content formats.

The first is to extend the existing resource types to include your own definition. This integrates well with the existing user interface and back-end data structure, but it is limited to content that can be treated similarly to other OpenCms types.

The second method is to add a new content definition. The OpenCms content definition API provides hooks for serving external data through OpenCms. It provides a generic framework for dealing with data that cannot be expressed well within the OpenCms VFS. While it does not impose many of the limits of resource types, it is far more complex and does not integrate well with existing CMS tools such as locking, permissions, and version control.

In this chapter, we will focus primarily on resource types, generating a new resource type for handling generic XML files. While I cover content definitions in a later section of this chapter, I have chosen not to include a full implementation of a content definition, since doing so would require lots and lots of code without offering even the basic functionality that we will see with our custom resource type.

While OpenCms often makes use of XML, there is no built-in type that facilitates storage of generic XML. The XML template type requires that the XML comply with the OpenCms XML template definition. So, we will create a new resource type, **genxml** (for 'generic XML'), which will store well-formed XML without regard for document types or schemas. In creating this, we will walk through the process of creating a new subclass of `com.opencms.file.CmsResourceType`, compiling it, inserting it into the OpenCms JAR file, and configuring OpenCms to use it. By the end of this section, we will have a new type incorporated into the Workplace and back office.

Coding a New Resource Type

The first thing to do is write the Java code for the new resource type. There are two ways of doing this. The first is to implement the `com.opencms.file.I_CmsResourceType` class. If you choose this way, make sure you also implement `java.io.Serializable` as well. All resource types must be serializable. Looking at the interface, you will notice that there are a couple dozen methods you must implement if you go this route. Implementing `I_CmsResourceType` and `Serializable` is a good choice if your content is going to diverge drastically from the basic OpenCms types. If it is not, though, a much easier approach is to extend one of the existing resource types.

A good candidate for extension is `com.opencms.file.CmsResourceTypePlain`. Since our generic XML documents will basically be formatted text files, the vast majority of the functionality of our resource type will exactly mirror that of `CmsResourceTypePlain`. In fact, we only need to override one method—the method responsible for creating new resources of this type.

```
package com.opencms.file;
import com.opencms.file.CmsResourceTypePlain;
import com.opencms.file.CmsResource;
import com.opencms.file.CmsObject;
import com.opencms.core.CmsException;
import java.util.Map;
/**
 * This class provides a generic XML (genxml) resource type.
 * It is in the com.opencms.file package due to constraints on
 * the CmsObject which it calls.
 */
public class GenericXmlResourceType extends CmsResourceTypePlain {
    public static final String C_TYPE_RESOURCE_NAME = "genxml";
    private static final String DEF_CONTENTS =
        "<?xml version=\"1.0\" ?>";
```

```
    /**
     * Creates a new "genxml" resource.
     * @param cms an instance of CmsObject
     * @param resourceName name of file in VFS
     * @param properties Hashtable of properties
     * @param contents File contents
     * @param parameter Additional information for
     * resource creation (unused)
     * @throws CmsException if there is an error with the
     * new file.
     */
    public CmsResource createResource( CmsObject cms,
                                       String name,
                                       Map props,
                                       byte[] contents,
                                       Object param)
                                       throws CmsException {
        if( contents.length == 0 ) {
            contents = DEF_CONTENTS.getBytes();
        }
        CmsResource res = cms.doCreateFile( name,
                                            contents,
                                            C_TYPE_RESOURCE_NAME,
                                            props );
        cms.lockResource( name );
        cms.writeProperty( name, C_PROPERTY_EXPORT, "true" );
        return res;
    }
}
```

The first thing to note in this class is the package. Rather than define it in our own package, as is the conventional practice in Java, we must keep this class in the `com.opencms.file` package. This is due to the fact that methods that our class accesses (namely those in `com.opencms.file.CmsObject`) are `protected`, and consequently cannot be accessed from classes outside the package. The OpenCms developers are changing the `CmsObject` and `CmsResourceType` APIs for the 6.0 release so as not to require this package constraint.

The `C_TYPE_RESOURCE_NAME` variable contains the string identifier for this class. Each resource type must have a unique resource name. The `DEF_CONTENTS` variable I defined is not necessary. It is used in the `createResource()` method to add default content. However, if you wish to leave the `contents` empty, you may do so.

As mentioned, the only method this class must override is `createResource()`. This method checks values, if necessary (here, I checked to see if `contents` is empty, adding default data if it is). Then it creates a new resource, locks it, and adds some default properties (if necessary). I only added one default property—I set export (`C_PROPERTY_EXPORT` from `com.opencms.core.I_CmsConstants`) to `true`. This sets the default export flag for genxml resources—genxml objects will be exported by default (see Chapter 8 for more on exporting). Once `createResource()` is done setting defaults, it returns the new `com.opencms.file.CmsResource`, initialized and locked.

Building the Resource Type

To compile this class, the OpenCms JAR file (`opencms.jar`) must be included in the classpath. Also, for the sake of simplicity, I want to 'unjar' the `opencms.jar` file and put my new class into the `com/opencms/file/` directory and then 'rejar' it.

One alternative to including this class in the `opencms.jar` is to place the compiled class(es) in their own JAR, and then include that JAR in the `/lib/` directory of your module. While this method of working can make debugging slightly harder (you will have multiple places to look for classes in the `com.opencms.file` package), it is more portable and doesn't require a custom `opencms.jar`.

> A tempting choice is to create a module named `com.opencms.file` and store a custom resource type in the `com.opencms.file/classes/com/opencms/file` subfolder. The problem with this method is that only one module can exist with this name, hence only one set of resource types can be added. If multiple module developers tried to implement resource types this way, there would be a namespace collision (multiple modules with the same names), and ultimately only one of the modules could be used per OpenCms instance.

Building with Ant

Here is an Ant script (`http://ant.apache.org/`) that compiles the class and then places it in the JAR:

```
<?xml version="1.0" ?>
<project name="GenericXML" default="dist" basedir=".">
    <description>
     Generic XML Build Script
    </description>
    <property name="src" location="src/"/>
    <property name="build" location="build"/>
    <property name="dist"   location="dist"/>
    <property name="docs"   location="docs"/>
    <!-- CHANGE ME: needs to point to opencms.jar -->
    <property name="opencms.libs"
        value="/home/mbutcher/opencms/lib"/>

    <!-- Jars -->
    <property name="lib.opencms"
      value="${opencms.libs}/opencms.jar" />
    <target name="init">
        <mkdir dir="${build}"/>
    </target>
    <target name="compile" depends="init"
         description="compile the source " >
        <!-- Compile the java code from ${src} into ${build} -->
        <javac srcdir="${src}" destdir="${build}"
        excludes="CVS,.svn"
        classpath="${lib.opencms}"/>
    </target>
```

```
    <target name="dist" depends="compile"
         description="rejar opencms.jar with custom file
                      package">
        <mkdir dir="${dist}/lib"/>
        <mkdir dir="${build}/opencms/"/>
        <unjar src="${opencms.libs}/opencms.jar"
               dest="${build}/opencms/"
               overwrite="false"/>
        <copy todir="${build}/opencms/com/opencms/file">
            <fileset dir="${build}/com/opencms/file"/>
        </copy>
        <jar
            jarfile="${dist}/lib/opencms-custom.jar"
            basedir="${build}/opencms"/>
    </target>
    <target name="clean"
         description="clean up" >
        <!-- Delete the ${build} and ${dist} directory trees -->
        <delete dir="${build}"/>
        <delete dir="${dist}"/>
    </target>
    <target name="doc" description="Run JavaDoc">
        <mkdir dir="${docs}"/>
        <javadoc packagenames="com.opencms.file.*"
            sourcepath="${src}"
            destdir="${docs}"
            author="true"
            version="true"
            use="true"
            windowtitle="Generic XML Library for OpenCMS">
            <doctitle><![CDATA[<h1>Generic XML Library</h1>
]]></doctitle>
        </javadoc>
    </target>
</project>
```

This build file should exist at the top level of your project. In the example, I've highlighted the one place where file path information was hardcoded. You will need to change this to suit your own configuration.

The beginning of the script simply sets all of the properties that will be used during the build process. After this, there are five targets. The `init` target handles any initialization that must be done before compiling. In this case, it just makes the build directory. After that, `compile` uses `javac` to compile the custom resource type. Note that it only requires `opencms.jar`. More complex resource types may require other JAR files or classes. If the compilation completes successfully, then `dist`, the most complex target, will be run.

After making a few necessary directories, `dist` unjars the contents of the old `opencms.jar` into the local build directory. Note that `overwrite` must be set to `false` because we will need to customize one of the OpenCms properties files in a later section. Then the new resource type is copied into the `com/opencms/file` directory of the OpenCms class tree and the whole thing is rejarred as `opencms-custom.jar`. The `clean` target removes all of the files created by `ant`, and the `doc` target runs **Javadoc.** Neither is run automatically, and each must be called explicitly (for instance, `ant doc`).

Editing the Properties Files

The opencms-custom.jar file is a replacement for opencms.jar—which contains all of the OpenCms Java classes, as well as a few properties files. Before our custom resource type is ready for use, though, we must make one change to the properties file build/opencms/com/opencms/workplace/workplace_en.properties. In this file, find the fileicon section and add the property fileicon.genxml=GenXML. If your workplace users will be using other languages, add a similar entry for each language's property file (e.g. workplace_de.properties for German language settings). We will use the fileicon.genxml property in the next section.

Once you've finished editing the properties files, run ant to rebuild opencms-custom.jar. Stop Tomcat (or whatever servlet engine you are using) and move $CATALINA_HOME/webapps/opencms/WEB-INF/lib/opencms.jar to a safe location outside the $CATALINA_HOME/webapps directory.

> Do not put the old opencms.jar in a place where Java or Tomcat might include it in the classpath. The Java classloader may use the wrong version of the classes or properties file.

Copy opencms-custom.jar into $CATALINA_HOME/webapps/opencms/WEB-INF/lib/ and start Tomcat. The next thing to do is create a new **restype** file in the VFS to tell OpenCms how to handle the new resource type.

Adding a Restype

Once Tomcat is running again, open a web browser and login to OpenCms. Navigate to /system/workplace/restypes/ and lock the file named plain. Copy plain to a new file named genxml (to copy, click on the file's icon and select copy from the popup menu). Once the new genxml file exists, open it in the sourcecode editor. This file provides OpenCms information on what actions can be performed on files of resource type genxml. Essentially, this file is used to generate dynamic JavaScript menus, and it is, in fact, just a long list of JavaScript function calls.

The first line of the file is the most important. It will look like this:

```
vi.resource[resource_id]=new res(
  "plain",
  "language_key(fileicon.plain) ",
  vi.iconPath+"ic_file_plain.gif",
  "explorer_files_new_othertype.html?initial=true&type=plain",
  true);
```

This will appear on one line in the editor, but I've added line breaks here to make it a little easier to read. We need to change this first line to be specific for genxml resource types.

- The first parameter, "plain", indicates what resource type to use. This should be changed to "genxml".
- The next parameter defines the human-readable name of the resource type, and it uses the fileicon.plain property from workplace_en.properties. Change this to fileicon.genxml to use the value we set in the last section.
- The next parameter determines which icon to put next to the file type when it appears in lists. You can use a predefined one or create your own. The directory for icons is /system/workplace/resources, and the ic_file_*.gif icons are the ones used for file icons. I created one called ic_file_genxml.gif and placed it in the /system/workplace/resources directory.
- The final parameter defines what URL is called to create a new page. In the default, all you need to change is the value of the type parameter, which should be set to genxml. For resource types that need to use a different creation page, you can use others or define your own in the /system/workplace/actions directory.

When rewritten, the line should look like this (without the line breaks):

```
vi.resource[resource_id]=new res(
  "genxml",
  "language_key(fileicon.genxml) ",
  vi.iconPath+"ic_file_genxml.gif",
  "explorer_files_new_othertype.html?initial=true&type=genxml",
  true);
```

Menu Items

The rest of the lines in the genxml file create menu items. All of them follow the same pattern. Let's look at the first one (the lock menu item) to get an idea of what is going on. Again, I have broken one line into several for the sake of readability.

```
addMenuEntry(  resource_id,
  "language_key(explorer.context.lock)",
  "lock.html?initial=true",
  "''",
  "rules_key(d d aaai dddd dddd dddd dddd)" );
```

The first parameter should always be resource_id.

The second parameter retrieves the human-readable name of the menu entry from the workplace properties files.

The third parameter is the URL for executing the menu item.

The forth, which is blank in this example, specifies the target window in the browser. OpenCms uses frames, and this parameter can specify the frame into which the URL for the previous parameter should be loaded. The most common value for this parameter, when it is set, is `"'_top'"`. It is imperative that the string for this parameter be surrounded by single-quotes (`'`) inside double quotes (").

The last parameter is the rules key.

Rule Keys

The rules key is used to determine how menu items should appear on the list. The rules are broken up into two single-flag sections and five rule sections containing four flags (From the preceding example: `d d aaai dddd dddd dddd dddd`). There are three possible flags:

- `a`: This flag means the menu item should be marked active. Active menu items will be clickable.
- `i`: This flag marks the menu item as inactive. It will be displayed in gray and will not be clickable.
- `d`: Presumably, `d` stands for 'deactivated'. Menu items marked with `d` will not be shown at all.

The first item in the list of rules determines the item's menu state in the Online project (i.e. when published). In the case of this example, the lock icon will not show up in the popup menus for the Online project. The second rule determines whether the menu should show up in the Offline project (or any sub-project) if the resource exists only in the Online project. Only a few commands ever mark this as anything other than `d`, as this is a rare state.

Each of the next five sets of keys determines highlighting states for a specific combination of lock status, lock owner, and currently active project.

- The first set (`aaai` in the example above) is used when no one has a lock on the file.
- The second set is used when the user has a lock on the file, and is in the same project in which the lock was created.
- The third set is used when someone else has a lock on the file in the same project as the current user's active project.
- The fourth set is used when the user owns the lock, but the lock was created in a different project.
- The fifth set is used when the lock is owned by another user and in a different project.

Now, each of these rules has four components. For instance, the first rule is made up of `aaai`. Each of these rules corresponds, in order, to one of the following states: **unchanged**, **changed**, **new**, **deleted**.

So, to phrase the first rule (`aaai`) in plain language, if no one has a lock on the file and the file is unchanged, changed, or new, the lock menu item will be activated. However, if the file is deleted, then the lock menu item will be grayed out and inactive.

For our purposes, we will leave all the rules as they appear, so there is no need to change any of these entries in the `genxml` file.

Adding Properties for the Resource Type

The next task is to create properties for our new file type. Go to the administration view and click Properties management. Find the section for genxml and add at least the following properties: `Title`, `Description`, `Keywords`, `export`. These four types are necessary for creating a new resource. You may add other properties as desired.

The last step in creating the new resource type is adding a short entry to the `registry.xml` file.

Editing the OpenCms Registry

In the `$CATALINA_HOME/webapps/opencms/WEB-INF/config/registry.xml` file, there is a section containing definitions for resource types, containing entries like this:

```
<restype>
    <name>plain</name>
    <launcherType>1</launcherType>
    <launcherClass/>

 <resourceClass>com.opencms.file.CmsResourceTypePlain</resourceClass>
</restype>
```

These entries tell OpenCms how to handle a request for a particular resource. The example above defines the behavior for the plain type (specified in the `<name>` element). The `<launcherType>` element indicates which launcher class should be used to load and deliver the class. Type 1, which we will use for our example, is the `com.opencms.flex.CmsDumpLoader` launcher, which simply returns the resource unchanged.

The common OpenCms launcher types are:

- 1 (`com.opencms.flex.CmsDumpLoader`): Delivers resources unchanged
- 3 (`com.opencms.flex.CmsXmlTemplateLoader`): Applies the XML template processor
- 4 (`com.opencms.launchers.CmsLinkLauncher`): Redirects to the appropriate resource
- 6 (`com.opencms.flex.CmsJspLoader`): Applies the JSP processor

In Chapter 7, we will define a custom resource launcher.

The <launcherClass> element can be used instead of <launcherType>. It requires a full classpath (e.g. com.opencms.flex.CmsDumpLoader). When it is empty, OpenCms will use the launcher specified in <launcherType>.

Finally, <resourceClass> defines the class that describes this resource type. For our example, we can just copy the contents of the <restype/> entry for plain and change the values of <name> and <resourceClass>:

```
<restype>
    <name>genxml</name>
    <launcherType>1</launcherType>
    <launcherClass/>
    <resourceClass>com.opencms.file.GenericXmlResourceType
       </resourceClass>
</restype>
```

Once you have completed the edits to the registry.xml file, restart your servlet engine. We are now ready to use the new resource type.

Using the New Resource Type

At this point, the new resource type has been added and should show up along with all of the other resource types. In the explorer view, when you click on the magic wand icon to create a new file, GenXML should be in the chooser list:

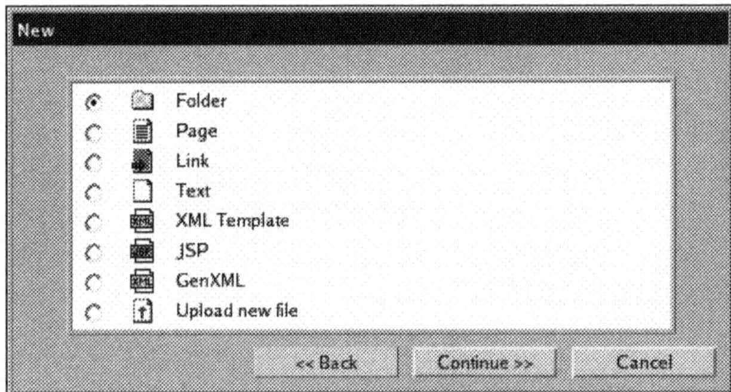

Note the presence of the new GenXML item. Once a new genxml resource is created, it should show up in the VFS along with the rest of your content.

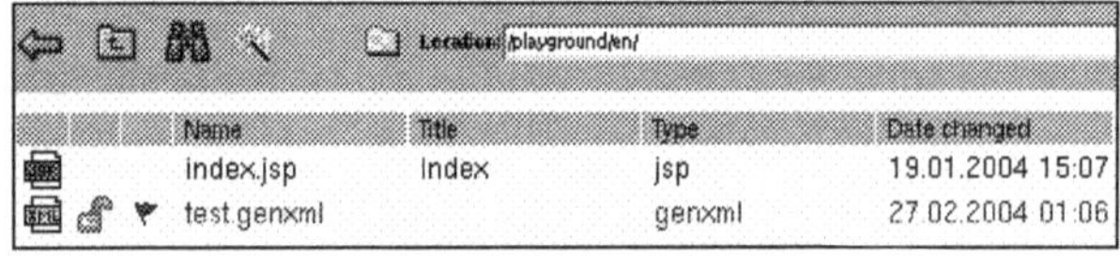

That is all there is to creating a simple resource type. In Chapter 6 (*Creating an OpenCms Module*) we will build a new module based around this resource type.

Resource types represent one way of extending OpenCms to handle specific types of content. They are relatively easy to develop and integrate well within the OpenCms framework. However, they are designed to handle simple single-file data. More complex content, such as relational database tables, may require a much more sophisticated method of managing content. In the next section, we will discuss the OpenCms content definition mechanism—an extension API designed to provide a gateway for integrating complex content into OpenCms.

Content Definitions

Content definitions offer another mechanism for extending the content types that OpenCms will support. Unlike resource types, which merely create a new type of document within the existing OpenCms architecture, a content definition allows you to create a complex, external content control mechanism that does not use the predetermined facilities of resource types. Phrased more simply, content definitions provide a way of storing data that is fundamentally different from existing OpenCms data, but controlling it through the OpenCms back office and publishing system.

The OpenCms developers created a **News module** (that has since been extended by a number of independent developers), which made use of content definitions to create a completely different type of content. This content is stored in non-OpenCms tables in the database, accessed by a separate pool of database connections, and managed by a custom set of back office classes.

Content definitions are not designed to integrate seamlessly into OpenCms. Content is not placed into the VFS, and the OpenCms access control and publishing architecture is only minimally linked with the content definition. Since this content is so isolated from the rest of OpenCms, developers usually have to develop custom editing applications in the administration view which, in turn, editors have to learn.

The API for developing custom content definitions is fairly complex and will require lots of custom coding, as well as thorough knowledge of OpenCms internals. Content definitions, in all of their complexity, can provide a way to get legacy content into OpenCms, but this is not a trivial process.

The Steps for Creating a Content Definition

While the size of the necessary code for producing a content definition prohibits inclusion in a book like this, I will outline the steps necessary for creating a content definition. The best source of information beyond this description is the sourcecode of the News module, which, at the time of this writing, was available from the official OpenCms site.

1. Determine how and where the custom content is to be stored. Usually, it is stored within the same database as the OpenCms content, though in different tables. However, it could just as easily be stored in different databases, flat files on the real file system, or some other storage mechanism.
2. Next, you will need to create a new module to house your content definition. This was discussed in the previous chapter.
3. Once this is done, you will need to write a class that extends the abstract class `com.opencms.defaults.A_CmsContentDefinition`. Basically, you will need to implement the constructors as well as a number of methods for adding and deleting content in your custom datasource. There are a host of getters and setters, as well as some status methods, that you will need to override as well. Since your data will have its own structure, you will need to add getter or setter methods for any specific tasks that your content definition will need to manage your content.

Important Methods

In this process, there are three methods that bear specific mention. The first is `getFieldNames()`. This method is called by OpenCms to find out what fields exist for the content in this content definition.

Here's a brief example from a content definition that handles generic XML data from a separate set of database tables:

```
/**
 * Gets a list of filed names for Back Office.
 * @param cms CmsObject instance
 * @return vector of field names.
 */
public static Vector getFieldNames( CmsObject cms ) {
    Vector n = new Vector();
    n.addElement( "Title" );
    n.addElement( "Description" );
    n.addElement( "XML_Namespace" );
    n.addElement( "Contents" );
    return n;
}
```

The `getFieldNames()` method returns a `java.util.Vector` of the names (as `String` objects) of these fields. Every field name of the content definition must be returned by this method.

The second method that I want to specifically address is `getFieldMethods()`. This is slightly more complex than the previous method, as it returns a `Vector` of methods that

OpenCms then can call explicitly. This is achieved by using Java's reflection mechanism to get the methods of the current class.

```
/**
 * Gets a list of methods for Back Office
 * @param cms CmsObject instance.
 * @return Vector of methods.
 */
public static Vector getFieldMethods( CmsObject cms ) {
    Vector methods = new Vector();
    try {
        methods.addElement(
           GenericXmlContentDefinition.class.getMethod(
            "getTitle",
            new Class[0]));
        methods.addElement(
           GenericXmlContentDefinition.class.getMethod(
            "getDescription",
            new Class[0]));
        methods.addElement(
           GenericXmlContentDefinition.class.getMethod(
            "getNamespace",
           new Class[0]));
        methods.addElement(
           GenericXmlContentDefinition.class.getMethod(
            "getContents",
            new Class[0]));
    } catch (NoSuchMethodException e) {
        System.err.println(e.toString());
    }
    return methods;
}
```

This makes the `getTitle()`, `getDescription()`, `getNamespace()`, and `getContents()` methods (all of which were custom-defined getters) available to OpenCms.

The last method I want to specifically mention works similarly to the above, though it requires some more explanation. OpenCms supports filtering the content retrieved from content definitions. To achieve this, content definition implementations must provide a list of methods for filtering content. Filters are responsible for taking a list of parameters and retrieving content based on those parameters. Often, they sort or restrict the content that is stored in the underlying database, though they may do much more complicated processing as well. The `getFilterMethods()` method, which must be implemented, returns a list of methods that perform these filtering operations. Here's a very simple example:

```
/**
 * Gets a list of filters.
 * @param cms CmsObject instance
 * @return vector of field names.
 */
public static Vector getFilterMethods( CmsObject cms ) {
    Vector filters = new Vector();
    try {
        filters.addElement(
```

```
                new CmsFilterMethod(
                    "List By XML Namespace... ",
                    GenericXMLContentDefinition.class.getMethod(
                        "getDocsByNamespace",
                        new Class[] {String.class}),
                        new Object[] {}
                ));
        } catch ( Exception e ) {
            System.err.println(e.toString();
        }
        return filters;
    }
```

This creates a `Vector` containing an instance of `com.opencms.default.CmsFilterMethod`. (In a real application, this would return at least half a dozen filter methods, not just one.) The constructor for the `CmsFilterMethod` takes a `String` containing the filter name, a `java.lang.reflect.Method` object containing the filter method, a `Class[]` array containing the classes for each of the parameters that must be passed into the method (in this case, a single `String` parameter), and an `Object[]` array containing the filter parameters. Using the `Object[]` array, you can pass instances of the classes in the `Class[]` array into the method.

In the example above, I have a method called `getDocsByNamespace()` that takes one `String` object (set in `Class[]{String.class}`). If I always want that namespace to be set to `http://example.com/myXmlNamespace`, I can set the value in the `Object[]` array as follows:

```
Object[]{"http://example.com/myXmlNamespace"}
```

Creating the content definition is only a fraction of the work, and once it is complete, you will need to write a custom back-office application, as well as classes and JSPs to format and deliver the content to the end user. While not discussed in the context of creating content definitions, these topics are covered in Chapters 6 and 7.

The fact that implementing a content definition is so absurdly complex has led the OpenCms developers to consider a new approach, and it is likely that OpenCms 6.0 will contain either a much revised implementation of content definitions or an altogether different extension mechanism.

The Virtual File System

Rather than store files under control of the CMS directly in the file system, OpenCms stores all the content in the database. Using a relational database (RDBMS) rather than the operating system's file system gives OpenCms three distinct functional advantages.

First, OpenCms code can make use of the RDBMS by creating richer metadata, relationships, and indexes than a standard file system could support. The tasks of a content management system are much more specialized than those of a general file system, and whereas the file system would be difficult to extend in such a way as to suit the specialized needs of a CMS application, a RDBMS provides all of the necessary tools for modeling, storing, and retrieving specialized content.

The second advantage of using an RDBMS is that access to the content can be controlled much more efficiently and securely. File-system-level access control falls under the domain of the operating system. This produces a problem: access control differs from OS to OS. The obvious example is the difference between Windows and UNIX-like operating systems. To make the situation more complicated, Java, aiming at platform neutrality, does not provide good facilities for dealing with file-level access. Rather than introduce the need to handle multiple unique operating systems, OpenCms uses the database and adds its own access control mechanisms within the database tables.

Additionally, the file system is available for use by other applications on the system. This creates uncertainty, as it is possible that other programs outside the CMS could access and alter the contents of these files without going through the procedures enforced by the CMS. Storing the information in the database minimizes the risk, as the resources in the database are not open for general use, and thus remain partitioned from other applications.

I have already briefly alluded to the third advantage of using an RDBMS, and that is platform neutrality. Java's well defined **Java DataBase Connectivity (JDBC)** mechanism provides a consistent method of dealing with information stored in databases. Since the core specification of SQL (Standard Query Language)—the de facto standard database manipulation language—has long been standardized and is implemented broadly, only minor changes must be made to allow OpenCms to communicate with varying database implementations (MySQL, SQL Server, and Oracle are all supported now). For more information on where database access classes reside, see the *Class Structure* section in this chapter.

In contrast with all of the advantages of RDBMS systems, though, the fact is that the file system approach to organizing data has become ubiquitous in the computing world. Traversing a file system is a basic skill of the novice computer user, while traversing a set of RDBMS tables, even if in a graphical presentation, is difficult even for experienced users. To take advantage of the ubiquity of the file system approach, OpenCms developers implemented a file system look-alike that structures and presents the information in the database so as to mimic the structure of the file system. This look-alike is called the Virtual File System.

> The term Virtual File System is also used in UNIX and Linux systems to refer to an abstraction layer removed from the physical storage media. The two meanings should not be confused—the VFS in OpenCms uses the RDBMS, while the VFS in UNIX or Linux is part of the underlying operating system and is, in fact, synonymous with what we generally call 'the file system'. In this book, I will refrain from using the term VFS in relation to the UNIX/Linux definition.

The similarities between the VFS and standard file systems are limited, though. Within the workplace, resources are always presented within the model of the file system. However, at the API level, the similarities are much less pronounced.

To access a file in the operating system's file system, for instance, Java code typically invokes a `java.io.FileReader` object, getting the contents of the file via calls to a `read()` method. In OpenCms, however, files (represented by the `com.opencms.file.CmsFile` class) are retrieved from an instance of the `com.opencms.file.CmsObject` object, and the entire contents of the file are stored in a byte array accessible with the `getContents()` method. This is not to say that one model is easier to work with than the other, but it does reflect the underlying difference between the VFS and the operating system's file system. (For an example of retrieving files from the OpenCms VFS, see *Getting the Contents of Other Files* in Chapter 4.) Since the VFS *does* follow the convention of referring to files in the context of a path (e.g. `/playground/myfile.txt`), locating and retrieving files is done in the familiar file system paradigm.

How Page Types Are Stored in the VFS

Another big difference between the VFS and a traditional file system is that OpenCms stores different resource types in different ways. Most notably, Page documents are split into two files and stored in separate locations within the VFS. The **controlcode** for the page contains information about *which* Java class is used for rendering the content, *which* template should be used to display the page, and *where* the actual content of the document is located. When you create a new file and give it a name, the file that you create actually contains only the controlcode. (To access the controlcode, left-click on the file's icon and select Edit controlcode.) The body of the document, however, is stored in `/system/bodies`—not in the location where you actually created a file. For instance, if you create a file of type Page in `/playground/myPage.html`, the actual contents of the file will look like this:

```
<?xml version="1.0" encoding="ISO-8859-1"?>
<PAGE>
    <class>com.opencms.template.CmsXmlTemplate</class>
    <masterTemplate>
        /system/modules/com.examle.site/templates/
        example-page-template.xml
```

```
    </masterTemplate>
    <ELEMENTDEF name="body">
        <CLASS>com.opencms.template.CmsXmlTemplate</CLASS>
        <TEMPLATE>
            /system/bodies/playground/myPage.html
        </TEMPLATE>
    </ELEMENTDEF>
</PAGE>
```

This is controlcode. Almost all of the contents of this file are remainders of the old XML template architecture that is being replaced by JSP, and thus you will probably never have to change anything in the controlcode file.

The highlighted portion of the above XML file—the `<TEMPLATE>` element and its contents—points to the location in `/system/bodies` where the actual contents of the page are located. If we open that file, `/system/bodies/playground/myPage.html`, in the sourcecode editor, it will look like this:

```
<xml version="1.0" encoding="ISO-8859-1"?>
<XMLTEMPLATE>
    <TEMPLATE>
      <![CDATA[
        <p>This is an example.</p>
      ]]>
    </TEMPLATE>
    <edittemplate>
      <![CDATA[
        <P>This is an example</P>
      ]]>
    </edittemplate>
</XMLTEMPLATE>
```

Inside the `<XMLTEMPLATE>` element, there are two different copies of the body. The first copy is in the `<TEMPLATE>` element. This copy has been cleaned by **JTidy** (an HTML formatter and validator)—note that the `<p>` elements are in lowercase, in conformance to the HTML 4.01 specification suggestion and the XHTML 1.0 requirement. The code in the `<TEMPLATE>` section is used to render the page for viewing.

The second section, `<edittemplate>`, contains the HTML as produced by the WYSIWYG or sourcecode editor. When you edit content through one of these editors, it is stored into the `<edittemplate>` section and then run through JTidy. JTidy's results are then written into the `<TEMPLATE>` section. However, the next time the editor is invoked, it operates on the contents of the `<edittemplate>` element. This can lead to some confusion, as JTidy may significantly change the content that it places in `<TEMPLATE>`, but these changes are not reflected back into the `<edittemplate>` section.

While directly editing the contents of body files is not recommended, JTidy's behavior occasionally necessitates editing the `/system/bodies` version of the template manually. If possible, however, you ought to try and produce code in the WYSIWYG or sourcecode editors that JTidy will not significantly alter (and any HTML 4.01-compliant documents should make it unscathed through JTidy).

When a Page is edited, both the controlcode file and the body file are modified, and, in fact, any time the lock is changed on the controlcode file, the change is automatically duplicated on the body file.

Resource Names and the VFS

When you are programming with OpenCms, you should be aware of a few discrepancies between the way VFS files are presented in the explorer view and how they may occasionally be referenced in JSP or Java code. In order to make this clear, I'll explain a few details of OpenCms internals.

All CMS files are instances of `com.opencms.file.CmsFile`, and all folders are instances of `com.oepncms.file.CmsFolder`. These two classes differ only in a few methods, but most of the functionality of both is provided by a common superclass: `com.opencms.file.CmsResource`. Each `CmsResource` is given a unique name. This is called the **Resource Name**. A Resource Name looks like a VFS path, but is in fact a superset of the VFS path information. For instance, the file named `myfile.txt` in the `/playground` folder would have the path `/playground/myfile.txt`, but the Resource Name `/default/vfs/playground/myfile.txt`.

The Resource Name contains one additional component, called the **Root Name** (`/default/vfs`, in this case). Only resources with Resource Names that begin with `/default/vfs` are considered to be part of the VFS. The purpose of this structure is to provide a method to easily extend the resource concept without requiring that resources be part of the VFS. All built-in resources have the `/default/vfs` Root Name, and are thus part of the VFS. Occasionally, you will encounter a method that returns a Resource Name rather than a VFS path. You can get the VFS path of the resource by removing the Root Name.

Here's a small piece of example code:

```
<%@ page session="false"
   import="com.opencms.flex.jsp.CmsJspActionElement,
           com.opencms.file.CmsObject,
           com.opencms.file.CmsResource"
%>
<%
CmsJspActionElement cms = new CmsJspActionElement( pageContext,
                                                    request,
                                                    response );
CmsObject cmso = cms.getCmsObject();
String rootName="/default/vfs";
String myAbsPath, myTitle;
CmsResource myResource;
// Here's our test String:
String resourceName = "/default/vfs/playground/myfile.txt";
```

```
if(resourceName.startsWith( rootName )) {
  myAbsPath = resourceName.substring( rootName.length() );
  // myAbsPath is now /playground/myfile.txt
} else {
  myAbsPath = resourceName;
}
myTitle = cmso.readProperty(myAbsPath, "title");
out.println("<h2>" + myTitle + "</h2>" );
%>
```

As you can see, this code simply strips off the Root Name if it is present and then attempts to get the title for the document. Since some methods deal with Resource Names and others with VFS paths, it is important to understand the difference.

Reading from and Writing to the VFS

Most VFS reading and writing operations are carried out automatically by OpenCms, and many of the JSP APIs (`com.opencms.flex.jsp.*`) handle all the details associated with dealing directly with the VFS. However, complex JSPs and Java classes often need to deal more directly with the VFS.

Both reading and writing require a handle to a `com.opencms.file.CmsObject` instance. Usually, this can be obtained from a `com.opencms.flex.jsp.CmsJspActionElement` with the `getCmsObject()` method. Diverging somewhat from the norm in object-oriented programming, the `CmsObject` methods tend to use `Strings` as keys for identifying objects. When dealing with the VFS, the `String` is usually the **VFS absolute path** (which is the Resource Name minus the Root Name).

The task of reading files is fairly straightforward and a variety of methods are available—mostly in the `com.opencms.file.CmsObject` class—that will retrieve files and their associated metadata (such as properties). One thing to watch out for, however, is file permissions. Development is usually done by a user with administrative privileges working in the Offline project. Consequently, the user will have access to all of the files in the VFS, and will have the security privileges needed to access Java methods that are flagged as 'admin only' (like `CmsObject.writeUser()`). Regular site visitors, however, do not have elevated privileges, and will not be able to access files to which they are not given permission, nor will they be able to execute JSP pages that contain code that requires higher security permissions. When you write applications, test them thoroughly in the Online project with a user account that has the same permissions as your visitors will have. Usually, the Guest account is ideal for these tests (since by default all users are Guest).

Another factor in the complexity of reading files is resource type. Reading a plain type is as simple as opening the `com.opencms.file.CmsFile` and calling `getContents()`. Sometimes a higher-level object can do the work. The CSV parser example that we developed in Chapter 4 read a plain file using only methods of `CmsJspActionElement`.

Binary, image, and JSP files all store their content in the same way, and thus the content for each of these types can be retrieved using `CmsFile.getContents()`. Here is an example 'View Source' JSP that displays the sourcecode for a JSP file, rather than rendering it:

```
<%@ page import="com.opencms.flex.jsp.CmsJspActionElement,
                 com.opencms.file.CmsObject,
                 com.opencms.file.CmsFile,
                 com.opencms.file.I_CmsResourceType"
%>
<%
CmsJspActionElement cms =
  new CmsJspActionElement( pageContext, request, response );
// view my own source. ;-)
String myFileName = cms.info("opencms.request.uri");
CmsObject cmso = cms.getCmsObject();
CmsFile myFile = cmso.readFile( myFileName );
/*
 * This checks to make sure the code is a JSP file. Since
 * CmsFile.getType() returns an int, we have to get the
 * int that correlates to the type "jsp" from an impl of
 * I_CmsResourceType.
 *
 * Yes, it is odd that the two methods have the same name.
 */
if( myFile.getType() ==
    cmso.getResourceType("jsp").getResourceType() ) {
  String myFileTitle = cmso.readProperty( myFileName, "title");

  StringBuffer sb = new StringBuffer();
  // Get CmsFile contents
  byte [] fileContents = myFile.getContents();
  // Encode any "<",">" and "&" in the JSP.
  for( int i = 0; i < fileContents.length; ++i ) {
    if( fileContents[i] == '<' ) {
      sb.append( "&lt;" );
    } else if (fileContents[i] == '>' ) {
      sb.append( "&gt;" );
    } else if (fileContents[i] == '&' ) {
      sb.append( "&amp;" );
    } else {
      // Definitely NOT Unicode friendly
      sb.append( (char)fileContents[i] );
    }
  }
  String fileSourceText = sb.toString();
  out.println( "<h1>Source of: " + myFileTitle + "</h1>" );
  out.print( "<pre>" + fileSourceText + "</pre>" );
} else {
  out.println( "<h2>" + myFileName + "is not a JSP.</h2>" );
}
%>
```

This code simply reads itself (or the source of whatever page includes it) and, if the document type is 'JSP', it prints the sourcecode.

> The `com.opencms.util.Encoder` class provides a static method `escapeHtml()`, designed to escape common HTML sequences in a way similar to the example we just discussed. However, its escaping was not sufficient for displaying the previous example code (it does not escape ampersand signs if they are part of HTML entities), so I have chosen to implement the simple for-loop escape sequence instead. In most cases, the `escapeHtml()` method is sufficient for displaying HTML without risking undesired behavior.

If similar code was called on a Page type, you would not see the body of the document, but would instead get the controlcode. Getting the actual contents of the file is a bit more involved. First you must get the controlcode, then the body file, and then the contents of the body file. This JSP prints the body of a file, but bypasses the template mechanism:

```
<%@ page import="com.opencms.flex.jsp.CmsJspActionElement,
                 com.opencms.file.CmsObject,
                 com.opencms.file.CmsFile,
                 com.opencms.file.I_CmsResourceType,
                 com.opencms.template.CmsXmlTemplateFile,
                 com.opencms.template.CmsXmlControlFile"
%>
<%
CmsJspActionElement cms =
  new CmsJspActionElement( pageContext, request, response );
String myFileName = "/playground/index.html";
CmsObject cmso = cms.getCmsObject();
CmsFile myFile = cmso.readFile( myFileName );
```

This code begins in much the same way as the earlier JSP source viewer example. After verifying that the type is Page, though, things look a bit different:

```
if( myFile.getType() ==
    cmso.getResourceType("page").getResourceType() ) {
  String myFileTitle = cmso.readProperty( myFileName, "title" );

  // Get the control code
  CmsXmlControlFile controlCode = new CmsXmlControlFile( cmso,
                                                         myFile
                                                        );
  // Get the name of the body file.
  String bodyFileName = controlCode.getElementTemplate("body");
  // Create a new CmsXmlTemplateFile object
  CmsXmlTemplateFile bodyFile =
    new CmsXmlTemplateFile( cmso, bodyFileName);

  // Yes, this is normal.
  String bodyContents = bodyFile.getTemplateContent( null,
                                                     null,
                                                     null );
  out.println( "<h1>" + myFileTitle + "</h1>" );
  out.print( bodyContents );
} else {
  out.println( "<h2>" + myFileName + "is not a Page.</h2>" );
}
%>
```

Rather than get the contents of `myFile` with the `getContents()` method, we construct a new `CmsXmlControlFile` object, which parses the control code with an XML parser and then provides convenient accessors for retrieving specific control codes. Primarily, what we are interested in is the `<TEMPLATE>` element inside the `<ELEMENTDEF name="body">` element. The `<TEMPLATE>` element contains the full path to the body file. `getElementTemplate("body")` returns the path as a `String`.

We create a new `CmsXmlTemplateFile` to represent the body file—this parses the body file (which is also XML) and provides a number of convenience methods for accessing specific parts of the XML. The only thing we want from the body file is the content of the `<TEMPLATE>` element, and we get that with the `getTemplateContent()` method. Odd as it may appear, calling this method with `null` for all three arguments is perfectly valid. In fact, the first two parameters are not used at all (though they probably were in earlier versions of OpenCms). The third parameter can be used to specify a named body, if one exists, but passing it `null` causes it to retrieve the default body, which is what we want. Once the JSP has the contents of the body, it just writes the title and the body to the output stream.

For the most part, the OpenCms API is designed to expedite file reading in any project. Writing files is a different story. The Online project is read-only. It does not allow any writing at all, and other than publishing the Offline project, there is no sanctioned method for updating content in the Online project. While OpenCms offers a number of methods to add, edit, and remove files, none of these can be used on files in the Online project. Form data handling, then, is not usually accomplished by writing the data into the CMS. Rather, developers have created modules (such as the **FormMail** module available on the OpenCms website) to deliver the data to another source.

Occasionally, developers will deliberately circumvent OpenCms security to allow writing to the CMS. This generally involves creating a location in the Offline project where a user with minimal permissions can write files. Then the application will temporarily log in as that user and write a file to the Offline project, and then log back in as the previous user.

Obviously an application like this has some risks, but if done carefully, it can work. Here are the rough steps in creating an application to handle writing files:

1. Create a new, low-privileged user. This user needs to be able to create files in a specific directory, but not to edit the rest of the CMS.
2. Create a directory into which the low-privileged user may write files.
3. Create the necessary forms and a JSP to handle the file submission.

The JSP should do the following:

- Read the user input and verify that the contents are legitimate. All the data checking should be done while still retaining the Guest user's permissions.

- Once the data is verified, use the `CmsObject.loginUser()` method to log in the user that is allowed to write files.
- Since files cannot be written to the Online project, the code must switch to the Offline project (or, if you would prefer, a specific project that you have created). You can use the `setCurrentProject()` method of `com.opencms.file.CmsRequestContext` to change projects. You can get a `CmsRequestContext` object with `CmsJspActionElement.getRequestContext()`.
- Create a new `com.opencms.file.CmsResource` and write to it. The exact process will differ depending on the resource type. For a Plain document, you can simply use the `setContents()` method of `com.opencms.file.CmsFile`. Creating a Page document, however, requires creating both the body and the controlcode files.
- Optionally, you may decide to publish the file (depending on the application). This can be done with the `CmsObject.publishResource()` method.
- Once the write is complete, switch back to the Online project and do a `CmsObject.loginUser()` for the **Guest** user.

Again, allowing a visitor to write to the CMS is a security risk. It is important to make sure that the user cannot take advantage of any permission elevation when the file is written. While it is possible to give the **Guest** user permission to write to an area of the CMS, such design is less desirable from a security standpoint.

Class Structure

This section provides an overview of the organization of the OpenCms packages. Developers will find this a useful introduction to the class structure of OpenCms.

The package structure for OpenCms follows the standard Java convention. Since the code was written before Alkacon acquired the `opencms.org` domain, they used `com.opencms` even though the product is maintained by the open source community. For OpenCms 6.0, many of the packages will be moved to an `org.opencms` package.

Most of the functionality that you, as a developer, will require for developing modules and JSPs is present in the `flex.jsp`, `file`, `defaults`, and `core` packages.

> Almost all OpenCms code is documented using Javadoc, Java's built-in tool for API documentation. However, OpenCms developers have only posted the Javadocs for the `com.opencms.flex.jsp` package. To get the rest of the Javadocs, you will need to download the sourcecode and run the `javadoc` tool

against the sources. In Appendix A, I have included an Ant `build.xml` that has a Javadoc target. If you are planning on doing any serious Java or JSP development with OpenCms, you will definitely need the Javadocs.

com.opencms.boot

As the name suggests, this package contains classes responsible for bootstrapping OpenCms during startup.

com.opencms.core

Classes in this package provide the operational mechanisms for OpenCms. For instance, the servlet implementation, `OpenCmsHttpServlet`, and its associated classes are in this package, as are classes for running OpenCms in a command-line mode (`CmsShell`).

As far as development goes, the most important classes in this package are `A_OpenCms` and `OpenCms`.

`OpenCms`, which runs as a singleton and extends the abstract class `A_OpenCms`, provides the true core of the platform. It handles events, manages the runtime, and does all of the logging. You can (and should) use the OpenCms logger to handle any logging messages that you need to send in modules or JSP code. Since the `OpenCms` instance is a singleton initialized during startup, sending a log message can be done like this:

```
import com.opencms.core.A_OpenCms;
....
  A_OpenCms.log( A_OpenCms.C_OPENCMS_INFO, "Task completed." );
```

To keep your code flexible, and to allow for possible alternative implementations of the abstract `A_OpenCms` class, you should use `A_OpenCms` rather than `OpenCms`.

The `I_CmsConstants` interface is also extremely useful, as it defines many of the constants used within OpenCms. Many OpenCms classes implement this to gain simple access to constants.

com.opencms.dbpool

This package includes all of the classes used for setting up the OpenCms database connection pool. This whole package is going away in the next version, so avoid working directly with it, if possible.

com.opencms.defaults

Roughly stated, this package provides classes that provide basic functionality required for extending OpenCms. Along with abstract classes to facilitate the development of back-office modules, content definitions, this package provides some nice tools to assist you in developing applications. For example, the `CmsMail` class provides a simple interface for sending mail from OpenCms.

> In order to use `CmsMail`, you must set values in the `registry.xml` file to provide `CmsMail` with mail server information. In particular, you must set values for the `<smtpserver/>`, `<smtpserver2/>`, and `<defaultmailsender/>` elements.

com.opencms.defaults.master

This package contains the master module for OpenCms. Essentially, the master module comprises the implementations of content definitions that OpenCms uses natively. If you are developing content definitions, this package provides useful examples and classes that can be easily extended.

com.opencms.file

This package contains classes that manage or represent resources within the CMS. Applications that deal directly with content will often use classes within this package, and we've already seen numerous examples involving classes from this package.

The `CmsObject` class is inescapable for OpenCms developers. It serves as the controller for access to the CMS. With over 270 public methods, it is a daunting class to work with. However, it is impossible to perform any complex tasks without using it. `CmsFile`, `CmsFolder`, `CmsResource`, and `CmsUser` are also frequently used classes from this package.

com.opencms.file.<database>

In order to support numerous databases, OpenCms developers abstracted database-specific code into separate packages. Consequently, none of the methods in the `com.opencms.file` package are database specific.

The `com.opencms.file.genericSql` package contains classes that provide baseline SQL database support, and then other packages (`mySql`, `mssql`, and `oraclesql`) provide database-specific optimizations for their respective platforms. In each of these directories, there is a properties file called `query.properties`, which contains all of the SQL used for handling transactions with that particular database. This file can be extremely helpful when debugging database issues.

Each of these database packages has a `CmsRequestBroker` and a `CmsDbAccess` class. The `CmsRequestBroker` class provides the database-specific logic that `com.opencms.file.CmsObject` requires.

Thus, many of the methods in `CmsObject` simply call corresponding methods in `CmsRequestBroker`. The `CmsDbAccess` class handles all database queries.

com.opencms.file.utils

This package has only one class, `CmsAccessFilesystem`, which provides access to the file system of the underlying operating system.

com.opencms.flex

The `Flex` package and all of its sub-packages are responsible for the JSP functionality in OpenCms. Classes in this base package handle loading and execution of JSP scripts. The Flex mechanism is discussed in more detail in Chapters 3, 4, and 8.

com.opencms.flex.cache

OpenCms includes a sophisticated caching mechanism for speeding the process of interpreting and executing JSP files. This package contains the classes that implement JSP caching. FlexCache is discussed in Chapters 3, 4, and 8.

com.opencms.flex.jsp

This package contains the classes used to provide the JSP scriptlet and tag implementations for OpenCms. It is by far the most commonly used package for OpenCms site development.

In the last chapter, we reviewed the functionality of this package in detail.

The `CmsJspActionElement` class provides basic OpenCms access to scriptlets, and is used frequently in OpenCms JSP scripts. `CmsJspNavBuilder` and `CmsJspNavElement` provide dynamic navigational elements. The remainder of the classes in this package define the `<cms:*/>` JSP tags that compose the OpenCms JSP taglib.

> The `com.opencms.flex.jsp` Javadoc API documentation is available as an OpenCms module. You can obtain this module from the official OpenCms website.

com.opencms.flex.util

This package provides a number of utility classes used by the Flex mechanism. Most of these classes are specific to the Flex cache.

com.opencms.htmlconverter

Only one class and one interface are present in this package, which handles transforming HTML. The `CmsHtmlConverter` handles running HTML through the JTidy HTML formatter and verifier.

com.opencms.launcher

Launchers are responsible for taking content of specific resource types and preparing that content for delivery to the client. Earlier in this chapter, in the section on creating resource types, we discussed assigning a launcher to a resource type in the `registry.xml` file. This package contains the default OpenCms launchers.

In Chapter 7, we will take a close look at launchers.

com.opencms.linkmanagement

This package provides the classes used for checking links within the CMS.

com.opencms.report

When you publish, export, or import in OpenCms, OpenCms displays progress in a dynamic textbox. The classes within this package are used to generate these reports.

com.opencms.template

Before OpenCms used JSP, it used XML templates. Controlcode files and the structure of Page types are a vestige of the old XML template functionality. This package provides a number of classes and interfaces for handling XML template files.

Accessing the information in Page documents will often involve using the `CmsXmlControlCode` and `CmsXmlTemplateFile` classes. Additionally, back-office modules still rely heavily upon the XML template language, and developing back-office classes will entail using members of this package as well.

If you are developing XML applications in OpenCms, you may find the `CmsXmlXercesParser` class useful for dealing with your XML documents.

OpenCms developers have already announced their plans to completely remove the XML template dependencies in the system, and it is likely that XML template functionality will exist only as an add-on in the 6.0 release of OpenCms. Unfortunately, though, they are still a necessary part of the OpenCms architecture.

com.opencms.template.cache

The Template Cache, also known as the Element Cache, was the precursor to the FlexCache. It still provides some caching for XML templates, but has been superseded by the FlexCache and should be considered deprecated (though it is not marked as such).

com.opencms.util

This package contains several useful utility classes, including the `Encoder` class, which contains methods for escaping and encoding various formats (for example XML, HTML, and ASCII).

The `Utils` class provides commonly used methods for displaying formatted date strings, sorting lists, checking if HTTPS has been used, and other miscellaneous activities.

com.opencms.workplace

The classes in this package provide all of the functionality to the Workplace and back-office tools. Various XML templates use these classes to perform their activities. In upcoming chapters, we will examine the back office and spend more time looking at the structure of these classes.

Summary

In this chapter, we have explored some of the more arcane aspects of the OpenCms architecture, and have looked at some of the key methods for extending the base functionality of OpenCms. We looked at creating custom document formats with resource types and encapsulating more complex data formats with content definitions. We looked at the VFS in detail, examining its design and discovering how to access files in the VFS. Finally, we took a brief glance at the OpenCms Java class hierarchy. In the next chapter, we will apply this knowledge as we create a full-blown module.

6

Creating an OpenCms Module

Modules provide a mechanism for extending the functionality of OpenCms with Java libraries and classes, JSP pages, and XML templates. Modules are designed to be easily distributed among OpenCms installations, and can provide functional elements ranging from portable content to sophisticated applications that interact with content in OpenCms. We have already encountered OpenCms modules. In this chapter, we are going to take an in-depth look at developing modules. Specifically, we will cover:

- Using modules
- Creating a module
- Adding templates, content, and JSP pages to the module
- Adding custom Java classes and libraries
- Scheduling tasks to run automatically
- Managing module dependencies
- Exporting and deploying your module

Using Modules

The purpose of a module is to provide a container, easily imported and exported, to hold extensions to OpenCms. The temptation is to consider these 'extensions' to be complex applications including dozens of files of Java code, XML templates, and JARs. While the module mechanism would certainly work well for such an extension, many modules contain only a handful of files—usually templates and JSP files. In fact, some of the modules Alkacon releases are composed entirely of Page documents designed to add documentation and help-text to the system. In Chapter 2, for instance, we installed the help system module, which contains the help text for OpenCms.

Rather than considering modules strictly from the perspective of providing additional code, consider them as vehicles for encapsulating data, be it code or content, that could be useful in situations other than the immediate context. In other words, when looking at a set of data that you think *might* be a good candidate for a module, ask yourself these two questions:

- Can this data be useful in other situations?
- Is it likely that I will have to move this data independently of the rest of the OpenCms installation?

If the answer to either of these questions is 'yes', you will benefit from putting the data in a module.

Sometimes the sparse amount of data may not seem to warrant a separate module. However, I have a few modules that each contain only a few files—a couple of JSPs or Java classes—and they have proved very useful in multiple projects.

There is one circumstance for creating a module that does not really match the above criteria. Each new OpenCms site will need a site-specific module (usually called the **site module**).

The Site Module

The site module contains information specific to the site. In the previous chapters, we constructed the `com.example.site` module for exactly this purpose. The site module contains templates, JSPs, Java classes, and custom libraries that are required for running the site, but aren't necessarily reusable or useful outside the context of the current site. Typically, site modules consist primarily of JSP templates, images, and CSS files; some support JSP scriptlets. While site-specific Java classes were once required for handling XML template files, OpenCms 5.0.x uses JSPs instead. In most cases, Java classes perform tasks can be generalized, and ought to exist in a regular module so that they can be reused in other projects.

In Chapters 3 and 4, we created the `com.example.site` module and used it for storing templates and scriptlets, thereby illustrating the use of a site module. In this chapter, we will be focusing on creating a functional extension to OpenCms using the custom resource type we created in the previous chapter. However, the processes involved in creating, managing, and deploying this module are readily applicable to the site module.

Creating a Module

In this section, we will create a new module and discuss typical module organization. In the last chapter, we created a generic XML resource type (genxml) for storing XML data. This module will provide **eXtensible Stylesheet Language Transformations (XSLT)** functionality for transforming XML into HTML.

> XSLT is an XML format standardized by the World Wide Web Consortium (W3C), the standards body responsible for HTML, XML, HTTP, and a host of other Internet-related technologies. XSLT files are XML documents that contain instructions on how to transform one type of XML into another type of XML—or HTML. For more information on XSLT, visit the W3C's website: `http://www.w3.org/Style/XSL/`.

To create a new module, go to the administration view and click on the magic wand icon. OpenCms will present a form to complete that looks something like this:

Create module

Package name: com.example.genericxml.xslt Version: 1

Module name: GenericXML XSLT module

Description

This module provides eXstensible Stylesheet Language - Transformations (XSLT) services to OpenCms. It uses the GenericXML (genxml) resource type.

Simple module type | Administration point | View

Export classes/ folder | Export lib/ folder

Maintenance event class

Publish event class

Author: M Butcher

Email: mbutcher@example.com

Date created: 04.03.2004

Ok | Cancel

We have already encountered this form in Chapter 4, when we created a site module. The Package name should contain a Java-compliant package name (in our case `com.example.genericxml.xslt`). This will become both the name of the module and the path to this module's Java classes. Version contains the version number of the module. Unless you have a good reason to do otherwise, it should always start out as 1 (or 1.0, if you prefer). Module name is the human-readable name of the module.

Description is a full description of what services the module provides. Often, when you create the module you only have a general idea of what the module will eventually do, so this field will contain only generic information. However, before you export the module (covered at the end of this chapter), it is a good idea to come back to the description and fill in some additional information. Change information, pointers to documentation, and licensing information are included here in the description, as there is really no other formalized place for such module information.

Underneath Description are two rows of checkboxes. The first checkbox is labeled Simple module type. It is checked by default and should remain checked. Un-checking it causes OpenCms to revert to a legacy module format that is (practically speaking) deprecated and unsupported.

The next checkbox, Administration point, indicates that this module will have an icon in the administration view. If checked, then OpenCms will automatically create the `administration/` directory in your module. In the next chapter, we will create a module with an administration interface. For this module, however, leave it unchecked. If you intend to create your own content definition (see the previous chapter) or provide a different mechanism for displaying CMS content than that which is built into OpenCms, you will need to check the View checkbox. Our module will take advantage of JSP pages for displaying information, so leave this unchecked.

The Export classes/ folder and Export lib/ folder checkboxes determine whether the `classes/` folder (which contains any custom Java classes) and the `lib/` folder (which contains any module-specific JAR files) are written from the VFS to the real file system. These files are written inside the unpacked OpenCms servlet directory—Java classes are written to `$CATALINA_HOME/webapps/opencms/WEB-INF/classes/`, and JAR files are stored in `$CATALINA_HOME/webapps/opencms/WEB-INF/lib/`.

Since Java classes and JARs cannot be loaded from the VFS, these checkboxes must be checked for any module that includes any Java code or JARs. Even if your module does not have any Java code at the outset, it is advisable to leave both checked. That way, should you add any code later, it will be correctly copied to the file system.

The Maintenance event class text field is reserved for modules that require extended functionality during various stages of module development (creation, modification, or deletion). As the label implies, the field should point to a valid Java class file in the module's `classes/` directory.

The maintenance class is useful for performing custom tasks on the module when it is imported, modified, or removed. For instance, if you need to do some extra clean-up work when the module is deleted, you can build a maintenance class with a `moduleWasDeleted()` method that will be run when the module is removed.

There are a few oddities about the way maintenance classes perform. Primarily, there is no interface to implement or abstract class to extend. This means that you must know *what* methods OpenCms is looking for (and correctly implement them), or else your class will be useless.

The registry processing code (`com.opencms.file.CmsRegistry`) is responsible for handling maintenance events, and it looks for only three methods within a given maintenance class:

- `public static void moduleWasUploaded( com.opencms.file.CmsObject cms )`: This method is called when the module is loaded (see below).
- `public static void moduleParameterWasUpdated( com.opencms.file.CmsObject cms )`: This method is called when one of the module's parameters is changed. Mainly, this occurs when you modify the module settings via the administration view's module management screen. You can use this method to execute custom code any time a module parameter is changed.
- `public static void moduleWasDeleted ( com.opencms.file.CmsObject cms )`: This method is called when the module is removed. While the name indicates that this is called *after* the module is deleted, it is actually called *before* the module is deleted. Thus, all of your module content will still be available when this method is invoked. This method is useful for performing custom clean-up tasks before a module is deleted. It is particularly useful if your module stores information outside of OpenCms.

Each of these methods is declared static—the `CmsRegistry` does not first construct the object. It only executes the applicable method.

Another oddity in the maintenance class structure is that in OpenCms 5.0.x, the first of the three methods is essentially broken because the module's class files are not written to the real file system before the `CmsRegistry` tries to execute the method. Consequently, the `moduleWasUploaded()` method will never be successfully called. Various developers have devised workarounds for this, but none of these fixes have made it into the official OpenCms yet.

The **Publish event class** textbox allows you to specify a Java class to be executed when one or more resources are published. Each time a file or project is published anywhere in the VFS, an OpenCms event is fired (the event ID is different depending on whether the publish was performed on a single file or an entire project). Unlike the maintenance class, creating an event listener is straightforward and standardized. Implement the `com.opencms.flex.I_CmsEventListener` interface and provide instructions for what to do when a publish event occurs. A basic publish event listener looks like this:

```
package com.example.genericxml.xslt;
import com.opencms.file.CmsObject;
import com.opencms.flex.CmsEvent;
import com.opencms.flex.I_CmsEventListener;
public class SampleEventListener implements I_CmsEventListener {
   /**
    * Register this event listener with the OpenCms singleton.
    */
```

```
    private PublishEventIndexUpdate() {
        A_OpenCms.addCmsEventListener(this);
    }
    /**
     * When an event (any event) is fired, this method will be
     * executed.
     */
    public void cmsEvent(CmsEvent event) {
        switch(event.getType()) {
            case EVENT_PUBLISH_PROJECT:
            case EVENT_PUBLISH_RESOURCE:
                // DO SOMETHING HERE
                break;
        }
        return;
    }
}
```

When this class is registered as an event listener, the `cmsEvent()` method will be executed every time an event is fired (regardless of the event). The switch statement determines *which* kind of event was actually fired. We only care about two: `EVENT_PUBLISH_PROJECT` (called when an entire project is published), and `EVENT_PUBLISH_RESOURCE` (called when a resource is published directly). In a normal implementation, matching `case`s would actually do something useful. For instance, our genxml module could (if we were really zealous) validate all XML documents to make sure they are well formed, alerting the administrator if any XML is invalid.

Again, these fields in the module creation dialog can be edited later, so you do not have to have the Java classes written before you can create a module. You may leave the fields blank now, and add the class information at a later time.

The Author and Email fields should be filled out with the name of either the organization or individual that created the module and an e-mail address for inquiries. The Date created field is automatically generated, so you shouldn't have to edit it. Once the necessary fields are completed, click OK to create the module. Our example should now be visible under `/system/modules/com.example.genericxml.xslt/` in the explorer view.

Navigating the New Module

A good portion, though not all, of the module structure is created automatically. When you view the new module, you should see the `classes/`, `default_bodies/`, `libs/`, and `templates/` folders. If you checked the View checkbox in the module creation screen, you will have a `view/` folder. Likewise, if you checked Administration point, you will have an `admin/` folder.

In addition to these, you will have to manually create three folders: `elements/`, `jsptemplates/`, and `resources/`. The explorer view for the module should look something like this:

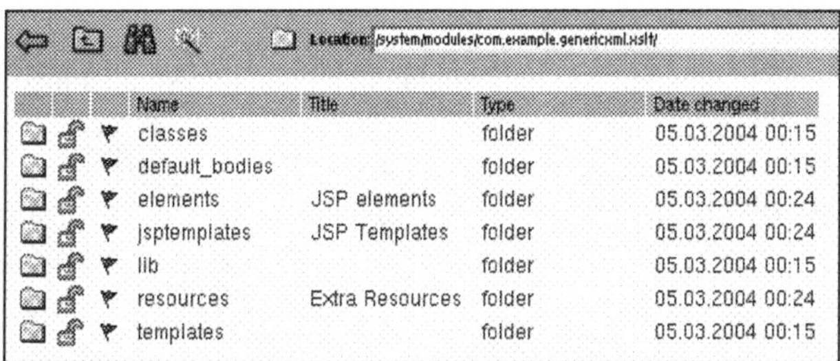

The `classes/` folder is for storing Java classes, and OpenCms will automatically create the folder structure for the package. So `classes/` will contain the following folder hierarchy: `com/example/genericxml/xslt/`.

In Chapter 3, we discussed creating 'default body' files that can be loaded from the WYSIWYG editor. These bodies can contain arbitrary layout information that can help editors create standard content without coding HTML. The `default_bodies/` folder can be used for storing module-specific default bodies. This is especially useful for site modules, though other modules can make use of this as well.

The `elements/` directory, which we had to create by hand, is used for storing JSP code—often in the form of scriptlets. While there is no requirement for this folder, it is the conventional place to store JSP info.

JSP template files should not go in `elements/`. Instead, they ought to be placed in the `jsptemplates/` directory. Again, this is a directory that, while conventional, is not created automatically by OpenCms. While it is not recommended, it is possible to put JSP templates in a different location, but the XML template stubs must point to the correct location of the JSP templates.

The `lib/` directory is reserved for JARs that contain Java classes and properties files. Normally, the contents of both the `lib/` and the `classes/` directories are written to both the VFS and the real file system—the latter is required for the Java class loader to find them. The Export class/ folder and Export lib/ folder checkboxes in the module creation dialog can be used to enable or disable the copying of these folders to the real file system. Just remember: If those boxes are left unchecked, the classes and libraries will *never* be loaded or executed by OpenCms.

Another directory that must be created manually is the `resources/` folder. This folder is the de facto location for images, CSS, JavaScript files, and other supporting elements. JavaScript files sometimes pose an exception—if the module makes use of numerous JavaScript files, developers may choose to add a `scripts/` folder specifically to house `.js` files.

As we have seen in previous chapters, the `templates/` folder is for XML templates files. For the most part, your XML template files will just point to JSP templates. While many other locations are determined by convention alone, the location of XML templates is hard-coded into OpenCms, so XML templates absolutely must be placed in the module's `templates/` directory. If they are placed elsewhere, OpenCms will not be able to find them.

Many developers choose to create a `docs/` *folder. This folder typically contains the README, INSTALL, TODO, and LICENSE files that are standard in UNIX software distribution.*

When a new module is created, its root folder (in this case `/system/modules/com.example.genericxml.xslt/`) and all of its subfolders will be locked. To unlock them all, you will need to go to the `/system/modules/` folder and choose Unlock and then Publish directly from the module's popup menu.

We have now finished creating the module. From here, we will turn to developing Java classes and importing both the classes and the supporting libraries, into our module.

Custom Classes and Libraries

Java classes and libraries can be used to add sophisticated functionality to a module. There are no specific caveats or constraints on classes and libraries—as long as they do not overtly conflict with existing code (for example, importing a different version of an existing library, such as Xerces), any code can be included in a module.

OpenCms does not offer any tools for developing the Java code inside the CMS. Unlike JSP files, Java code must be written and compiled outside OpenCms, and then the resulting `.class` or `.jar` files must be imported. Any time this executable content is added or modified, you must unlock and publish the files so that the code will be copied from the VFS to the real file system, where the Java classloader can find it. Then, you will need to restart the servlet container so that the classes will be loaded.

Our module will contain the code necessary for applying an XSLT stylesheet to an XML document, transforming it into an HTML document. The following `CmsXslTransformer` class uses Java's built-in **Java API for XML Processing (JAXP)** to get the Java Virtual Machine's XML implementation—with Tomcat, this is usually the **Apache Xalan** (XSL processor) and **Xerces** (XML Parsers, DOM) libraries.

The following code handles XSL transformations:

```
package com.example.genericxml.xslt;
import java.io.ByteArrayInputStream;
import java.io.OutputStream;
import java.io.Writer;
import javax.xml.transform.Source;
import javax.xml.transform.Result;
import javax.xml.transform.Transformer;
```

```
import javax.xml.transform.TransformerFactory;
import javax.xml.transform.TransformerException;
import javax.xml.transform.TransformerConfigurationException;
import javax.xml.transform.stream.StreamResult;
import javax.xml.transform.stream.StreamSource;
import com.opencms.core.CmsException;
import com.opencms.file.CmsObject;
import com.opencms.file.CmsFile;
public class CmsXslTransformer {
    private CmsObject cms;
    private Transformer transformer;
    // Don't want this to be called at all.
    private CmsXslTransformer() {}
    public CmsXslTransformer( String xsltStylesheet,
                              CmsObject cms )
            throws CmsException {
        this.cms = cms;
        try {
            TransformerFactory tf =
                TransformerFactory.newInstance();
            CmsFile xsltFile = cms.readFile( xsltStylesheet );
            Source s = this.getCmsFileSource( xsltFile );
            this.transformer = tf.newTransformer( s );
        } catch ( TransformerConfigurationException tce ) {
            throw new CmsException(
                "Cannot create XSLT transformer.", tce );
        } catch ( TransformerException te ) {
            throw new CmsException(
                "Cannot use XSLT transformer.", te );
        }
    }
    public void transform( CmsFile file, Result res )
            throws CmsException {
        Source source = this.getCmsFileSource( file );
        try {
            this.transformer.transform( source, res );
        } catch ( Exception e ) {
            throw new CmsException( "Failed to transform file",
                                    e );
        }
        return;
    }
    public void transform( String filename, OutputStream out )
            throws CmsException {
        CmsFile myFile = cms.readFile( filename );
        StreamResult res = new StreamResult( out );
        this.transform( myFile, res );
        return;
    }
    public void transform( String filename, Writer writer )
            throws CmsException {
        CmsFile myFile = cms.readFile( filename );
        StreamResult res = new StreamResult( writer );
        this.transform( myFile, res );
        return;
    }
    protected Source getCmsFileSource( CmsFile myFile )
            throws CmsException {
```

```
            ByteArrayInputStream bis =
                new ByteArrayInputStream( myFile.getContents() );
            StreamSource source;

            try {
                source = new StreamSource( bis );
            } catch ( Exception e ) {
                throw new CmsException(
                    "Error parsing " + myFile.getResourceName(),
                    e );
            }
            return source;
        }
    }
```

The constructor for `CmsXslTransformer` retrieves the XSLT file from the OpenCms VFS using the `CmsObject` passed into the constructor. The protected `getCmsFileSource()` method does the work of retrieving the file from the VFS and then putting the file contents into a `StreamSource` object that the transformer classes can use.

Then, the constructor creates a new `javax.xml.transform.Transformer`, which will be responsible for transforming XML documents. The three `transform()` methods perform the same task: they retrieve a file from the VFS, transform it using the `Transformer` object created by the constructor, and then write the results to the specified output. The `transform( String filename, Writer writer )` method is particularly useful for JSP pages, as it can write to the `JspWriter` object, `out`, that is within the context of every JSP page.

Once the class is written, it must be compiled in the regular file system. There is no mechanism in OpenCms for taking a Java source file and compiling it—the compiled class files must be uploaded into OpenCms. In order to get this code to compile, you will need to make sure that the `opencms.jar` is in the classpath.

When compilation is complete, go to the OpenCms explorer view, navigate to the `/system/modules/com.example.genericxml.xslt/classes/com/example/genericxml/xslt/` folder, and click on the magic wand icon to create a new file. Choose the **Upload new file** item and click **Continue**. Set the file type to **binary** (there is no Java class type) and then click **Finish** to upload the file. Once created, the file will show up as locked and unpublished. Unlock and publish the file and then restart the servlet container so that OpenCms can load the new classes.

> One major divergence in OpenCms from typical Java programming technique is the nearly ubiquitous use of only one exception for the entire platform—the `CmsException`. In addition to being thrown during any OpenCms-specific failure, other exceptions are usually caught and wrapped in `CmsExceptions`, and then rethrown.

> Dealing with this sort of exception handling technique can be very frustrating, as it circumvents the general idea behind the hierarchical organization of exceptions found in Java. However, `CmsExceptions` are often given an integer ID, corresponding to a constant in `I_CmsConstants`, that can help identify the true source and reason for the exception. Herein, I have followed the OpenCms conventions for exception handling, and only `CmsExceptions` are thrown.

Adding Libraries

Tomcat and many other servlet engines include a class that implements the `javax.xml.transform` portion of JAXP. However, some servlet engines may not. On those platforms, you will need to include an XSL processing library, such as Xalan (`http://xml.apache.org/xalan-j/index.html`), in the module's `lib/` folder.

The process of adding a library is almost identical to adding a class—the difference being that all JAR files are stored in the `lib/` folder instead of the `classes/` folder. For instance, if you need to add `xalan.jar`, go to the `/system/modules/com.example.genericxml.xslt/lib/` folder, click on the magic wand icon and upload a new binary file, unlock the JAR file, publish it, and then restart the servlet container.

> Do not upload another version of Xalan if one already exists. It can cause unpredictable results. If you do not know if you have an implementation of a transformer, test the preceding code first before uploading any libraries. If you see exceptions stating that there is no available implementation of the `javax.xml.transform` classes, you may upload Xalan or another XSL library.

Adding Content

Along with adding compiled code in the form of classes and JARs, a module should also contain any other resources needed for utilizing the code. As I stated at the beginning of this chapter, many modules do not contain any compiled code, but are made up entirely of documents, templates, and JSP pages. As we've seen in Chapter 4, adding content to a module is no different than adding content to any other location in the VFS. Simply stated, anything that exists in the module's directory (in this case `/system/modules/com.example.genericxml.xslt/`) will be exported with the module. It is also possible to attach content in other parts of the VFS to the module, and we will do that in the *Managing the Module* section later.

Before we get to that, though, we will create some XML content to transform, the XSLT stylesheets for transformation, and a JSP page that will do the transformation, using the class we just created.

Creating a Simple XML Document

XML documents can be complex, requiring sophisticated and large XSLT stylesheets for translation. But since our focus here is on the OpenCms module architecture, and not XML or XSLT, we will create a very simple XML document and a bare-bones stylesheet for translating it into HTML.

Since the XML content is likely to fall under editorial control, it should be stored under the root folder rather than in the module folder. So we will create the /xml/ folder. Inside it, we will create a basic XML document. In the previous chapter, we created a genxml file type, which is meant to identify XML data. However, you can also use a Plain type, as it allows just about any text content, including XML and HTML.

```
<?xml version="1.0" ?>
<basic>
  <name>XML Content</name>
  <body>This is an example of some basic XML content.</body>
</basic>
```

This document only contains three elements—the root element, <basic/>, a <name/> element, and a <body/> element. Now we need to create an XSLT stylesheet to transform this simple XML file into an HTML document.

A Place for XSLT Templates

Our new module makes use of XSLT files, so it makes sense for us to create another folder in the module directory (/system/modules/com.example.gericxml.xslt/), named xslt/. We will create a new XSLT template in this folder. Again, you may use the genxml type we created in the last chapter, or you can simply use the built-in Plain file type. Here is a simple XSLT stylesheet:

```
<?xml version="1.0" ?>
<xsl:stylesheet version="1.0"
  xmlns:xsl="http://www.w3.org/1999/XSL/Transform"
  xmlns="http://www.w3.org/TR/xhtml1/strict"
  >
  <xsl:output method="html" indent="yes"/>
  <xsl:template match="/">
    <html>
      <head>
        <title><xsl:value-of select="/basic/name"/></title>
      </head>
      <body>
        <h1><xsl:value-of select="/basic/name" /></h1>
        <p><xsl:value-of select="/basic/body"/></p>
      </body>
```

```
    </html>
  </xsl:template>
  <xsl:template match="*"/>
</xsl:stylesheet>
```

XSLT makes heavy use of XML namespaces, as any XSLT file will contain at least two sets of XML elements: the XSLT element set (or sets—there can be more than one) and the elements used for the transformation and output of the source document. In this case, the source will be transformed into HTML.

The root element is `xsl:stylesheet`, where `xsl` is the name for the `http://www.w3.org/1999/XSL/Transform` namespace. HTML is declared the default namespace and has no prefix. In other words, any elements or attributes that begin with `xsl:` are XSLT instructions; the rest is just HTML.

> Namespace declarations in XSLT stylesheets are mandatory, so you will need to make sure to include the `xmlns` attributes in the root element. The URLs for XSLT and HTML are defined by the W3C and must be typed correctly, or else the XSLT processor will process the contents incorrectly. Every W3C XML and HTML format has a unique namespace. In fact, every XML format ought to have its own namespace, though certainly not all do.

The next element in the stylesheet specifies how the results will be written.

```
<xsl:output method="html" indent="yes"/>
```

Since we are transforming the XML to HTML, the method is set to `html`. The default output method is XML, but traditional HTML (with the exception of XHTML) does not always qualify as well-formed XML, so the `html` method must be explicitly set. If `indent` is set to yes, the output will be formatted in an easy-to-read format with lots of whitespace and line breaks. Otherwise, the stylesheet engine will use only the minimal amount of whitespace.

XSLT stylesheets function by reading the source document and, at each element, trying to find a template in the stylesheet to apply to the particular element. In the preceding stylesheet, there are two templates: `<xsl:template match="/" />`, which matches the root element, and `<xsl:template match="*"/>`, which matches any element at all—`match="*"` means that any element (expressed by *) should be considered a match. The latter template is a catchall, and doesn't do anything. It is there because some XSLT processors require it. The `<xsl:template match="/" />` element, on the other hand, does all of the work in this stylesheet. The `match` attribute contains the / XPath expression, which—just as a UNIX file system path refers to the root directory—refers to the root element of the XML document. Consequently, this template will be executed as soon as the XSLT processor hits the first element.

The template defines the HTML document that will be written. During processing, the <xsl:value-of/> elements are replaced with the information from the source XML document (the simple XML document we just created). In the HTML <title/> element, the <xsl:value-of select="/basic/name"/> element indicates that the text in the <name/> element inside the <basic/> element ("XML Content") should be placed here. Like <xsl:template/>'s match attribute, the select attribute of <xsl:value-of/> uses an XPath statement to identify the target element from the source XML. The XPath expression /basic/name points to a piece of XML that looks like this:

```
<basic>
  <name>Some Content Here</name>
</basic>
```

When the value-of expression is evaluated, it will take the text inside of /basic/name and insert it into the resulting document. So this fragment of an XSLT stylesheet, <title><xslt:value-of select="/basic/name"/></title>, will become <title>XML Content</title>.

Inside the HTML body, there are two more <xsl:value-of/> elements—one that places the value of /basic/name inside the <h1/> element, and another that places the value of /basic/body inside the <p/> element.

Now, we will write a JSP that will take the source XML and transform it with the XSLT stylesheet, sending the results to the browser.

JSP Elements

JSP elements, stored in the module's elements/ folder, contain reusable pieces of code that can be easily integrated into other JSP pages. On occasion, they are completely stand-alone pages, but are more often designed for inclusion in another JSP.

We need a JSP element to take the contents of an XML document and transform them with the XSLT that we created.

```
<%@ page import="com.opencms.flex.jsp.CmsJspActionElement,
                 com.opencms.file.CmsObject,
                 com.example.genericxml.xslt.CmsXslTransformer"
%>
<%
CmsJspActionElement cmsjsp =
    new CmsJspActionElement( pageContext,request, response );
String style = request.getParameter( "xslt" );
String source = request.getParameter( "source_xml" );
CmsObject cms = cmsjsp.getCmsObject();
CmsXslTransformer trans = new CmsXslTransformer( style, cms );
trans.transform( source, out );
%>
```

This is fairly straightforward. We get the name of the stylesheet, style, and the name of the source XML document, source, from the request parameters.

We create a new `CmsXslTransformer`, and then `transform()` the `source` document, writing the output to the `JspWriter out` object that exists within the scope of all JSPs.

Now that we have a JSP element, we can create a simple JSP file in the `/playground/` folder.

```
<%@ page session="false" %>
<%@ taglib
  prefix="cms" uri="http://www.opencms.org/taglib/cms" %>
<cms:include
  file="/system/modules/com.example.genericxml.xslt/elements
                                                  /xsltrans.jsp">
  <cms:param name="source_xml">/xml/basic-content.xml</cms:param>
  <cms:param name="xslt">
    /system/modules/com.example.genericxml.xslt/xslt/sample.xslt
  </cms:param>
</cms:include>
```

This simple JSP includes the JSP element we created, and then passes it two parameters—`source_xml`, which points to the source XML file, and `xslt`, which points to the XSLT stylesheet. Rather than explicitly define these parameters here, you could pass them in as part of the GET string (by appending `?source_xml=/path/to/myfile.xml&xslt=/path/to/mystyle.xslt` to the URL).

Loading this new JSP will now produce an HTML document resulting from the transformation:

```
<html xmlns="http://www.w3.org/TR/xhtml1/strict">
<head>
<title>XML Content</title>
</head>
<body>
<h1>XML Content</h1>
<p>This is an example of some basic XML content.</p>
</body>
</html>
```

The XSLT has substituted information from our source XML document into the `<xsl:template/>` and has written it out as HTML.

XSLT processing can be memory and processor intensive, and having the transformation run for every single request can be an unnecessary performance bottleneck. In the next section, we'll use an automated task to convert the XML documents to HTML, and then write the results into separate files in the VFS.

Adding a Scheduled Task

OpenCms provides a mechanism, similar to cron in UNIX, for running particular tasks at an appointed time. The primary user interface to this tool is in the 'scheduled tasks' section of the administration view. In this section, we will create a new task to convert batches of XML to HTML using the `CmsXslTransformer` class we created earlier.

To accomplish our task, we will need to create two classes—one to do the batch transforming and one to implement the `com.opencms.core.I_CmsCronJob` interface. Technically, these could be merged into one class, but since we may want to reuse the batch transformation code elsewhere, it is good to keep functionality split.

The BatchTransformer Class

The first class, `BatchTransformer`, will be responsible for transforming a directory of files using a single stylesheet, and then writing the resulting files to another directory.

```
package com.example.genericxml.xslt;
import com.opencms.core.CmsException;
import com.opencms.core.A_OpenCms;
import com.opencms.file.CmsObject;
import com.opencms.file.CmsResource;
import com.opencms.file.CmsFile;
import javax.xml.transform.stream.StreamResult;
import java.io.ByteArrayOutputStream;
import java.util.Vector;
import java.util.Hashtable;
import java.util.List;
import java.util.Iterator;
public class BatchTransformer {
    private CmsObject cms;
    private CmsXslTransformer cmsTrans;
    private boolean isLogging = false;
    private String outType = "plain";
    // Don't want this to be called at all.
    private BatchTransformer() {}

    public BatchTransformer( String xsltStylesheet,
                             CmsObject cms )
            throws CmsException {
        this.cms = cms;
        this.cmsTrans = new CmsXslTransformer( xsltStylesheet,
                                               cms );
    }

    public int transform( String inDir, String outDir )
            throws CmsException {
        Vector files = this.cms.getFilesInFolder( inDir );
        return this.transform( files, outDir );
    }
    public int transform( List cmsFiles, String outDir )
            throws CmsException {
        Iterator it = cmsFiles.iterator();
        int counter = 0;
        CmsFile file;
        ByteArrayOutputStream baos;
        StreamResult result;
        while( it.hasNext() ) {
            file = (CmsFile) it.next();
            // Need to write files, and there is no JAXP
            // wrapper for VFS.
            baos = new ByteArrayOutputStream();
```

```
            result = new StreamResult(baos);
            cmsTrans.transform( file, result );
            // Now the baos should have the contents of the HTML.
            if( baos.size() > 0 ) {
                this.createNewFile( file,
                                    baos.toByteArray(),
                                    outDir );
                ++ counter;
            }
        }
        return counter;
    }
    public void setVerbose( boolean verbose ) {
        this.isLogging = verbose;
        return;
    }
    public boolean getVerbose() {
        return this.isLogging;
    }
    protected CmsFile createNewFile( CmsFile original,
                                     byte[] contents,
                                     String outdir )
            throws CmsException {
        String newName = original.getName() + ".html";
        String origName = original.getResourceName();
        String origPath = original.getAbsolutePath( origName );

        String title = this.cms.readProperty( origPath,
                                              "Title" );
        String desc = this.cms.readProperty( origPath,
                                             "Description" );
        if( title == null || title == "" ) {
            title = "Untitled";
                                }
        if( desc == null || desc == "" ) {
            desc = "Tranformed file.";
                                }
        try {
            // If the file exists, delete it.
            // If file doesn't exist, call to lock will
            // throw a CmsException.
            // There is no method for checking if a file exists.
            this.cms.lockResource( outdir + newName, true );
            this.cms.deleteResource( outdir + newName );
            this.cms.unlockResource( outdir + newName );
            this.cms.publishResource( outdir + newName );
            if( this.isLogging ) {
                A_OpenCms.log( A_OpenCms.C_OPENCMS_INFO,
                               "Deleted " + outdir + newName );
            }
        } catch ( CmsException e ) {
            // must create new file.
            if( this.isLogging ) {
                A_OpenCms.log( A_OpenCms.C_OPENCMS_INFO,
                               "Failed delete of" + outdir +
                               newName +
                               ". Exception: " + e.toString() );
            }
        }
```

```
        CmsResource newFile;
        Hashtable props = new Hashtable();
        props.put( "Title", title );
        props.put( "Description", desc );
        // This will throw CmsException if it fails.
        newFile = cms.createResource( outdir,
                                      newName,
                                      this.outType,
                                      props,
                                      contents );
        if( this.isLogging ) {
            A_OpenCms.log( A_OpenCms.C_OPENCMS_INFO,
                           "Created " + outdir + newName );
        }
        return (CmsFile) newFile;
    }
```

The `BatchTransformer` constructor creates a new `CmsXslTransformer` that will be used for all of the transformations. Each of the `transform()` methods iterates through a list of files in the source folder, transforms the file, and then calls the `createNewFile()` method to dump the transformed contents into a file in the VFS. The files will be dumped into the directory specified in the call to `transform()`, and the new files will have the same names as the source files, but with `.html` appended.

The `createNewFile()` method first checks to see if the file already exists. Since there is no method in OpenCms to facilitate checking for the existence of files, the only way to find out is to attempt to manipulate the file. If an exception is thrown, that indicates that there is no file by that name. The problem, of course, is that the exception could be thrown for other reasons (for instance, if the file exists, but is corrupt). OpenCms developers are going to fix this behavior in the next release.

If no exception is thrown when the file is accessed via `cms.lockResource()`, the file is removed, and the removed file is then published, which has the effect of removing the file from the **Online** project as well as all of the **Offline** projects (all other projects are actually subprojects of Offline).

If a `CmsException` is thrown, the assumption is that the file does not exist. The method continues on to create the new `CmsFile`. It uses the properties of the original file to create the `Title` and `Description` properties of the transformed file, and then puts the results of the XSLT transformation into the `CmsFile`. Note that the newly created file is not unlocked or published.

The CronBatchTransformer Class

Now, we need a wrapper class that will implement the `I_CmsCronJob` interface and handle running the `BatchTransformer`.

```
package com.example.genericxml.xslt;
import com.opencms.core.I_CmsCronJob;
import com.opencms.core.CmsException;
```

```
import com.opencms.file.CmsObject;
import java.util.HashMap;
public class CronBatchTransformer implements I_CmsCronJob {
    // Names of the params.
    public static String PARAM_SOURCE_DIR = "source_dir";
    public static String PARAM_DEST_DIR = "dest_dir";
    public static String PARAM_STYLESHEET = "xslt";
    public String launch( CmsObject cms, String params )
            throws Exception {
        HashMap paramMap = parseParams( params );
        String sourceDir, destDir;
        if( !paramMap.containsKey( PARAM_SOURCE_DIR )) {
            throw new CmsException( "No source directory set." );
        } else if( !paramMap.containsKey( PARAM_DEST_DIR )) {
            throw new CmsException(
                "No destination directory set." );
        } else if( !paramMap.containsKey( PARAM_STYLESHEET )) {
            throw new CmsException( "No XSLT Stylesheet set." );
        }
        String style = (String) paramMap.get( PARAM_STYLESHEET );
        sourceDir = (String) paramMap.get( PARAM_SOURCE_DIR );
        destDir = (String) paramMap.get( PARAM_DEST_DIR );
        // We need to be in the Offline (4) project.
        cms.getRequestContext().setCurrentProject( 4 );
        BatchTransformer bt = new BatchTransformer( style, cms );
        bt.setVerbose( true );
        int count = bt.transform( sourceDir, destDir );
        return "Created " + Integer.toString( count )
            + " documents.";
    }

    private static HashMap parseParams( String params ) {
        if( params == null || "".equals( params ) ) {
            return new HashMap();
                                        }
        String sep1 = ","; // Separates params
        String sep2 = "="; // Separates name/value
        HashMap results = new HashMap();
        String [] args = params.split( sep1, 0 );
        String [] nameVal;
        int i, j = args.length;
        for (i = 0; i < j; ++i) {
            if( args[i].length() > 2 ) {
                nameVal = args[i].split( sep2, 2 );
                if( nameVal[0].length() >= 1 )
                    results.put( nameVal[0], nameVal[1] );
            }
        }
        return results;
    }
}
```

The `CronBatchTransformer` implements the `launch()` method of `I_CmsCronJob`. OpenCms passes the `launch()` method an instance of a `CmsObject` and a string that contains the contents of the parameter string specified in the scheduled tasks screen (we'll look at that in detail in a moment).

The `parseParams()` method simply parses that parameter string according to a few simple rules: commas (`,`) separate arguments and the equals (=) sign separates the name from the value in any given parameter. Once the parameters are parsed, the `launch()` method checks to make sure that all three parameters—`source_dir`, `dest_dir`, and `xslt`—are set. If they are not, a `CmsException` is thrown and the task is aborted.

- The `source_dir` parameter specifies *which* folder the raw XML files exist.
- `dest_dir` indicates *where* the transformed files should be written.
- `xslt` indicates *what* stylesheet will be used to transform the XML files.

Next, the active project is set. By default, scheduled tasks run in the Online project. However, we want to work in the Offline project, where we can add and remove files. Unfortunately, we cannot simply refer to the project by name, but must do so by project ID. Project 4 is the Offline project.

Once operating in the correct project, the `launch()` method creates a new `BatchTransformer`, which transforms all of the files in `source_dir` and writes them to the folder specified by `dest_dir`.

Finally, the `String` returned by `launch()` will be written to the OpenCms log file. Unless an exception is thrown, the message should say 'Created N documents', where N is the number of documents created.

Just as with the `CmsXslTransformer` class, both `BatchTransformer` and `CronBatchTransformer` should be compiled and loaded into the `classes/com/example/genericxml/xslt/` folder in the module, and then the resources should be unlocked and published. Finally, the servlet container must be restarted to load the new classes.

> If you have numerous files to load into the VFS and they all share the same destination folder, you can zip them into a single file and load the zip file. In the OpenCms file-selector dialogue, there is a checkbox for unzipping the file. If you check this, the zip file will be unpacked, and each of its files will be written into the VFS.

Scheduling a Task

The next step is to schedule our new task. Go to the administration view and click on Scheduled tasks. You will see a textbox with the following heading:

```
Syntax: minute(*|0-59) hour(*|0-23) day(*|1-31) month(*|0-11) day of
week(*|0-6) user group startclass parameter
```

The Scheduled tasks screen works in much the same way as a UNIX cron table. There are nine columns in this cron table, separated by spaces. The first five specify the time that the task is to be run. The legend here indicates the order of the columns: `minute`, `hour`, `day`, `month`, and `day of week`. Each of these columns takes an integer value. Obviously, not all of these can (or should) be completed for any given task—`day` and `day of week`, for instance, are mutually exclusive. So, if you do not wish to use a particular column, simply place an asterisk (*) in the column.

The next two columns specify *which* `user` and `group` OpenCms will use to execute the task. This can be used to enforce security rules on automated tasks. On a production system, it is wise to run a task with a user and group with fewer permissions than an admin user. This can protect the content from accidental damage. However, when you write your cron classes, you must be proactive in catching exceptions thrown by access violations.

> It is often desirable to catch some exceptions and keep on processing, rather than let a single access violation stop an entire task. This can be tricky, though, as OpenCms objects almost ubiquitously throw the same `CmsException`, and as we have seen, exceptions are often used in lieu of simple test functions (like testing to see if a file exists).

The eighth parameter, `startclass`, defines the class that will be executed when the task is run. This class must implement `I_CmsCronJob`. When the task is started, this class will be loaded and initialized, and its `launch()` method will be executed.

How an I_CmsCronJob Is Executed

`launch()` is passed two arguments. The first is an instance of `CmsObject`, and the second is the entire contents of the last column in the cron table—the parameter column. The parameter column consists of alphanumeric characters excluding spaces (which are used as column delimiters) and line breaks (which are used as record separators). The `com.opencms.core.CmsCronScheduleJob` class, which is responsible for executing scheduled tasks, makes no effort to parse this parameter string. Instead, it is up to each cron class to do its own parsing. The `parseParams()` method we created in the `CronBatchTransformer` class reads parameter strings of the form `name1=value1,name2=value2` where commas (`,`) separate parameters, and equals signs (=) delimit the name and the value. However, you may choose to use any method you find suitable, as long as the parameter string does not contain spaces or line breaks.

Here is my entry for running the XSLT transformer code we created:

```
15 1 * * * Admin Administors
com.example.genericxml.xslt.CronBatchTransformer
source_dir=/xml/,dest_dir=/html/,xslt=/system/modules/com.example.gen
ericxml.xslt/xslt/sample.xslt
(Note: the above should be on one line.)
```

This task will run at 1:15 am as the `Admin` user in the `Administrators` group. It will execute the `launch()` method of `CronBatchTransformer`, passing it the parameter string `source_dir=/xml/,dest_dir=/html/,xslt=/system/modules/com.example.genericxml.xslt/xslt/sample.xslt`.

> Often, OpenCms administrators report errors in the log file that state that the cron table is corrupt. The most likely cause for this is an empty line at the end of the cron table. The OpenCms cron scheduler cannot handle blank lines. Simply go into the Scheduled tasks screen and delete the blank lines to fix the problem.

Once the entry is in the cron table, it will be run as scheduled. Changes to the cron table do not require the server to restart. The output of cron scripts is written to the main OpenCms log (viewable with the Logfile viewer in the administration view), and after every job, you should see a message in the log file indicating the status of the task:

```
[05.04.2004 15:35:10] <opencms_cronscheduler> Successful launch of
job com.opencms.core.CmsCronEntry{35 15 * * * admin Administrators
com.example.genericxml.xslt.CronBatchTransformer
source_dir=/xml/,dest_dir=/html/,xslt=/system/modules/com.example.gen
ericxml.xslt/xslt/sample.xslt} Message: Created 2 documents.
```

If the task fails with an exception, the exception will be written to the log file, and the failure will be noted.

Now we have a functionally complete module. Here, we will turn to topics relating to managing and deploying the module itself.

Managing the Module

For the most part, the tasks for managing a module do not differ substantially from the creation wizard we walked through in the beginning of this chapter. The Module management task in the administration view provides access to the module management software. The Module management screen lists all of the modules installed on the system. Just as with files in the explorer view, clicking on the module's icon brings up the popup navigation menu for that module.

In the popup menu, there are four entries: Administrate, Properties, Export, and Delete. Delete should be self-explanatory—executing it deletes the entire module, including content stored outside the module, but explicitly specified in the module's `additionalresources` (which we will return to later in this chapter). We will cover Export in the next section. In this section, though, we will cover the other two.

Administrate

Choosing the Administrate item will bring up a screen that ought to look familiar—it is identical to the module creation screen that we walked through at the beginning of this chapter, and behaves identically. Use this screen to update critical information about the module before you export it. For instance, each time a new version of the module is released, the Version field in this screen should be updated to indicate that. In addition, if you add an administrative point, a view, or maintenance and publishing classes, you should update the information here so that those classes are associated with this module.

The Dependency Screen

Clicking Continue will bring up the module dependency screen:

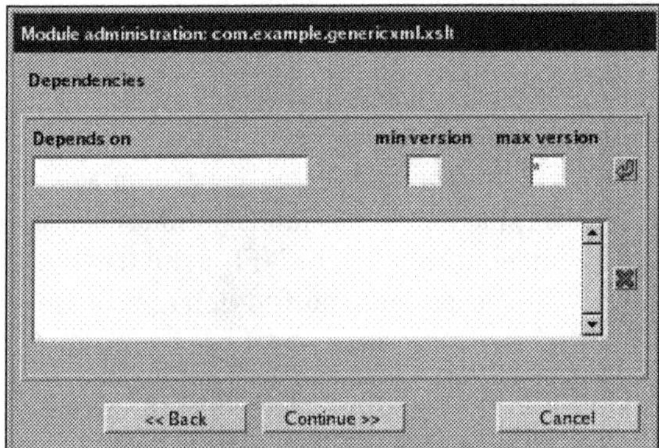

If this module requires another module in order to function correctly, fill in the Depends On, Min Version, and Max Version fields of the form, and add the dependency to the list. When the module is imported into another system, OpenCms will run a dependency check to ensure that it has the required modules. This dependency check is also run when someone attempts to delete a module—a module will not be deleted if other installed modules require it.

The Depends On field should contain the full name of the module—for example, `com.example.genericxml.xslt`. Min Version and Max Version should contain version numbers. The asterisk (*) value can be used to allow any version value. If, for instance, Min Value is 1.0 and Max Value is *, any version greater than or equal to 1.0 will be allowed. Clicking the blue arrow icon adds the dependency to the list in the text area below. Clicking Continue will bring up the module properties dialogue.

The Module Properties Screen

Like files and folders, modules can have properties. However, there are only a few predefined properties for modules, and really, only one particular property is used: `additionalresources`. Consider the folder we created for storing XML documents, `/xml/`. Since it is a likely candidate for editing, we put this folder in the root of the VFS along with the rest of the content. However, we may want this folder to be included with our module, making it easy to deploy our XML documents along with the framework for transforming them into HTML via XSLT. Using the `additionalresources` parameter, we can associate the `/xml/` folder with this module.

While using `additionalresources` can provide a simple way of putting module content outside the module directory, it can add unnecessary complexity and confusion. For instance, if we associate the `/xml/` directory with the module, then any new content that is created inside the `/xml/` folder will automatically become associated with the module. If the module is exported, that content will go with it. If the module is deleted, that content will be deleted as well.

> Judicious use of the `additionalresources` property can add significant features to the module (for instance, the OpenCms tutorial modules use this method to put the tutorial text in the content portion of the VFS). But use this property carefully—it can cause unexpected and hard-to-debug problems if misused.

The module properties list for our XSLT module is empty. Use the **New** button to create a new property. You will notice that this property-creation dialogue is more complex than the corresponding property screen for files and folders.

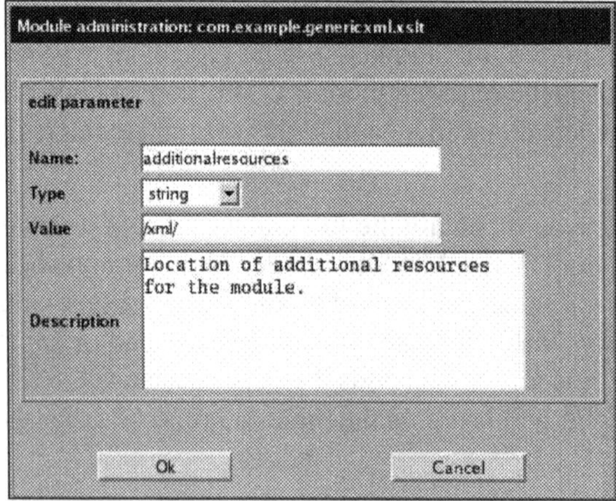

Name should be `additionalresources`. Type indicates the format of the data in the value. For the most part, this consists of the primitive types plus string (corresponding to `java.lang.String`). For `additionalresources`, string is the appropriate type. The Value textbox should contain the name of the directory, `/xml/`, which we are associating with the module.

> If you need to specify multiple paths in the `additionalresources` parameter, use semicolons to separate the values. Example: `additionalresources: /xml/;/extras/`.

The optional Description field allows you to make a brief note about the kind of data stored in the parameter. This is useful if you need to define your own properties for a new module. Clicking OK will create the new parameter.

Once you have created the new property, the previously empty box will now have an entry showing the new property.

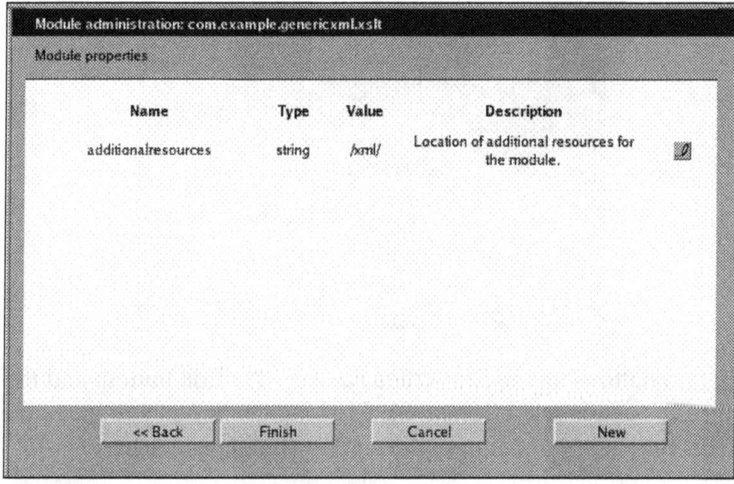

To edit the property, click the pencil icon on the right. Otherwise, clicking Finish will write your changes to the VFS (actually, most are written already, and the Finish and Cancel buttons appear to function identically).

Properties

Returning to the module's popup menu, the second item in the menu is Properties. Essentially, it provides a slightly different view of some of the data in the Administrate wizard we just walked through.

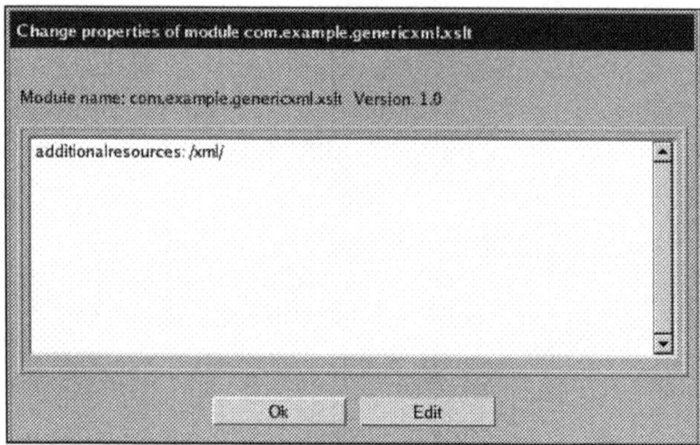

The first dialogue lists the module's properties. You should see the `additionalresources` property in the box. Highlighting the property activates the Edit button, which, when clicked, will open a very simple dialogue that will show you the information about the property, including type and description, but will only allow you to change the value.

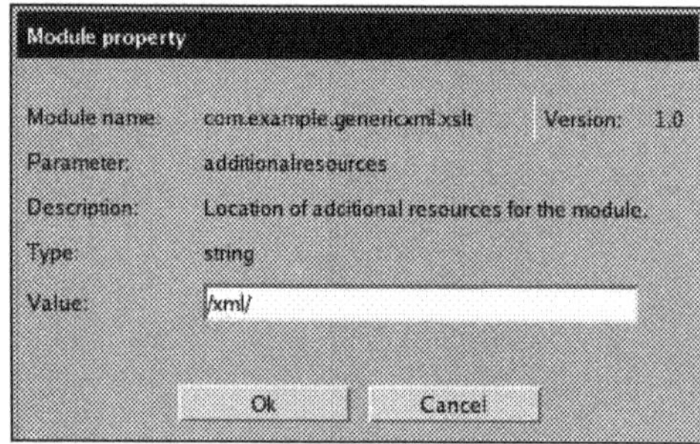

There are only two buttons on the Properties screen—the Edit button, and the Ok button (which should have been labeled Continue). Clicking Ok brings you to another stripped-down view—this time of the module's information and dependencies.

The dialogue that follows is provided for convenient viewing, but is read-only. It simply pulls the information from the first two screens of the Administrate wizard into one place. Oddly, this screen also has two buttons—Ok, which will return to the Module management screen, and Parameter, which brings up... properties again! Essentially, it works like a 'back' button, though the name is misleading.

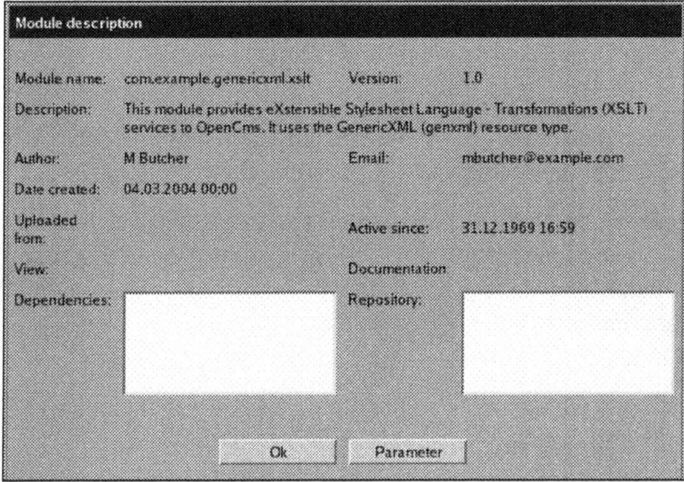

Now we've looked at setting custom module properties. In order for most of these properties to be useful, your code will need to be able to access the parameters and manipulate the stored data.

Accessing Module Parameters from JSP Pages

If you are writing custom modules, module properties provide a convenient method of storing module-specific information. But retrieving them is a little different than retrieving the properties that are attached to individual resources.

Module parameters are written into the registry file in `$CATALINA_HOME/webapps/opencms/WEB-INF/registry.xml`. Consequently, all you have to do to retrieve a property is read it from the registry:

```
<%@ page import="com.opencms.file.I_CmsRegistry,
                 com.opencms.core.A_OpenCms" %>
<%

String mod_name = "com.example.genericxml.xslt";
String param_name = "additionalresources";

I_CmsRegistry registry = A_OpenCms.getRegistry();

String add_res = registry.getModuleParameterString( mod_name,
param_name );

out.println( add_res );

%>
```

The preceding code reads the additionalresources property from the com.example.genericxml.xslt module and prints the value.

The JSP first retrieves a copy of the registry. To do this, it uses the getRegistry() method of the com.opencms.core.A_OpenCms singleton class, which returns an object that implements the com.opencms.file.I_CmsRegistry interface.

The getModuleParameterString() method of the I_CmsRegistry object returns the value of the parameter param_name (additionalproperties, in this case) from the module with the name mod_name (com.example.genericxml.xslt, in this case). Setting the value of a parameter can be done just as easily, using the setModuleParameter() method defined in the I_CmsRegistry interface.

In the next section, we will move on to the topic of exporting the module. Before you export the module, you may want to revisit the Administrate screen for your module and make sure the basic information, including version and description, is up to date.

Exporting and Deploying the Module

The Export feature automatically packages the module into a single zip archive, prepared for import into another system. To export a module from the Module management screen in the administration view, click on the module's icon and select Export from the popup menu. You will be prompted to confirm that you want to export the module. Clicking Ok will begin an export process that looks similar to publishing a project. The last line in the list of messages should say something like ... the module has been exported, indicating that the files from the module were packaged into a single archive and written to the real file system.

By default, modules are exported to $CATALINA_HOME/webapps/opencms/WEB-INF/export/modules/, where they are named as [module-name]_[version].zip; for example, com.example.genericxml.xslt_1.0.zip. The zip file contains all the files necessary for importing this module into another OpenCms server—including the contents of the module directory, some metadata stored in an XML manifest file, and resources specified with the additionalresources property.

Installing the module on another system is as simple as copying the module archive to *that* server and running the module installation wizard as we did in Chapter 3.

Summary

In this chapter, we covered the process involved in creating a complete module, including Java code, JSPs, and content. We also explored the process of managing and exporting the module. The module feature of OpenCms is a powerful way to extend the generic

CMS capabilities of the server. The examples given here should provide a basic introduction to building modules, as well as the general development guidelines for successfully coding against OpenCms APIs. However, we have only scratched the surface here.

The diversity of modules that already exist for OpenCms, ranging from documentation to special content types, to complete functional elements like online calendaring or site searching, attest to the flexibility and potential of the module mechanism. The OpenCms developers have expressed excitement at the wealth of module development, and are continuing improvements to the module mechanism. It is likely that this modular framework will continue to be a major foundation for development and extension of OpenCms.

7

Advanced Modules

In the previous chapter, we created a module for transforming XML documents to HTML using XSLT stylesheets. In this chapter, we will look into a few of the more advanced possibilities available in the module mechanism. We will add an administration point to the module, providing an entry in the administration view for transforming XML documents at the click of a button. We will also create a custom launcher class for customizing the way OpenCms delivers content of the generic XML resource type we created in Chapter 5.

In this chapter, we will cover:

- Creating an administration point for a module
- Using JSPs for creating an administration screen
- Editing XML templates
- Creating a custom launcher class

Adding an Administration Point

Many advanced modules will have some tasks that need to be performed by an administrator. We can integrate module administration into the existing administration view by creating an **administration point**.

We already have an existing module, `com.example.genericxml.xslt`, to which we can add an **administration point**. In the last chapter, we created a scheduled task to run a batch transform of the XML files. However, it would be nice to be able to run the command with the click of a button, instead of waiting for the task to run. In this chapter, we will implement such a screen in the administration view.

The first thing to do is configure the module for an administration point. To do this, switch to the administration view and go to Module management. Choose Administrate from the popup menu of the `com.example.genericxml.xslt` module. On the first screen of the module administration wizard, check the Administration point box, and then continue through the rest of the wizard, clicking Finish on the last screen.

In the explorer view, you should now see an `administration/` folder under `/system/modules/com.example.genericxml.xslt/`. This folder is used for storing the contents that will be displayed in the administration view.

Creating Icons

Before continuing on to create the administration screens, we need to create a directory for icons, and then create an icon for our application. Create a folder called `pics/` in `/system/modules/com.example.genericxml.xslt/`. You will need an icon for the administration menu. Typically, these icons are 32 pixels by 32 pixels. The file must be a GIF file. My GIF file is called `xsl-admin.gif`. It is also a good idea to create an inactive version of your icon. This icon will be used when the task should be marked as unavailable. This icon must have the same name as the other icon, but with an `_in` suffix; for example, `xslt-admin_in.gif`. Typically, the inactive icon is created by converting the color icon to grayscale.

Adding a Properties File

The next thing to do is create a properties file for administration point properties. This file, called `workplace.properties`, must be created in the base of the classes hierarchy, `classes/com/example/genericxml/xslt`. If you are supporting multiple languages, you should create one properties file for each language, naming it `workplace_en.properties`, where `en` is replaced by the ISO language code—`fr` for French, `de` for German, etc.

The only thing we need in the properties file is a property for the name of our administration point. Here is an example:

```
genericxml.administration.icon.xslt=XSLT Administration
```

The property name can be whatever you want, but it is wise to make sure that it will not clash with that of another property in OpenCms. A typical convention is to use the module name, followed by `administration.icon` and a short name for the menu.

Unlock and publish the properties file. You will also need to restart the servlet container so that the properties file is read.

> If you do not restart (or if you make a typo in the properties file), and you finish creating the administration point, the caption to the image icon will look something like this: ??? `genericxml.administration.icon.xslt` ???.

> If you restart and still see the error message, double-check the spelling and syntax in the properties file.

Anytime you make changes to the properties file, you will need to unlock it, publish it, and restart the servlet container. We are now ready to create the main administration point directory.

Creating Administration Point Folders

You will recall that a folder named `administration/` was automatically created for us by the module administration wizard. Inside `administration/`, you must create one folder for each icon you want to display in the administration view. Each of these folders must have several OpenCms properties (the sort that are stored in OpenCms, not in the Java properties file) that instruct OpenCms how to display the icon.

For the application at hand, we will create a folder named `XSLT/`. When creating a folder in the `administration/` folder, we use the same wizard as we would to create a folder anywhere else in the VFS. A word of caution here! When creating this folder, we have to do a few things differently than usual. Instead of creating a *new* wizard for these screens, the OpenCms developers used the *same* wizard, with the properties being used for different purposes. The result is that the property named title is actually used to hold information about the image icon.

The usual fields should be completed according to the following guidelines:

- Name should be the name of the administration screen; XSLT in our case.
- Title is not the title of the administration point. Rather, it is the name of the GIF file (minus the extension) that we saved in the `pics/` directory; for example, our image was named `xslt-admin.gif`, so this field should be set to xslt-admin.
- Navigation Text (which corresponds to the `NavText` property) should be set to the name of the Java property we created in the `workplace.properties` file—`genericxml.administration.icon.xslt`.
- Position in navigation functions normally. It controls *which* position in the navigation this icon will occupy. Normally, it is best to leave the default value. You can change it later by editing the folder's `NavPos` property.

Once you create the folder, you will be prompted to create an `index.html` page. Click Cancel, as we will be creating a JSP page instead.

Adding Additional Properties

There are two additional properties that you can set by editing the properties by hand: `visiblemethod` and `activemethod`. The `visiblemethod` property determines whether the administration point will be visible, while the `activemethod` property determines whether the administration point will be active (clickable). Unlike most properties, these two take the full name of a Java method that takes no parameters and returns a boolean value.

The `com.opencms.workplace.CmsWorkplaceDefaults` class has a number of methods that are useful for these two properties.

`com.opencms.workplace.CmsWorkplaceDefaults.isOnlineProject`, for instance, will return `true` only if the current project is online. If `activemethod` used this method, then the icon would only be marked active when the Online project is selected.

`com.opencms.workplace.CmsWorkplaceDefaults.isNotOnlineProject` does the opposite. The icon would be marked inactive (grayed out) when the Online project is selected.

> You must leave the parentheses off of the method name when specifying the `activemethod` and `visiblemethod` property values.

Both `activemethod` and `visiblemethod` are optional, and default to visible and active respectively if not set. For our application, we will set `activemethod` to `com.opencms.workplace.CmsWorkplaceDefaults.isNotOnlineProject`.

Of course, it is also possible to create custom classes that can perform other checks—perhaps customized to your specific projects or groups—and control the visibility or activation of an administration icon. The code in `com.opencms.workplace.CmsWorkplaceDefaults` provides some good example methods, and you may find reading the sourcecode beneficial.

Creating an Administration JSP

We now have a folder for our administration point. Inside that folder, we create a new JSP named `index.html` (note that the extension should be `.html`, not `.jsp`).

We want to create a page that will allow us to specify a stylesheet, a source directory, and a destination directory (just like the scheduled task in the last chapter) and then run the XSLT transformation on the fly.

The JSP Code

Instead of splitting the application into multiple pages, we can handle the whole transformation with one JSP file that includes both the form and the code for processing the form values. Aside from being more efficient to code, it also presents a simple user interface.

Here is the beginning of the code for the `index.html` JSP:

```
<%@ page session="false"
    import="com.opencms.flex.jsp.CmsJspActionElement,
            com.opencms.file.CmsObject,
            com.opencms.core.CmsException,
            com.example.genericxml.xslt.BatchTransformer"
%>
<%
  String xslt = request.getParameter("xslt");
  String srcDir = request.getParameter("sourcedir");
  String destDir = request.getParameter("destdir");
  CmsJspActionElement cmsjsp =
      new CmsJspActionElement( pageContext, request, response );
  String baseUrl = cmsjsp.link( "/system/workplace/" );
%>
<html>
<head><title>XSLT Admin</title></head>
<script>
adminUrl = "<%= baseUrl %>action/administration_head.html';
</script>
<body
  onload="window.top.body.admin_head.location = adminUrl;">
<h1>XSLT Administration</h1>

<form method="GET" target="_self">
  XSLT Stylesheet: <input type="text" name="xslt" /><br/>
  Source Dir: <input type="text" name="sourcedir" /><br/>
  Destination Dir: <input type="text" name="destdir" /><br/>
  <input type="submit" value="Submit" />
</form>
```

This first section of code shows both the HTML form and the JSP scriptlet (above the HTML) that fetches the values submitted by the form.

The HTML form simply defines three fields: one for the XSLT stylesheet, one for the source directory, and one for the destination directory.

> In this example, I have hardcoded the labels (`XSLT Stylesheet`, `Source Dir`, `Destination Dir`), but if I needed to support multiple languages, I would store the labels in the `workplace.properties` file discussed earlier. Using the techniques discussed in Chapter 4, the appropriate language could be inserted dynamically based on the user's preferences.

When this form is completed, it will submit three parameters: `xslt`, `sourcedir`, and `destdir`. The JSP code (after the page declaration) fetches the values of the request parameters and puts them in `String` objects. A new `CmsJspActionElement` is created and the `baseUrl` string is created to simplify creating links.

After the initial scriptlet block, the HTML document is created. In the header, there is a very short JavaScript section followed by the <body> tag:

```
<script>
adminUrl = "<%= baseUrl %>action/administration_head.html";
</script>
<body
  onload="window.top.body.admin_head.location = adminUrl;">
```

The script simply sets the `adminUrl` variable for later use. Remember: <%= `baseUrl` => is a JSP scriptlet equivalent to <% `out.println( baseUrl );` %>. `adminUrl` is used in the `onLoad` event handler in the <body> element. When the page is loaded, the value of the variable `location` in one of the other HTML frames (`top.body.admin_head`) is set to the value of `adminUrl`. Essentially, this is setting a variable for the script that determines where the blue back button should go. If this statement is left out, the back button will be deactivated.

Below the form, we need to add the rest of the page—a scriptlet for handling the XSLT transformation code:

```
<%
  if( xslt != null && srcDir != null && destDir != null ) {
    CmsObject cms = cmsjsp.getCmsObject();
    boolean filesExist = true;
    try {
      cms.readFile( xslt );
      cms.readFolder( srcDir );
      cms.readFolder( destDir );
    } catch ( CmsException e ) {
      out.println( "<b>Stylesheet, Source and Destination "
        + "must exist in VFS" );
      filesExist = false;
    }
    if( filesExist ) {
      BatchTransformer trans =
        new BatchTransformer( xslt, cms  );
      int numProcessed = trans.transform( srcDir, destDir );
      out.print( "<p>Processed " );
      out.print( numProcessed );
      out.print( " Files. Output was written to "
                 + destDir
                 + ".</p>");
    }
    out.println( "<script>" );
    out.println( "document.forms[0].xslt.value = '"
                 + xslt
                 + "'" );
    out.println( "document.forms[0].destdir.value = '"
                 + destDir
                 + "'" );
```

```
        out.println( "document.forms[0].sourcedir.value = '"
                     + srcDir
                     + "'" );
        out.println( "</script>" );
    }
%>
</body>
</html>
```

This scriptlet begins by making sure that all three of the parameters are set. Next, it uses the try/catch method discussed in the last chapter to see if `xslt` references an existing `CmsFile`, and `srcDir` and `destDir` reference existing `CmsFolders`. If the three parameters are valid, a new `BatchTransformer` is created and the files in the `srcDir` folder are transformed and written to the `destDir` folder.

Underneath the transform code, there is a short dynamically generated JavaScript that sets the values of the three form fields to the values that the JSP received in the request. This is done as a convenience.

The Administration Point in Action

When you switch to the administration view and click on the XML icon, you should see something like this:

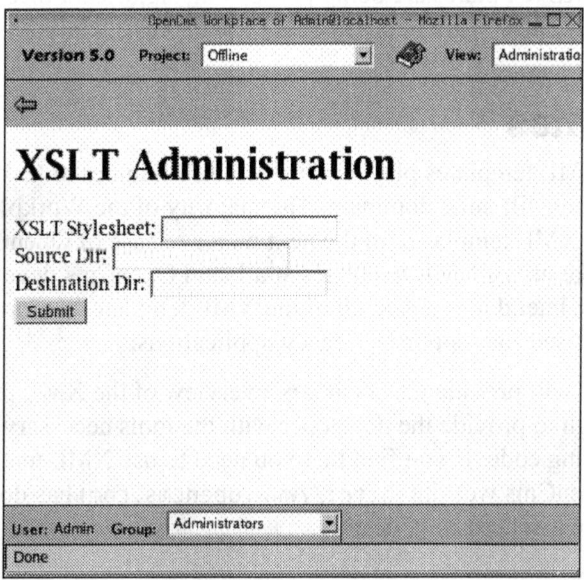

When you complete the form and run it, you should get a simple message displaying the number of files that were transformed:

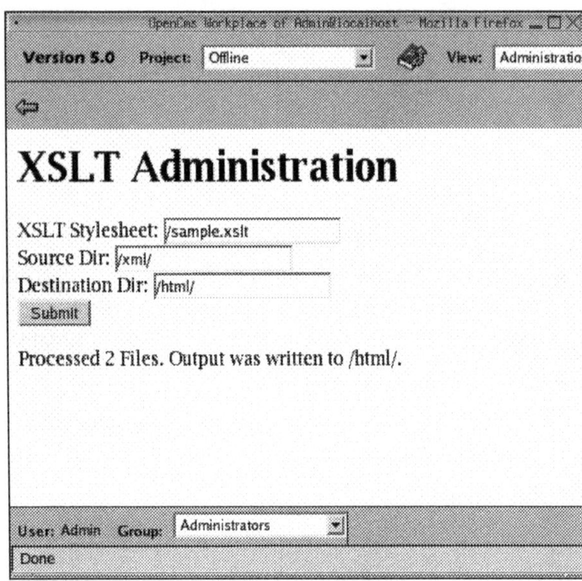

At this point, we have completed a simple administration point. From here, we will continue on to examine the proprietary (and deprecated) OpenCms XML template language. While XML templates are being phased out, significant pieces of OpenCms—specifically the Workplace—still make frequent use of XML template technology.

XML Templates

In OpenCms 5.0, XML templates play a minor role in a number of tasks, but there is one area in which they are still quite dominant. The majority of the Workplace is still implemented using XML templates. In the next major release of OpenCms, the core system will not make use of XML templates at all, and OpenCms developers have announced that they intend to relegate all of the XML template support code to a separate module that can be used for supporting legacy applications.

With this in mind, I will provide just a cursory overview of the XML template mechanism—enough to provide the developer with the tools necessary to interact with, fix, or modify existing code. If you find that you need to use XML templates more extensively, the OpenCms website (`http://www.opencms.com`) has documents that explain the template mechanism in detail.

How XML Templates Work

Essentially, there are three XML template types used for rendering a page:

- The frametemplate defines the structure of the page. Typically, the frametemplate will contain the HTML structural tags, such as <html/>, <head/>, and <body/>.
- The contenttemplate contains the content that will be placed into the frametemplate. For Page resources, a contenttemplate also has a sub-template for the body. This sub-template is typically stored in the /system/bodies folder.
- The mastertemplate ties the other two together, correlating a Java class to each of the other templates. The Java classes are used to retrieve dynamic information. These classes extend the com.opencms.template.CmsXmlTemplate class, and, in regard to the Workplace, are in the package com.opencms.workplace.

When a page that uses XML templates is called, OpenCms reads the contenttemplate to find the mastertemplate, which it uses to dynamically load the Java classes and then render the frametemplate and the contenttemplate.

Editing XML Templates

As the name implies, XML template files are written in XML. The HTML that they contain is wrapped inside <![CDATA[ ]]> sections. For instance, consider this fragment of a contenttemplate that when run creates a simple HTML page with one dynamic message retrieved from the workplace.properties file:

```
<?xml version="1.0" encoding="ISO-8859-1"?>
<WORKPLACE>
<TEMPLATE name="file">

<![CDATA[
  <html>
    <head>
      <title>
        ]]>
          <LABEL value="example.title" />

        <![CDATA[
      </title>
    </head>
    <body>
      ]]>
        <METHOD name="getBody"/>

      <![CDATA[
    </body>
  </html>
]]>
</TEMPLATE>
</WORKPLACE>
```

Everything in CDATA sections (highlighted) is HTML that must be escaped in CDATA to prevent the XML parser from errantly parsing it. The other elements, `<WORKPLACE>`, `<TEMPLATE>`, `<LABEL>`, and `<METHOD>`, are all XML template elements.

In XML templates, there are three functional elements that you will encounter frequently, two of which are present in the preceding section:

- `<LABEL value="some.property.string"/>`: This element is used to retrieve a value from a properties file. In the Workplace, it is almost always the `workplace.properties` files.
- `<METHOD name="someMethod"/>`: This element executes the named method in the class that has been correlated with this template. If the template was associated with the `com.example.workplace.ExampleTemplate` class, the `ExampleTemplate.someMethod()` would be executed and its contents written into the template. It is possible to pass a `String` parameter to the method by enclosing the parameter inside the `<METHOD>` element. For example, `<METHOD name="someMethod">myParam</METHOD>`.
- `<PROCESS>elementName</PROCESS>`: This element takes the value of another element, named `elementName`, and includes it in place of the `<PROCESS>` element. The example we just saw would try to find an `<elementName>` element and include its contents.

The Structure of the Workplace XML Templates

The Workplace XML templates and all supporting files are stored in the VFS under the `/system/workplace` folder. They are laid out as follows.

The action Folder

The `action/` folder contains files for the functional elements of the Workplace. Most of the files in this folder are simple XML templates that define the class and `mastertemplate` to use in handling an action.

The administration Folder

The `/system/workplace/administration/` folder works just like the `administration/` folder in a module. Each directory in the folder represents an icon in the administration view, and within each of those folders are all of the XML templates and JSP files necessary for that administration point.

The help and locales Folders

These folders are used to store text for the help and localization subsystems.

The resources Folder

The `resources/` folder contains all the supporting resources (primarily images) that the Workplace requires.

The restypes Folder

We examined the `restypes/` folder in Chapter 5 when we created a new resource type. Each of the files in this folder contains JavaScript for displaying context and popup menus for resources based on the file's type. These files are then included in other XML templates before they are sent to the client.

The scripts Folder

OpenCms makes use of a tremendous amount of JavaScript. Much of it is stored inside individual XML template files, but some libraries of functions have been extracted into stand-alone files, which are in this directory.

The templates Folder

This folder contains all of the XML templates for displaying the workplace (excluding the templates that are in the `administration/` folder). These files, `frametemplates`, provide the look and feel information for each screen in the Workplace. Often, files in this folder will be correlated with identically named files in the `actions/` folder; this greatly simplifies the process of trying to correlate the two.

Most of the time, if you are trying to modify the layout of a workplace screen, you will be working in the `templates/` folder.

The /system/login Folder

Finally, it bears mentioning that one piece of the workplace code is stored outside the workplace directory—primarily for security reasons.

The `/system/login` folder contains the XML templates and necessary supporting files for handling authentication to the OpenCms Workplace.

At this point, you should have the necessary tools to add a custom administration point to your module, even if it entails tying into the legacy XML template code. Now, we will turn our attention from administration points to another tool for advanced modules: custom launchers.

Creating a Custom Launcher

In Chapter 5, we created a custom resource type, generic XML, which was designed specifically for storing arbitrary XML data. Since creating that resource type, we have developed a JSP to handle XSLT translations on the fly, a scheduled task to transform an entire directory of XML files to HTML using a given stylesheet, and an administration point that runs the same process on demand.

While each of these is useful, another solution to the problem would be to have OpenCms recognize *when* a file was a genxml document and, if there was an associated XSLT file, automatically transform the file on the fly. In this situation, there would be no additional maintenance aside from creating the XML files and one or more stylesheets.

In this section, we will create a class that implements the `com.opencms.launcher.I_CmsLauncher` interface for processing the contents of a particular resource type, and we will add this class to our XSLT module. This is an example of how a module can extend the capabilities of the OpenCms system.

The Basic Idea

When a Page type resource is requested, OpenCms retrieves the Page, the body, the XML template, and the JSP template, and uses them all to render the final document. When a Plain type resource is requested, OpenCms delivers the resource as-is and doesn't attempt to modify the file contents at all. When a JSP page is requested, the JSP is compiled and executed. In each of these three cases, OpenCms handles the request differently.

In Chapter 5, we created a custom generic-XML (genxml) resource type. We configured OpenCms, in `registry.xml`, to handle requests for genxml documents the same way it handles requests for resources of the Plain type. However, it is possible to create a custom launcher for the resource type that will process genxml documents in a different manner.

The launcher that we will implement will read an XML file. If the XML file has the `xslt` property set, pointing to an XSLT file in the VFS, then the launcher will transform the XML using that stylesheet. If no stylesheet is set, the launcher will simply return the XML as-is.

OpenCms uses a dynamic class loader to load all of the launcher classes; so, creating a new launcher is straightforward: implement `com.opencms.launcher.I_CmsLauncher`, put it in a module, configure the registry, and restart OpenCms.

Implementing a Launcher

The `I_CmsLauncher` interface defines four methods:

- `clearCache()`: This method is used by XML template classes for clearing the template cache. In applications such as ours, which do not rely upon the XML template mechanism, there is nothing that this method must do.
- `getLauncherId()`: Every launcher has a specific ID. In the `registry.xml` file, resource types are correlated to the launcher based on this ID. The ID is an integer, and, to avoid conflicts with OpenCms, it should be higher than 10.
- `initLauncher()`: This is the most important method of the interface. When OpenCms receives a request to render a resource using this launcher, it will call this method. Essentially, this method will handle the processing of information and the subsequent writing of that information to the output stream.
- `setOpenCms()`: This method provides a way of setting the instance of `A_OpenCms`. When the new launcher is created, this method is immediately called. Some of the launchers (most notably, the abstract `A_CmsLauncher` class that many of the other launchers extend) do nothing when this method is executed. They directly use the `A_OpenCms` singleton instead of storing a local reference to the instance.

Our launcher will transform XML to HTML on the fly using XSLT transformations. Here is the code for the launcher:

```
package com.example.genericxml.xslt;
import java.io.OutputStream;
import java.io.ByteArrayOutputStream;
import java.io.IOException;
import javax.servlet.http.HttpServletResponse;
import com.opencms.core.A_OpenCms;
import com.opencms.core.CmsException;
import com.opencms.launcher.I_CmsLauncher;
import com.opencms.file.CmsObject;
import com.opencms.file.CmsFile;
public class CmsXslLauncher implements I_CmsLauncher  {
    private A_OpenCms ocms;
    public static int C_TYPE_XSLT = 21; // Launcher Type ID
    public static String PROP_XSLT = "xslt";
    public void clearCache() {
        return;
    }
    public int getLauncherId() {
        return this.C_TYPE_XSLT;
    }
    public void initlaunch( CmsObject cms,
                            CmsFile file,
                            String templateClass,
                            A_OpenCms openCms )
                            throws CmsException {
        if ( openCms != null ) {
```

```
            this.ocms = openCms;
        }
        // It is possible that setOpenCms() was called.
        if ( openCms == null ) {
            throw new CmsException( "OpenCms class not set." );
        }
        if ( file == null || cms == null ) {
            throw new CmsException(
                "CmsFile and CmsObject are required." );
        }
        // Get the original servlet response --
        // use this to set headers.
        HttpServletResponse res = (HttpServletResponse)

cms.getRequestContext().getResponse().getOriginalResponse();
        // Get the servlet output stream.
        OutputStream out;
        try {
            out = res.getOutputStream();
        } catch ( IOException ioe ) {
            throw new CmsException(
                "Could not get output stream." );
        }
        // See if 'xslt' property is set.
        String fname =
            file.getAbsolutePath(file.getResourceName());
        String xsltTemplate = null;
        try {
            xsltTemplate = cms.readProperty( fname, PROP_XSLT );
        } catch ( Exception e ) {
            // This is not an error.
        }

        if ( xsltTemplate == null ) {
            // Send plain XML.
            byte [] contents = file.getContents();
            if ( contents == null || contents.length == 0 ) {
                throw new CmsException( "File is empty." );
            }
            res.setContentType( "text/xml" );
            try {
                out.write( contents );
            } catch ( IOException ioe ) {
                throw new CmsException(
                    "Error writing data.", ioe );
            }
        } else {
            // Do transform and send HTML.
            res.setContentType( "text/html" ); // Set MIME type
            CmsXslTransformer transformer =
                new CmsXslTransformer( xsltTemplate, cms );
            ByteArrayOutputStream bos =
                new ByteArrayOutputStream();
            transformer.transform( fname, bos );
            try {
                out.write( bos.toByteArray() );
            } catch ( java.io.IOException ioe ) {
                throw new CmsException(
                    "Error getting output for " +fname );
```

```
                }
            }
            return;
        }
        public void setOpenCms(A_OpenCms openCms ) {
            this.ocms = openCms;
            return;
        }
    }
```

This class simply implements the four methods defined in `I_CmsLauncher`. The first method, `clearCache()` does nothing, as this class is not caching XML template code. The `getLauncherId()` method simply returns the ID for this launcher. The ID is stored in the `C_TYPE_XSLT` variable. We will use that ID when we edit the registry in the next subsection.

> There is no set methodology for choosing an ID for a resource type. Generally, you should choose an ID greater than 10, since various values between 1 and 10 are used by OpenCms. Since every resource type must have a unique ID, you should also check your `registry.xml` file to see the existing IDs before choosing an ID for your resource type.

The third method, `initLaunch()`, provides most of the functionality of this class. Remember: `initLaunch()` is called every time a request is given to this launcher—that is, OpenCms executes this method every time a request for content with this launcher ID is made.

In the parameters passed into `initLaunch()`, the `String templateClass` is not used at all—this is intended for use by the XML template mechanism. The instance of `A_OpenCms` is usually used for logging; in the preceding code, nothing is being logged.

After checking the parameters, the method retrieves the original `HttpServletResponse` object. Since we are going to set the Content-Type HTTP header, we must use this object instead of one of the output streams in OpenCms.

Once we have the output stream, the method attempts to get the `xslt` property for the `CmsFile`. If there is no template, the method gets the raw XML contents of the file, sets the Content-Type to the MIME-type `text/xml`, and then writes the file to the servlet's output stream. The client will receive the raw XML data.

However, if the `xslt` property is set, then instead of returning the raw XML data, the method creates a new instance of the `CmsXmlTransformer` class that we created in the last chapter, and then transforms the `CmsFile` with the stylesheet retrieved from the `xslt` property. The process of actually writing the content is a little bit convoluted. Rather than simply writing the contents of the transformation to the servlet output stream, we write them to a `ByteArrayOutputStream` and then pass its contents to the servlet output stream all at once:

```
transformer.transform( fname, bos );
try {
    out.write( bos.toByteArray() );
} catch ( java.io.IOException ioe ) {
    throw new CmsException(
        "Error getting output for " +fname );
}
```

This is done so that the servlet can get the entire contents of the output stream at once, calculate the length of the message that will be sent to the client, and set the HTTP Content-Length header. While it is possible to set most servlet containers into a 'streaming' mode that does not count the length before sending the response, it is usually better to do a little buffering here in order to set the correct HTTP headers. This will assist clients as well as proxies—both of which expect the Content-Length header.

Finally, the `setOpenCms()` method simply sets the object's reference to an instance of `A_OpenCms`.

After compiling this code, the class should be placed in the module's `classes/` folder along with the other classes we wrote in the previous chapter. As usual, you will need to unlock and publish the class file. But before restarting the server, edit the registry to configure the new launcher.

Editing the Registry

When we initially created our new resource type, we had to edit the `registry.xml` file, adding genxml to OpenCms' list of supported types. The entry looked like this:

```
<restype>
    <name>genxml</name>
    <launcherType>1</launcherType>
    <launcherClass/>
    <resourceClass>
        com.opencms.file.GenericXmlResourceType
    </resourceClass>
</restype>
```

By setting the `launcherType` to `1`, we instructed OpenCms to use the text processing launcher (`com.opencms.launchers.CmsDumpLauncher`) for handling requests for content of type genxml. Now, we need to configure it to use our new launcher class:

```
<restype>
    <name>genxml</name>
    <launcherType>21</launcherType>
    <launcherClass>
        com.example.genericxml.xslt.CmsXslLauncher
    </launcherClass>
    <resourceClass>
        com.opencms.file.GenericXmlResourceType
    </resourceClass>
</restype>
```

Notice that the `launcherType` is now set to `21`, the value of the `C_TYPE_XSLT` variable in our launcher class.

The value of the launcher ID is stored per file in the OpenCms database. When you change the value of the `launcherType` element, OpenCms does not make any changes to content in the database. Consequently, old genxml files will still use the old plain text launcher, while new genxml files will use the `CmsXslLauncher`.

> To change the files in bulk, you will need to modify the database with something like the following:
>
> ```
> update CMS_RESOURCES
>   set LAUNCHER_TYPE = 21
>   where RESOURCE_TYPE = 9;
> ```
>
> Where `RESOURCE_TYPE` is the ID for the genxml type and `LAUNCHER_TYPE` corresponds to `C_TYPE_XSLT`.

While `launcherClass` is now explicitly set, this shouldn't be strictly necessary, since OpenCms will use the `launcherType` to determine which class to use.

There is another change we need to make in the registry file. A dozen lines after the `<restype>` section is the `<launchers>` section, which provides a list of launchers that are initialized (referred to as **known launchers** in the OpenCms code). You will want to add the new launcher to this list:

```
<launchers>
    <launcher1>com.opencms.flex.CmsXmlTemplateLoader</launcher1>
    <launcher2>com.opencms.flex.CmsDumpLoader</launcher2>
    <launcher3>com.opencms.launcher.CmsLinkLauncher</launcher3>
    <launcher4>com.opencms.flex.CmsJspLoader</launcher4>
    <launcher5>com.exmaple.genericxml.xslt.CmsXslLauncher
    </launcher5>
</launchers>
```

The new element is named `<launcher5>`, where the `5` is simply an increment from the previous launcher element. Adding the launcher to this list ensures that the launcher is properly initialized when OpenCms starts.

At this point, restart the servlet engine so that the new launcher is loaded.

Testing the Launcher

Once the servlet container is restarted, we can create a new file to test out the new launcher. We will create a simple document in the `/playground/` folder that can use the stylesheet we created in Chapter 5:

```
<?xml version="1.0" ?>
<basic>
  <title>Launcher Test</title>
  <body>This document tests the new CmsXslLauncher.</body>
</basic>
```

Once the new file is saved, we need to set the `xslt` property to point to our XSLT stylesheet file:

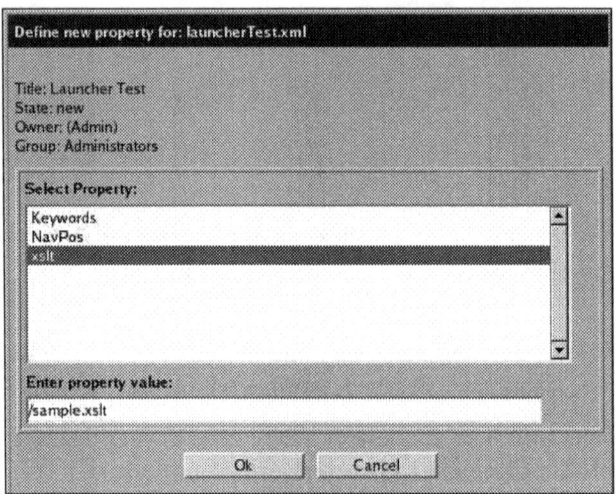

Now, requesting the new `launcherTest.xml` page should render the XML document using the `/sample.xslt` stylesheet that we specified in the properties file. The end result should look something like this:

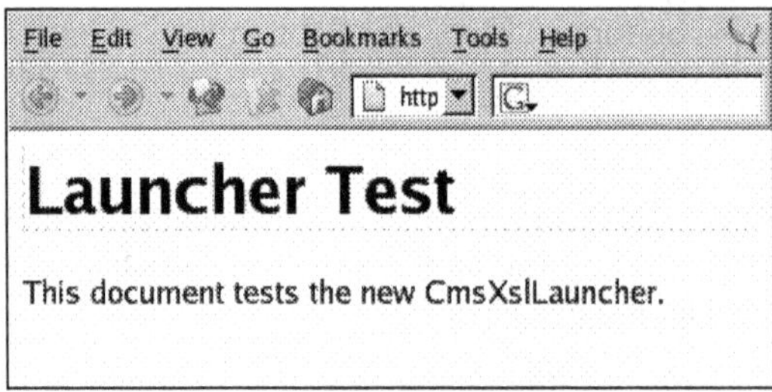

If an XML file does not have an XSLT file associated with it through the `xslt` property, it will simply be rendered as XML. For instance, this is what the `launcherTest.xml` file would look like if we removed the `xslt` property (display of unstyled XML varies by platform. This screenshot uses a Mozilla-based browser).

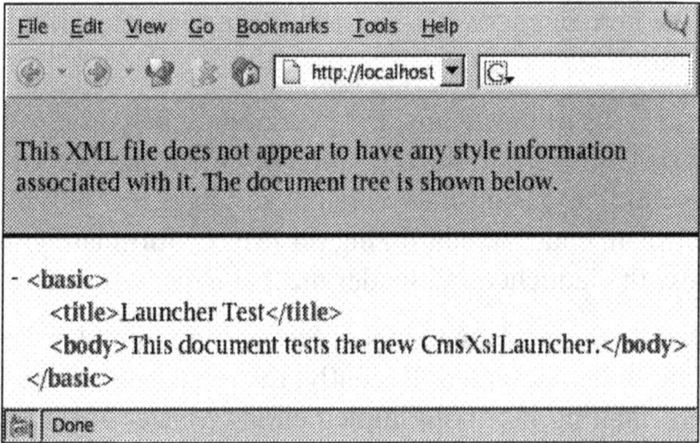

Our new launcher should be capable of handling any type of XML file.

Other Considerations

The launcher we created in this chapter is simple and stands alone. It does not need to be incorporated into either the XML template system or the JSP rendering system. However, other launchers may require much more integration into those other subsystems. In these cases, you may want to take different approaches to developing launchers.

Creating XML-Template-Based Launchers

If your launcher needs to leverage XML template code, implementing the `I_CmsLauncher` interface can be a rather arduous method of creating a launcher, as you will need to create a significant amount of XML-template-specific code. However, there is an abstract class that contains much of the code necessary for handling XML-template-based launchers: `com.opencms.launchers.A_CmsLauncher`. Unfortunately, it is scoped to the package, and so can't be accessed by external classes. However, simply extending the `CmsXmlLauncher` class in the same package and overriding the `launch()` and `getLauncherId()` methods should provide a sufficient workaround.

Creating Resource Loaders

JSPs can include other resources (we looked at the `<cms:include/>` tag in Chapter 4). Elements that must be included in JSPs must implement the `com.opencms.flex.I_CmsResourceLoader` interface. This particular interface, like `I_CmsLauncher`, is fairly straightforward, containing only five methods that must be implemented. In fact, the interface looks similar to the Java servlet specification.

However, the catch here is that if you want to use the class as a launcher too, you will have to implement the `I_CmsLauncher` interface in addition to this one, which can be a little confusing. Alexander Kandzior, the founder and lead developer of OpenCms, suggests extending the `com.opencms.flex.CmsDumpLoader` class if the class needs to be a launcher *and* a resource loader.

As is the case in other areas of OpenCms, the overlapping behavior of these two approaches is due, in a large part, to the transition of OpenCms from the XML template mechanism to JSP technology, and future versions of OpenCms will move away from the deprecated XML template code, standardizing on JSP. Unfortunately, in this specific case, it is unclear how the launcher and loader mechanisms will evolve.

Already, we've looked at some advanced tools for creating modules, but there is one concept left that ought to be addressed. Recently, there has been some hubbub on the OpenCms developers' mailing list about implementing Master Modules. To close this chapter, we will take a look at the Master Module concept.

Master Modules

In Chapter 5, we looked at content definitions as a way of adding support for adding complex external data sources to OpenCms. In OpenCms 5, the developers added a significant extension to the content definition concept. This extension, called Master Module, was intended to alleviate the need to create separate tables in OpenCms for storing non-native data. The Master Module mechanism provides features, such as locking and publishing, that are available to built-in OpenCms types, but not to content definitions. In addition, Master Modules were supposed to be much simpler to create than content definitions. However, rather than becoming less complex, Master Modules added even more complexity to the already complex content definition mechanism.

As a result, OpenCms developers gave up on the idea. They did not supply documentation or even (as far as I know) release any code that used the API. But since the code is open source, external developers have discovered the API and have begun developing against it.

The official stance on the Master Module concept is that it is deprecated and will be removed from future releases. Furthermore, the OpenCms developers are actively discouraging use of the API.

To add to the confusion, some independent developers have used the term Master Module as a synonym for content definitions. This is not accurate, and some of the programs floating around under the Master Module moniker are actually just examples of content definitions.

In short, while there is still some hype about the concept of the Master Module, developers are discouraged from implementing it. If you need to add support for complex external data sources, you should use content definitions instead.

Summary

The OpenCms module mechanism provides the flexibility for adding complex logic and tasks to the base OpenCms system. In this chapter, we extended the module from the previous chapter, adding advanced functionality such as an administration point and a custom resource launcher. But even here we have exploited only a fraction of the potential in module programming.

The module mechanism has proven itself an effective way to extend OpenCms, and future versions of OpenCms are expected to add even more interoperability with OpenCms modules. As developers continue to release new modules, OpenCms itself is becoming a more sophisticated platform for enterprise-level content management tasks.

8

Deploying an OpenCms Solution

In the last few chapters, we have focused our attention on developing code and content for the OpenCms platform. Now, we will return to the administrative aspect of managing OpenCms. In this chapter, we will examine the issues surrounding the deployment of an OpenCms solution. In this chapter, we will cover:

- Serving static versus dynamic content
- Static exports
- User authentication and management
- Backup and recovery
- Performance tuning

Serving Static versus Dynamic Content

In OpenCms, there are three ways of serving published content:

- Serving statically from the OpenCms servlet
- Serving dynamically from the OpenCms servlet
- Exporting from OpenCms and serving from another web server

In this section, I will describe the first two cases, explaining the relative advantages of each. In the next section, I will discuss the option to statically export and serve the content from another server.

Up to this point, we have performed all of our tasks (except for logging in) as a system user of OpenCms. Most of our work has been conducted through the Workplace tool, and other than testing material, we have not done much with the public side of OpenCms.

By nature, the Workplace is dynamic. Files and folders are created, locked, edited, unlocked, and removed; templates are created and updated. In short, the CMS itself is in a state of flux. However, once resources are published, the published copies become static. Until another publish event, a resource in the Online project remains the same.

Published Resources

Published resources cannot be edited. They are intended for consumption by an audience, not for manipulation by editors. Other than viewing, there is not much that can be done with a published resource inside the workplace view of the Online project.

In previous chapters, we focused primarily on the process of creating and managing content in the Offline projects. Now, we will deal with content that has been published—content in the Online project.

In this chapter, we will discuss static and dynamic resources as well as exported content. These concepts are meaningful for resources that are published to the Online project.

As we have seen, OpenCms operates as a Java HTTP servlet and can as such handle HTTP requests itself. In addition to providing access to the Workplace, the OpenCms servlet can also act as the main provider of the published content of the CMS. In fact, the base URL of OpenCms, `http://localhost:8080/opencms/opencms/`, loads the index page (`index.html` or `index.jsp`) from the Online project.

There are two different ways of serving content from OpenCms: static and dynamic. After discussing these two ways, we will look at static exports—the last of the three types I mentioned.

Static Serving

In the static mode, a resource is rendered into its final form when it is published and then this final form of the resource is stored on the file system. For instance, a file of type Page will be placed into its template when it is published, and the resulting file will be written as an HTML file in the `$CATALINA_HOME/webapps/opencms/export/` directory in the file system. Plain files will be written as-is; JSP files will be executed once and the result will be written to a static file.

When an exported file is requested (again, this is in the Online project through the public interface), the file is served as-is directly from the file system. No parsing or interpreting of the file takes place. Consequently, this greatly expedites serving these pages, but at the cost of any dynamic behavior. This can become particularly troublesome with JSP templates that actually execute included JSP pages. When a JSP is published, OpenCms simulates a request for the JSP. The JSP is then executed in this simulated environment and the results are written to a static file. However, this simulated environment may not contain all the information that would be available from a real request, and an export of a

JSP document may result in template errors (`[jsptemplate] ???`) or Java stack-traces if the JSP doesn't have all the information necessary to do its job. Consequently, statically exporting files that rely on dynamic JSP elements often entails detailed debugging and code rewriting. Remember: JSP templates are used for Page documents, and the code in (or included by) the JSP template will go through this export process.

Dynamic Serving

In contrast to a static file, one marked dynamic will be processed by the CMS at run time. When it is published, the content will be moved to the Online project, but its contents will not be written to the underlying file system. When OpenCms receives a request for a dynamic resource, it will process the resource in real time. For instance, if a Page document is requested, OpenCms will retrieve the page and its template, execute the template code, and return the results. JSP templates with dynamic elements work much better in this environment. However, executing pages on the fly does have performance drawbacks.

Fortunately, the static versus dynamic dichotomy does not mean that all the site's contents must collectively be marked either dynamic or static. A system-wide setting controls the default behavior, but individual files can be labeled with the `export` property, and you can configure the default policies for exporting.

The Export Property

Explicitly setting the `export` flag for a file is done through the file's properties dialog. `export` is a boolean value—it must either be `true` or `false`. If it is `true`, OpenCms will attempt to write a static rendering of the file to the underlying file system during a publish event. If `false`, the page will be executed dynamically. The default behavior depends on the settings in `opencms.properties`. It should be noted that certain settings in the `opencms.properties` file will override the file's `export` property. For instance, if `staticexport.enabled` is set to `false`, the file's `export` property will be ignored.

> If the `export` property is not explicitly set for a file, it will inherit the parent folder's `export` setting. If that is not set, then it will use the settings for `static.default.export` in the `opencms.properties` file.

When files are exported, they have a slightly different URL from non-exported resources. The path portion of the URL goes from `/opencms/opencms` to `/opencms/export`. Essentially, when OpenCms sees the latter URL, it loads the file directly from the file system without checking the database. Occasionally, this behavior can be confusing, as exported items can be retrieved with either URL, while non-exported items will give an error if requested with the `/opencms/export` path.

Changing Export Settings

As mentioned, there are several possible options configurable in the `opencms.properties` file located in `$CATALINA_HOME/webapps/opencms/WEB-INF/config/`. If you change these options, you will have to restart OpenCms for the changes to take place. Changes are not made retroactively either, so you may have to republish files in order to get them to use the new settings. If you turn on support for exporting files, you will have to republish your files in order for them to be written to the underlying file system.

The first relevant flag in `opencms.properties` is `staticexport.enabled`. If set to `true`, it will allow static exports. If this is set to `false`, it will disallow all static exports—the entire site will run dynamically, and any file-specific export directives will be ignored. Unless you know for sure that you will never want static files, it is best to leave this value set to `true`.

The second flag, `staticexport.default.export`, determines the default behavior for resources that do not have the `export` property explicitly set. It supports two incongruous values: `true`, which uses static export, and `dynamic`, which uses dynamic execution. While the `opencms.properties` file documents other settings, it also notes that none of the others are functional.

The `staticexport.default.export` option is set to `true` by default. In this case, resources are written to the file system during a publish, unless they have an `export` property set to `false`, in which case they are executed dynamically when requested by an end user. Conversely, if `staticexport.default.export` is set to `dynamic`, only pages with `export` set to `true` are exported to the file system.

> There is one major exception to exporting rules. JSP pages are exported only if the `export` property is set to `true`—even when the `static.default.export` property is set to `true`. The assumption behind this behavior is that JSP pages are dynamic by nature and should not be rendered statically unless the property is set. However, exported pages sometimes fail to correctly link back to the dynamic JSP pages, using the path to `/opencms/export` instead of `/opencms/opencms`, so make sure to do a thorough test of new JSP pages when they are initially published.

Determining settings for `staticexport.default.export` can be difficult. A rule of thumb, though, is that if your site uses a lot of dynamic JSP code, you ought to set this property to `dynamic`. As noted earlier, though, this will significantly increase the load on the server, as it will have to query the database and then execute the relevant OpenCms servlet and JSP code. Tuning the FlexCache, as described in Chapter 4, can help reduce overhead. Also, setting the `export` property to `true` on documents that are definitely static, like plain files, images, etc., can noticeably reduce load. Sometimes strategically configuring frequently requested documents such as the home page to be loaded statically can help too, if such pages do not rely upon dynamic elements.

If your site does not use elements that are necessarily dynamic, then setting `staticexport.default.export` to `true` may be a good solution. If your site (and particularly any of your JSP templates) relies on JSP scriptlets for user login, processing forms, or even time-stamping pages, then setting the default export property to `false` is probably not a good idea. However, if the documents remain static, exporting can be very helpful. When making this decision, pay careful attention to your JSP templates. If `staticexport.default.export` is `true`, then by default all of the elements in the JSP templates will be rendered into static HTML when published.

You may also want to consider exporting all the resources and serving them statically from a different web server, such as Apache.

Static Export

Static export takes the idea of statically serving documents one step further than serving static documents from OpenCms—it removes the dependency of the documents on OpenCms. In short, it exports the contents of the Online project into an entire self-sufficient website that can be served from a run-of-the-mill web server. Most resources are rendered statically, though you still must manually set the `export` property for JSP pages.

Successfully implementing a static export of this type can be a little tricky. First of all, your site must have very little JSP code, and that which exists must be able to be rendered into static HTML during the publishing cycle (for instance, the site navigation that we examined in Chapter 4 could be safely rendered into HTML for a published project, since its output will always be the same for a published project).

Configuring for Static Export

Generally speaking, static exports are done in the same manner as configuring the site for serving static resources. In the `opencms.properties` file, `staticexport.enabled` and `staticexport.default.export` should both be set to `true`. There are a few other parameters that can streamline the process of static exports.

Export Path Settings

The `staticexport.path` property can be used to set an alternative path to which the export will write. The default, as we have seen, is `export/`, which will write to `$CATALINA_HOME/webapps/opencms/export`. You may specify an absolute path instead.

Export URL Settings

Then there are four `url_prefix_*` properties. These properties are used to determine how URLs (primarily, `<cms:link/>` elements and calls to the `CmsJspActionElement.link()` method) will be rewritten during the export process. `url_prefix_export` determines the URL prefix for the resources being exported. By default, it uses `/opencms/export`. However, if you are moving these files to another server, you may prefer a shorter path structure. `url_prefix_http` and `url_prefix_https` are used to point exported pages back to dynamic pages. Mainly, these are only used when OpenCms will continue serving the static resources. The `url_prefix_servername` property is used to supply the server name to HTTPS URLs.

After the `url_prefix_*` settings, there are a number of rewriting rules for specifying exactly how to rewrite links and paths. Most of these are written using the ORO regular expressions library (`http://jakarta.apache.org/oro`), which is compatible with Perl 5 regular expressions. Change these only if you know what you are doing. In most cases, it is not necessary to alter these at all.

Using Relative Links

Further down in the properties file, you will find the `relative_links_in_export` property, which is `false` by default. Setting it to `true` will rewrite URLs with relative paths instead of absolute. In other words, URLs will look like `href="myfile.txt"` instead of `href="/opencms/export/myfile.txt"`. Be careful about setting this property to `true` if you have altered the rewriting rules.

Again, if you change anything in the `opencms.properties` file you will have to restart OpenCms for the changes to be loaded.

> Simply changing the export rules will not cause OpenCms to republish content that has already been published. Unless changed in one of the Offline projects, published content will not be republished to the Online project during a publish event. Major changes to the export configuration may require you to touch all of the files that need to be exported. A JSP is provided at the end of this section to automatically touch files—otherwise, the task must be done manually by locking, touching, and unlocking each file.

Running a Static Export

To export the files, go to the administration view, change the active project to Online, and click the Static Export icon. This icon is marked as inactive in any other project, so you must be in the Online project for the export to run.

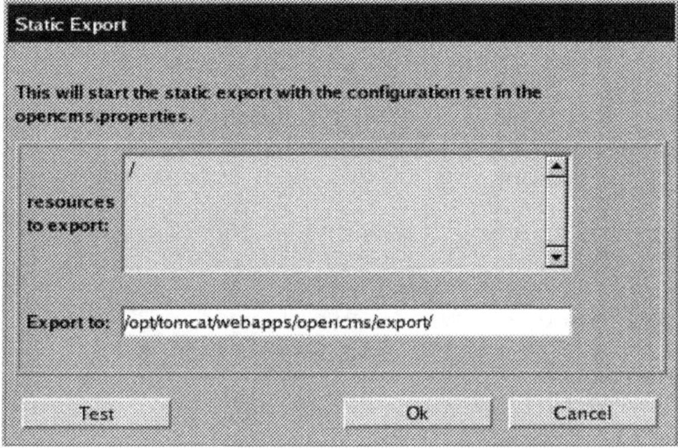

In the static export dialog, all the text fields are read only. They collect their information from the `opencms.properties` file. The **Test** button at the bottom opens a dialog for testing regular expressions on file names, and is not particularly useful unless you are changing the rewrite rules in the `opencms.properties` file. Clicking **Ok** will run the export, writing all files to the directory specified in **Export to**.

Essentially, the static export performs the same routine as publishing an entire project (where all of the files have been marked as changed) for a static site. Moving the exported site to another server is as simple as copying the files under the export directory to the desired destination. Initial setup of an external site can take a while simply to get the path information sorted out. If you statically exported JSP files or used other non-standard file extensions, you will either have to rename the files or map the extension to a known MIME type in the web server configuration files. Remember to manually set export properties for JSP files or other files that won't export automatically.

> If you are planning on exporting files statically, you may want to consider suffixing all of your JSP files with `.html` instead of `.jsp`. OpenCms doesn't use the extension to determine file-type information (it uses the file's resource type), and it will save you the trouble of having to configure the web server to serve `.jsp` files as static HTML.

Touching All Files in the VFS

On rare occasions, such as changing the export settings, you may have to republish everything in the VFS. Since OpenCms will only publish files that have been modified since the last publish event, it can be difficult to republish all files according to the new export rules.

Here is a short script that will touch all of the files in the CMS, effectively marking them for publication during the next publish event. This script should be run with great care.

Any files that are open when this script is run can lose data, and the editors will be kicked out. Also, the process is resource intensive, and can take a long time. It's best to do this only when you must.

```
<%@ page import="com.opencms.file.*,
                 com.opencms.flex.jsp.CmsJspActionElement"
%>
<html><head><title>Touch All Resources</title></head>
<body>
<h1>Touch All Resources in VFS</h2>
<p>WARNING: Make sure all users are logged out, as
they will lose their work if they have files open
during this operation.</p>
<p>This may take a while.</p>
<%
CmsJspActionElement cmsjsp =
  new CmsJspActionElement( pageContext, request, response );
CmsObject cms = cmsjsp.getCmsObject();
long timestamp = 0;
try {
  cms.lockResource( "/", true );
  cms.touch( "/", timestamp, true );
  cms.unlockResource( "/" );
} catch (Exception e) {
  out.println("<h2>Touch failed.</h2>");
  e.toString();
}
%>
<h2>Done</h2>
</body>
</html>
```

This script is very simple. It creates a new `CmsObject`, locks the root directory, touches everything in it, and then unlocks it.

Once this script is run, you will have to publish the Offline project. Since everything is going to be republished, it will take a while. Once this is done, any changes you made to the export configuration should have taken effect. Again, take care when using this script. Misusing it can cause loss of data.

Web User Authentication and Management

In Chapter 3, we looked at creating and managing user accounts for the OpenCms Workplace. In this section, we'll look at managing accounts for end users—those that do not need access to the OpenCms Workplace.

If you are using a statically exported site, you will need to use an external form of authentication, such as your web server's HTTP Auth mechanism. Because of the limitations of the OpenCms authentication mechanism, it may be easier to manage authentication through the web server itself. Consult your web server's documentation to learn more about this.

However, if you are using OpenCms, you can use its existing authentication code to manage authentication of external users. In this section, I will focus on using the built-in OpenCms authentication mechanism.

How OpenCms Handles Authentication

OpenCms is strongly centered on the concept of users and groups. All CMS tasks, including simple content display, require user and group information. In other words, there is a user and group associated with every transaction with OpenCms.

The Guest User

If no user is explicitly logged in, OpenCms automatically uses the Guest user account and the Guest group. Guest cannot login to the CMS Workplace, and has only read-access to files (unless you specifically assign it write permissions). Likewise, the Guest account can only see the Online project. In short, the Guest account is designed to allow anonymous visitors to see the published website.

CMS Users

To get to the Workplace, a visitor is forced to authenticate with a different ID. If the username and password are correct, the visitor is logged in and assigned his or her default settings, such as default group, project, view, etc. At this point, the user is considered a **CMS User**—that is, he or she has permission to use the Workplace.

At this point, there are two types of user. The guest user, which masks any number of possible anonymous visitors, is confined to the public side of the OpenCms site. The CMS Users are logged in and have permissions to work in the Workplace—even if those permissions are read-only or restrict them to a particular project.

Often, it is necessary to have a user type that must log in to the site, but cannot access the Workplace at all. Membership-based sites, for instance, would require this sort of functionality. Users would have to log in to see the published site content, but would not take part in the content management process at all—they would just use the contents of the published Online resources. To this end, there is a third type of user—the **Web User**.

Web Users

Structurally speaking, a Web User is similar to a CMS User. In fact, both are stored in the same table in the database. A visitor can be only one or the other at any given time, as they are mutually exclusive—you are either a CMS User or a Web User. However, the crucial difference between the two is how they are treated by OpenCms security. As mentioned, Web Users do not have access to the Workplace.

Many of the functions in the OpenCms API cannot be executed by a Web User (of course, the same goes for the Guest user).

As you may recall from our discussion in Chapter 3, CMS Users cannot manage their own accounts unless they are in the Administrators group. This effectively prevents users from being able to change their own permissions and give themselves more privileges.

Web Users, however, may create and manage their own accounts. Since they have no real permissions in the CMS other than reading the published contents, there is much less danger in letting these users create accounts. With this feature, it is possible to create online registration applications and management tools for website members.

The main caveat behind using Web Users is that even though they are fully supported in the API, there are absolutely no tools built into the Workplace for handling Web Users. So, in order to effectively use Web Users, you will have to develop custom tools for handling them.

The OpenCms developers have expressed interest in adding a suite of tools for Web Users, but their focus is on developing version 6.0 of OpenCms, and it is unlikely that they will actively work on anything in the near future. However, they have requested submissions from interested members of the community, so it is possible that a standard Web User module may surface.

Since there is no built-in code, we will look at the OpenCms APIs for creating and authenticating Web Users. While this still falls short of a fully functional solution, it should provide the groundwork for building a good custom implementation.

Creating Web Users

Membership-based sites often allow visitors to sign up for membership. The following is a basic form for creating a new user:

```
<form method="POST" action="create_user.jsp">
  First Name: <input type="text" name="fname" /><br/>
  Last Name: <input type="text" name="lname" /><br/>
  User Name: <input type="text" name="uname" /><br/>
  Email: <input type="text" name="email" /><br/>
  Password: <input type="password" name="pw1" /><br/>
  Password (Again): <input type="password" name="pw2" /><br/>
  <input type="submit" value=" Create Account "/>
</form>
```

This simple form gets the basic user information and sends it to the `create_user.jsp` page, which looks like this:

```
<%@ page session="false" %>
<%@ taglib prefix="cms"
  uri="http://www.opencms.org/taglib/cms" %>
<cms:include property="template" element="head"/>
<cms:include
```

```
file="/system/modules/com.example.site/elements/create_webuser.jsp"
/>
<p>Your account was created successfully.</p>
<cms:include property="template" element="foot" />
```

All this JSP does is include the `create_webuser.jsp` file, which contains a scriptlet for adding a new Web User to the OpenCms database. Note that the `template` property for this JSP page is set. As we saw in Chapter 3, the `<cms:include property="template" />` elements retrieve information from the JSP template file referenced by the file's `template` property.

The create_webuser.jsp Scriptlet

The `create_webuser.jsp` is responsible for checking the input and then creating the user's new account.

```
<%@ page import="com.opencms.flex.jsp.CmsJspActionElement,
                 com.opencms.core.CmsException,
                 com.opencms.core.I_CmsConstants,
                 com.opencms.util.MailUtils,
                 com.opencms.file.CmsObject,
                 com.opencms.file.CmsUser,
                 java.util.Hashtable"
%>
<%
String firstName = request.getParameter("fname");
String lastName = request.getParameter("lname");
String userName = request.getParameter("uname");
String email = request.getParameter("email");
String password1 = request.getParameter("pw1");
String password2 = request.getParameter("pw2");
String group = "Guests";
CmsJspActionElement cmsjsp =
    new CmsJspActionElement( pageContext, request, response );
CmsObject cms = cmsjsp.getCmsObject();
// Test each field
if ( userName == null || "".equals(userName) ) {
  throw new CmsException( "User Name is required." );
} else if ( email == null || "".equals(email) ) {
  throw new CmsException( "Email is required." );
} else if ( password1 == null || "".equals( password1 ) ) {
  throw new CmsException( "Password is required." );
} else if ( password2 == null || "".equals( password2 ) ) {
  throw new CmsException( "Password Again is required." );
} else if ( !MailUtils.checkEmail( email )) {
  throw new CmsException( "Email address must be valid." );
} else if ( !password1.equals( password2 )) {
  throw new CmsException( "Passwords do not match." );
} else if ( password1.length() < 7 ) {
  throw new CmsException(
    "Password must be at least 7 characters." );
}
// Set default values for optional params.
if ( firstName == null ) {
  firstName = "";
}
```

```
if ( lastName == null ) {
  lastName = "";
}
// Hashtable for custom parameters
Hashtable params = new Hashtable();
CmsUser user = cms.addWebUser( userName,      // Username
                               password1,     // Password
                               group,         // Default Group
                               "Web User",    // Comment
                               params,        // Params Hashtable
                               I_CmsConstants.C_FLAG_ENABLED
);
user.setFirstname( firstName );
user.setLastname( lastName );
user.setEmail( email );
cms.writeWebUser( user ); // Write changes to DB.
%>
```

The first thing this scriptlet does is retrieve all of the necessary parameters from the built-in `request` object. Then, it creates the `CmsJspActionElement` and fetches the `CmsObject` that we will need for creating users.

Once it has done that, it checks all the required fields (note that these do not include the first and last name fields, which are optional). If one of the parameters does not meet the requirements, the JSP throws a `CmsException`, which will display the error dialog box to the end user. While this is the standard way of handling errors, you may find it desirable to make the error output a little more attractive.

There is no code to check for the existence of a user. This code is absent for two reasons. First, there is no function for checking to see if a user exists. Second, users with low privileges (like Guest and Web Users) must supply a valid password to use the `CmsObject.readUser()` and `readWebUser()` methods. So, instead of being able to proactively check, we must rely on the exception thrown by `CmsObject.addWebUser()`.

After the required parameters are checked, the optional parameters, `firstName` and `lastName`, are initialized, and an empty `java.util.Hashtable` is created. The `Hashtable` can be used for storing arbitrary name/object pairs. OpenCms uses it for storing configuration information. Frequently, developers use the `Hashtable` for storing additional contact information such as addresses and phone numbers. The `Hashtable` object is serialized and stored in the database, so make sure that anything you put in the `Hashtable` implements `java.io.Serializable`.

Next, a new `CmsUser` is created by executing the `cms.addWebUser()` method. `addWebUser()` takes six parameters: user name, password, initial group ('Guests' in our case), a comment, the parameters `Hashtable`, and an integer called `flags`.

The `flags` parameter should use one of two constants: `I_CmsConstants.C_FLAG_ENABLED` or `I_CmsConstants.C_FLAG_DISABLED`. The first flag marks the user's account as activated, and will allow the user to log in and use the account. The other flag will leave the user's information in the database, but will not allow the account to be used.

Again, the `addWebUser()` method will throw a `CmsException` if it cannot create the user. This could be caused by the existence of a duplicate user name, but it may occur for other reasons as well.

Once the new `CmsUser` object has been created (and the initial user added to the database), we set three more properties for the user:

```
user.setFirstname( firstName );
user.setLastname( lastName );
user.setEmail( email );
```

These mutator methods only change the current object. In order to get the changes to propagate into the database, we also have to run `cms.writeWebUser()`.

> The information for both CMS Users and Web Users is stored in the `CMS_USERS` table in the database. There is another table, `CMS_WEBUSERS`, which may sound as if it ought to hold information for Web Users. This table is unused and is slated for removal in future releases of OpenCms.

Authenticating Web Users

Authenticating Web Users, like creating Web Users, requires a certain amount of work. There are no built-in authentication mechanisms that restrict viewing of published resources based on Web User settings.

Here I will demonstrate a simple mechanism for testing for authentication, but this method will only work for dynamic pages. It uses a JSP scriptlet in the template for handling authentication. Exported pages will render the scriptlet at publishing time, and will not rerun it for each request, so the code will not provide any authentication for exported pages.

The first thing we need is a scriptlet for logging Web Users into OpenCms:

```
<%@ page import="com.opencms.flex.jsp.CmsJspActionElement,
                 com.opencms.core.CmsException,
                 com.opencms.file.CmsObject,
                 com.opencms.file.CmsUser"
%>
<%
CmsJspActionElement cmsjsp =
  new CmsJspActionElement( pageContext, request, response );
CmsObject cms = cmsjsp.getCmsObject();
String username = request.getParameter( "username" );
String password = request.getParameter( "password" );
boolean logout = "true".equals(
  request.getParameter( "logout" ));
```

```
if( logout ) {
  // Log in Guest
  cms.loginUser( cms.anonymousUser().getName(), "" );
}
if( username == null || "".equals( username )) {
  String currentUser = cmsjsp.user( "name" );
  if( currentUser != null &&
      ! "".equals( currentUser ) &&
      ! "guest".equals( currentUser.toLowerCase() )) {
    // User is logged in.
    out.println( "You are logged in as " + currentUser );
  }
} else {

  try {
    cms.loginWebUser( username, password );
    out.println( "You are logged in as "
      + cmsjsp.user( "name" ));
  } catch( CmsException e ) {
    out.println( "Login Failed." );
  }
}
%>
```

This script looks for three parameters: `username`, `password`, and `logout`. The first two are used to log a new user in. The third is used to log the user in as Guest. Since there is no logout function and every visitor *must be* logged in, logging a user in as Guest is the closest we can come to actually logging someone out of the system.

If `username` is null or blank, the user is not trying to log in. In this case, we just check to see if the user is already logged in. `CmsJspActionElement` has a useful method for accessing user properties, and we use `cmsjsp.user( "name" )` to get the name of the currently logged-in user. If the currently logged-in user isn't Guest (or is empty), we print out the user's name.

If the `username` parameter is set, we assume that a visitor is logging in. To log in a Web User, we use the `loginWebUser()` method, which differs in security settings from the `loginUser()` method that is also in the `CmsObject`. `loginWebUser()` is used for authenticating Web Users, while `loginUser()` should only be used to authenticate a CMS User. If the login attempt is successful, it prints out a simple message. Otherwise, it prints an error message.

Using the Authentication JSP

This scriptlet must be called from another JSP document. The following document has a form for logging in:

```
<%@ page session="false" %>
<%@ taglib prefix="cms"
  uri="http://www.opencms.org/taglib/cms" %>
<cms:include property="template" element="head"/>
<cms:include
  file="/system/modules/com.example.site/elements/auth.jsp"/>
```

```
<form method="POST">
  Username: <input type="text" name="username" /><br/>
  Password: <input type="password" name="password" /><br/>
  <input type="submit" value="Login"/>
</form>
<a href="?logout=true">Logout</a>
<cms:include property="template" element="foot" />
```

This simple JSP includes the scriptlet we created above, and then provides a simple form for entering the user name and password, as well as providing a 'log out' link at the bottom. Using this form, a visitor can log in to OpenCms as a Web User.

Since the Web User and CMS User concepts are so similar in OpenCms, users logged in as CMS Users will have all of the privileges of Web Users—the system will see them as being logged-in users. However, they will not be able to log in using this form, which will only log in Web Users (the `loginWebUser()` method will not authenticate a CMS User). A CMS User will have to log in using the built-in Workplace login screen or some other custom screen that uses the `loginUser()` method to authenticate.

Restricting Access through a Template

Now, we can restrict access to certain resources to allow only users who are already logged in. Checking to see if a user is logged in can be done with a small scriptlet of a few lines:

```
<%@ page import="com.opencms.flex.jsp.CmsJspActionElement,
                 com.opencms.file.CmsObject"
%>
<%
String LOGIN_PAGE = "/playground/login.jsp";
CmsJspActionElement cmsjsp =
  new CmsJspActionElement( pageContext, request, response );
CmsObject cms = cmsjsp.getCmsObject();
String currentUser = cmsjsp.user( "name" );
if( currentUser == null &&
    "".equals( currentUser ) &&
    "guest".equals( currentUser.toLowerCase() )) {
  response.sendRedirect( LOGIN_PAGE );
}
%>
```

This scriptlet tests to see if the current user is set, and if that user is someone other than Guest. Since Guest is the only anonymous user, this test should be sufficient (again, there is no `isLoggedIn()` method or equivalent). If the visitor is not logged in, the scriptlet redirects to the location specified in the `LOGIN_PAGE` string—in this case, the JSP we created above.

Placing this code at the top of a JSP template's head area, for instance in a 'members only' template, makes it easy to quickly add authentication requirements to any particular page. Setting access permissions on a template does not protect types of data that do not render through a template (like images).

Like many aspects of OpenCms, you can extend the base ideas here and create much more complex and powerful authentication mechanisms. Using the permissions settings in the workplace, for example, you can restrict resources to members of a particular group, and then assign your Web Users to that group. By turning off the 'read' permissions for 'others' (the third group of permissions), you can restrict users of other groups (including the Guest user in the Guest group) from reading the page.

> When creating a group specifically for Web Users, be careful about the value of that group's parent group. A child inherits the permissions of its parent, so you can inadvertently grant a group too many permissions. The best way to avoid mistakes is to not set a parent group for any groups designed to hold Web Users.

OpenCms will reference permissions before displaying information about a resource, so dynamic navigation, for instance, will display only resources that the current user has permission to view. In other words, OpenCms will adjust dynamic menus based on the permissions of the current user. This can greatly simplify management of resources for a membership-driven website.

In the next section, we will move to another important topic for deploying and managing an OpenCms server: backing up and recovering OpenCms.

Backup and Recovery

A significant aspect of successfully implementing a content management system is providing a way to protect the data inside the CMS. A good backup and recovery mechanism is crucial for any CMS system. In this section, we will look at the facilities OpenCms offers for backing up and recovering the repository.

Backing Up the Database

Since OpenCms runs on top of an RDBMS, much of the OpenCms data can be backed up via the database's backup mechanism. For instance, MySQL offers the `mysqldump` and `mysqlhotcopy` command-line utilities for running database backups. Backing up the OpenCms tables is a good idea for a few reasons:

- The task of backing up a database is often very easy to do from a cron script or scheduled task during a nightly backup process. This strategy fits in with the commonly implemented backup strategies. As we will see in a few moments, a full backup of OpenCms takes some manual work.

- A database backup captures all the information in the OpenCms tables. Some data in the database is not actually backed up by OpenCms tools, so a database backup is really the only way of getting a direct snapshot of the exact information in the database.
- Restoring a database backup can be better, depending on the nature of the failure. For instance, if database files are corrupted, it is much easier to restore from a dumped copy of the database. However, in the event of a catastrophic disk failure, it is probably easier to restore from an OpenCms backup.
- For large sites, RDBMS backup tools are often much more expedient. OpenCms, running inside of a Java servlet container, has more memory constraints, but RDBMS servers can manage their memory much more efficiently.

Restoring data that's backed up from the tools included with the database will be entirely dependent on the specific RDBMS. You will need to consult your RDBMS documentation to find out more on such procedures.

Running just a database backup will *not* capture all of the data necessary for running OpenCms. Configuration files, classes, and libraries, which are all stored in the real file system, will be missed by the backup program. Therefore, it is a good idea to back up all of the files in the `$CATALINA_HOME/webapps/opencms` directory as well.

Backups from Within OpenCms

Using RDBMS tools is one way of backing up OpenCms, but another method is to use the tools built into OpenCms for this purpose. The advantage of these tools is that they are specifically tailored to OpenCms. The backup and restore operations can both be run within the Workplace.

To run a backup, go to the administration view in the Workplace and choose Database management. Export will collect some or all of the files in the VFS (depending on how you configure it) and compress them into a ZIP file. This file can later be imported into OpenCms using Import.

> The term 'export' is overused in OpenCms. The static exporting that we discussed at the beginning of this chapter performs a markedly different function than an export from Database management. A static export creates output intended for the browser, applying templates and running code where necessary. The Export feature in the Database management tool exports the raw data—templates, JSPs, and all—into the file system.

The Export and Import tools are intended to be general purpose, and a savvy administrator may use these tools to transport content from one OpenCms instance to another. However, they are well suited to the task of backing up OpenCms resources.

Performing an OpenCms Database Export

To back up the entire VFS (plus users and groups), click on the Export icon.

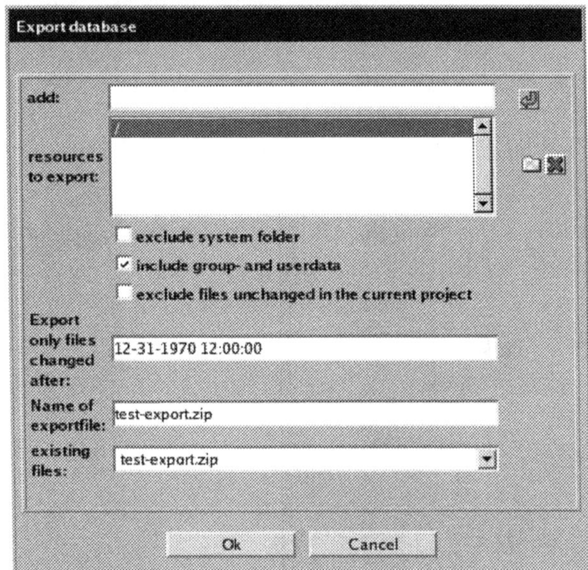

Type / in the add textbox and click the blue arrow to add it to the resources to export list. For a backup, include the system folder (so uncheck the box), user and group data (keep the second box checked), and include all data and not just the changed files (uncheck the last box). Note that by unchecking the exclude system folder box, you will export all of the modules and workplace files in `/system/` as well as the content. Leaving the box checked, on the other hand, will not completely ignore the `/system/` folder—it will still export the `/system/bodies/` and `/system/galleries/` folders.

To export all files, leave the Export only files changed after textbox in its default state. On some browsers, the JavaScript checking application gives a date format error regardless of the actual date format. Leaving this field blank will work around that bug and achieve the same effect.

You may either type a name in the Name of exportfile box or select an existing file from the list below it. Selecting an existing file will overwrite that file with the new data. Clicking Ok will export the files in a manner similar to publishing a project or exporting a module.

Just as is the case with a native database export, the Export tool only backs up data in the database. You will still need to make sure that resources located on the real file system—particularly the `opencms.properties` and `registry.xml` files—are backed up as well.

Backing Up Large Sites

The OpenCms export process uses a large amount of memory, and the larger the site, the more memory it will require. It is not uncommon for export processes for large sites to consume *all* the memory allocated to the JVM, and then abort because it does not have enough memory left.

The main way to work around this issue is to back up data per folder rather than all at once. Instead of exporting the `/` (root) folder, consider exporting two or three directories at a time. Each of these will have to be written to a separate export file. Unfortunately, this will result in some duplication of data (for instance, users will be backed up once for every export operation), but the duplication is not harmful.

The Backup Files

The output of the export is written to a ZIP file, which can get quite large if the `/system/` directory is exported. The structure of the contents of the ZIP file is largely analogous to the structure of the VFS. Based on our example, where we exported the VFS root, the base of the ZIP file corresponds to `/`. Files that appear at the base of the VFS, `index.jsp` for instance, appear at the root of the file. In my export, the `/xml/`, `/html/`, and `/playground/` folders created during the course of this book all exist at the base of the ZIP, as does the `/system/` folder. However, there is an extra file and an extra directory that did not exist in the VFS.

The `manifest.xml` file is created during the export process. It is an XML file that describes each of the files exported from the VFS. This is how the export procedure preserves metadata such as title, description, timestamp, and permissions. Not all of the information about resources is retained in the manifest file though. It does not preserve information about the lock or publishing state of the file, for instance. This is important because an export is done not from the Online (published) project, but from the Offline project. Thus, when the zipped file is imported, resources that are not ready for publishing may become indistinguishable from those already published.

> Project definitions are not exported. Consequently, any projects defined prior to the export will be lost during the export and import process.

In addition to the `manifest.xml` file, a directory named `~userinfo/` is created. This directory has `.dat` files that contain the information for each CMS User. The information in `~userinfo/` is used for restoring users and groups to the CMS.

> Web Users are not backed up during the export process. To back up all users, you will need to back up the `CMS_USERS` table in the database.

One of the biggest problems with the export method of backing up the CMS is that it must be done by hand. However, using the techniques we discussed in Chapter 6, it should be fairly straightforward to implement the `I_CmsCronJob` interface and create a simple object that calls `CmsObject.exportResources()`. Then, by adding an entry in Scheduled tasks, you can have OpenCms run exports at regular intervals.

Importing an Export Zip File

Restoring the backup should be simple and straightforward. Click on the Import icon and select the appropriate file; the data will be imported back into the VFS.

Users and Groups

User and group data will be imported first. The import process for these varies slightly from the import process for resources. If a user or group from the import file does not exist in OpenCms, the import will create the necessary user or group from the information contained in the `manifest.xml` file and the files in `~userinfo/`.

However, if the user or group already exists in OpenCms, the import will not change anything. So, if the settings for the users and groups in the import file are different from those in OpenCms, no changes will be made to OpenCms. This is not the case for CMS resources.

Resources

After user and group data has been imported, OpenCms imports the resources in the ZIP file. It uses a slightly different method for determining how to import each resource.

- If the resource exists in the import file but not in OpenCms, the file is created.
- If the resource exists in the import file *and* OpenCms, the import file overwrites the existing resource. The import process does not check timestamps or make any attempt to determine which file should be considered authoritative. It always overwrites the existing resource with the resource in the import file—even if they are the same.
- If the resource exists in OpenCms, but not in the import file, it is left untouched.

When the import is complete, all imported files will be locked by the user who ran the import, and will be marked as updated and needing to be published. This is true even if the resource in the import was identical to the resource in OpenCms. You will likely need to unlock the imported resources and publish them as desired once the import is complete.

Performance Tuning

OpenCms, written in Java and running as a servlet, is a resource-intensive application. Because of the nature of the content management process, OpenCms uses many synchronized objects—the cost of synchronization is decreased performance. While a fast processor and lots of memory are necessary for good performance, there are some small software adjustments that can help squeeze a little more performance out of the system. One of the easiest and most common ways to increase the performance of a Java application is to adjust the memory settings for the JVM as already discussed in Chapter 2. Let's move on to discuss the other ways.

Database Tuning

OpenCms supports several databases, including SQL Server, MySQL, and Oracle. Each database has different methods of tuning, and there are books and manuals that deal with this subject for each of them. However, there are a few common performance issues that continually come up in OpenCms discussions, and I will talk about those here.

MySQL

The most common issue with MySQL is its size limit on incoming data. By default, the limit is two megabytes, and many OpenCms modules contain JAR files (which are imported into the database) that are larger than this. To work around this limitation, edit the line in the MySQL configuration file, `my.cnf` (usually in `/etc` on UNIX-like OS):

```
[mysqld]
...
set-variable     = max_allowed_packet=2M
```

Setting it to something like `6M` should do the trick for OpenCms modules; I've seen administrators set this as high as 1 GB! Whenever you set variables in `my.cnf`, you will need to restart the database.

Since OpenCms is primarily developed and tested on MySQL, the default settings are good, and specific tuning of database parameters is not usually necessary. The MySQL manual at `http://www.mysql.com` has a section on tuning the database that highlights specific ways to increase database speed in a way that is transparent to applications that connect to the database. If you are looking to further improve database response times, that is a good place to start.

Oracle

By far, the most talked about issue with Oracle and OpenCms is a bug in the JDBC `DriverManager` that causes Oracle to deadlock under high traffic. Several different approaches have been taken to fixing the issue, and a few patches have been contributed to the OpenCms developers' mailing list. However, there does not seem to be a simple workaround for this issue. This issue seems to surface primarily on higher-traffic sites.

SQL Server

As the OpenCms developers will readily admit, SQL Server is the least tested of the supported databases. Even in the 5.0.1 release, some of the SQL Server queries do not function correctly. Consequently, if you are running SQL Server, you may need to apply some patches to the SQL properties file in the `com.opencms.file.mssql` package.

Rene van't Veen has submitted a patch to the OpenCms Bugzilla (`http://opencms.org/bugzilla`) as part of bug number 91. If you need the patch, you can obtain it from: `http://www.opencms.org/bugzilla/show_bug.cgi?id=91`.

The patch operates on only one file—the `query.properties` file in `com/opencms/file/mssql/`. All it does is replace two bad SQL statements that expected the wrong number of arguments.

Installing the patch is easy. You do not need to edit the OpenCms sourcecode to fix it—simply editing the file under the `$CATALINA_HOME/webapps/opencms/WEB-INF/classes/` directory and restarting the servlet container should work.

I have also heard some developers say that they increased performance by replacing the straight SQL statements with stored procedures. Geoff Winkless, an active contributor to the OpenCms community, reported to me that he noticed that 95% of the execution time for OpenCms queries was spent compiling the SQL statements. After transitioning to stored procedures, he noticed huge performance improvements. Geoff's modifications are available from the OpenCms developers' list archives: `http://mail.opencms.org/pipermail/opencms-dev/2004q1/009733.html`.

Doing this sort of modification, though, requires a lot of work (and could be a maintenance headache when doing upgrades).

OpenCms Tuning

At the beginning of this chapter, we looked at using static and exported resources as a way of improving speed. However, those methods require a significant trade-off—dynamic functionality is lost. In almost all cases, it is beneficial to have image files exported. Similarly, JavaScript, CSS, and other supporting files are rarely modified by OpenCms, and ought to be exported simply to provide faster service.

FlexCache

In Chapter 4, we looked at using the FlexCache mechanism for improving the performance of JSP pages. This is probably one of the easiest and most beneficial methods of improving the speed of dynamic content. JSPs are cached in a compiled state, which means that two major performance hits are avoided with cached JSP code: the file does not need to be retrieved from the databases, and the file does not need to be compiled again.

There are a few FlexCache properties that can be modified in the `opencms.properties` file. Mainly, these have to do with the amount of space and the number of entries allowed in the cache. These settings are discussed in Chapter 4.

Page Streaming

In addition to the cache properties, it is also possible to turn on page streaming by setting the `stream` property for a resource. This is set on a per-resource basis by adding the property in the file's property list. If `stream` is set to `true` (the default is `false`), the output from a JSP will not be buffered, but will instead be sent directly to the client. This may not actually boost the speed of OpenCms, but it will send a response to the client as soon as some data is written to the output stream, rather than writing the entire page before sending the data. The client will then perceive quicker response times and be able to begin using the page while it is still in the process of loading. Larger pieces of content will definitely benefit from setting `stream` to `true`.

One drawback of page streaming is that HTTP headers must be written before any content is sent to the client. This means that content types, redirects, and other HTTP headers must be set at the very beginning of the code. This can break an application that, for instance, sends a redirect when it encounters a content-rendering error.

Efficient Coding

One final aspect of OpenCms optimization that bears mentioning is the coding of Java and JSP code. In general, the same sorts of rules that apply to standard applications apply to coding in OpenCms. Keep JSPs short and fairly simple. Complex code should be migrated to Java classes, which do not require on-the-fly compilation like JSPs do.

OpenCms makes frequent use of synchronized objects, and this will slow down the system. Where possible, avoid using `Vectors` and `Hashtables` in your own code so that your code doesn't contribute to the slowdown caused by synchronization. On rare occasions where an object may be in memory for a while, but accessed only by a single thread, it may actually make sense to move the data from the synchronized data structure returned by an OpenCms method to another data structure that is not synchronized, such as an `ArrayList` or `HashMap`.

Other Resources

At the beginning of the book, I speculated that the primary problem that any content management system encounters is the seemingly infinite number of organizational procedures that persons and groups use to manage their content. While I have tried, in this book as a whole, to address the common ground that most of us will share, I know that every implementation will diverge from this common ground in one way or another.

Since OpenCms is an open-source product with an international user base, the community built around the product is a fantastic resource, with new information being created every day. While I have mentioned these resources throughout this book, it seems fitting to note them here at the conclusion.

The OpenCms website is an obvious destination for official information on OpenCms. The official binary and sourcecode releases of OpenCms can be obtained from this site, as can a number of modules:

```
http://www.opencms.org/
```

The OpenCms developers list serves as a general list for discussion of all aspects of OpenCms:

```
http://www.opencms.org/opencms/en/development/mailinglist.html
```

A searchable archive of the mailing list is also available:

```
http://www.opencms.org/opencms/en/development/mailinglist-
archive.html
```

There is also a second interface to the mailing list archives. It uses a different search engine, so you may get different search results:

```
http://news.gmane.org/gmane.comp.cms.opencms.devel/
```

Issues and bugs are tracked in the OpenCms Bugzilla:

```
http://www.opencms.org/bugzilla/
```

The 'unofficial' OpenCms forums are a good place to find information on specific topics. Sample code is often posted to this forum, as well:

```
http://www.opencms-forum.de/
```

There is an 'unofficial' list of OpenCms modules and tutorials. This site often has code that has not made it into the official OpenCms module repository:

```
http://opencms.al-arenal.de/
```

Summary

In this chapter, we looked at some of the issues that arise during the deployment of an OpenCms server. We looked at dynamic and static methods for serving resources, exporting a site for serving from another web server, backing up OpenCms, and tuning OpenCms. With these things mastered, you should be ready to publish your website and go live with OpenCms.

Building OpenCms from Source

This appendix covers the process of building OpenCms 5.0.x from source. Occasionally, OpenCms developers make changes to the sourcecode, but do not release a new version of the binary, and you may need to rebuild the sourcecode from scratch in order to incorporate those fixes into your instance of OpenCms. While the examples throughout this chapter are done using Linux, they should be applicable to the Windows environment as well. In this appendix, we will cover:

- Getting the OpenCms 5.0.1 source
- Checking out the 5.0.x sourcecode
- Building with Ant
- Generating Javadocs

What You Will Need

To build OpenCms, you will need the following:

- The **Sun J2SDK**, preferably version 1.4.1 or 1.4.2. If you are running OpenCms, you already have this. `http://java.sun.com/`
- The **Apache Ant** build tool. `http://ant.apache.org/`
- A **CVS** client if you want to build from the latest source. `http://www.cvshome.org/`
- The **OpenCms 5.0.1 sourcecode release**. `http://www.opencms.org/opencms/en/download/index.html`
- The **OpenCms sourcecode from CVS** (if you want to build the latest version). `http://www.opencms.org/opencms/en/development/cvs.html`

Getting the OpenCms Source

Before you can build OpenCms, you will need a copy of the official OpenCms 5.0.1 sourcecode release. This file has all the sourcecode for building OpenCms, and in addition, has the entire set of supplemental JAR files that are needed for building the source.

> You need the OpenCms 5.0.1 source release even if you intend to build from the CVS branch. The source release contains all the external JAR files that you will need to successfully build any 5.0.x version. Those JAR files are not included in the CVS repository, so you will need the source release for CVS builds.

Get the sourcecode from the OpenCms website:

`http://www.opencms.org/export/download/opencms/opencms_src_5.0.1.zip`

Once you have downloaded the source, create a directory (for example, `opencmsSRC`) and unzip the file into that directory:

```
>cd opencmsSRC
>unzip opencms_src_5.0.0.zip
```

If you want to work with the newest version in the OpenCms 5.0.x branch, continue on to the next section. Otherwise, you may skip down to the *Building OpenCms with Ant* section.

Checking Out the Source from CVS

To check out the sourcecode from the official OpenCms CVS repository, you will need a CVS client. Clients for many different platforms are available from `http://www.cvshome.org`, as is installation and configuration documentation. Install and configure your client per the documentation.

> Instructions here are for the cvs command-line program. For other clients, you may need to consult the manual to find out how to do an anonymous checkout.

Create a directory into which you will put the CVS checkout. As I named the source release directory `opencmsSRC/`, I will name this directory `opencmsCVS/`. Change directories to the `opencmsCVS/` directory.

Follow these steps to check out the latest version of OpenCms 5.0:

```
>export CVSROOT=":pserver:anon@cvs.opencms.org:/usr/local/cvs"
>cvs login
>cvs -z3 co -r branch_5_0_x opencms
```

When you are prompted for a password, enter `anon`.

Worthy of note in the above example is the `-r branch_5_0_x` flag. The OpenCms CVS repository contains all recent versions of OpenCms, including the unstable and untested development version, which will eventually evolve into a production-quality release candidate for OpenCms 6.0. Running the latest unstable OpenCms installation is not what we want to do. Instead, we only want to work with patches to the 5.0.x tree. In CVS parlance, we are working with the 5.0 branch, which the OpenCms developers aptly named 'branch_5_0_x'. Using the `-r` flag and the branch name ensures that we get just the files that are related to OpenCms 5.0, and not the new experimental code.

> The 5.0.x branch contains only patches and fixes for the 5.0 series of OpenCms releases. Only minor changes are made to the code, and the API doesn't fluctuate much. The other current branch, 5.3.x, is much different than the 5.0 releases. It contains new libraries and functionality—some of it incomplete or broken. Eventually, 5.3 will evolve into 6.0. There will be no formal release of the 5.3 tree—it is only for development. If you are looking to get involved in developing or beta-testing future OpenCms releases, you may choose to work with the 5.3 branch, but it is not stable enough for use as a server.

After the CVS checkout is done, you should have a directory named `opencms/` with contents that look something like this:

```
> ls
   CVS         doc  history.txt   license.txt  patches  src-modules
   todo.txt    build.xml  etc  install.html  modules    src      test
   web
```

Once you have the project checked out, you will need to copy the `ExternalComponents/` directory from the source release to your new CVS tree:

```
> ls -d1 opencms*
   opencmsCVS
   opencmsSRC
> cp -a opencmsSRC/ExternalComponents opencmsCVS/
> ls -1 opencmsCVS/ExternalComponents/
   Tidy.jar
   activation.jar
   fesi.jar
   jakarta-oro-2_0_6.jar
   jug.jar
   mail.jar
   mysql-connector-java-2_0_14-bin.jar
   servlet.jar
   xerces-1_4_4.jar
```

Now, the new CVS checkout has all the JARs necessary for running a build.

Building OpenCms with Ant

Ant, another project from the Apache Foundation, is a Java build tool. Increasingly, IDEs, developer kits, and even operating systems are including Ant with their wares. However, if you do not have Ant already, you will need to get it from `http://ant.apache.org/`. Follow the instructions on the website to install and configure Ant for your platform.

Just as Tomcat uses the environment variable `JAVA_HOME`, so does Ant. Make sure this variable is set correctly before attempting to run the build.

At this point, we should have everything we need to build OpenCms. Change directory into `opencms`:

```
cd opencmsCVS/opencms
```

In this folder you will see a file called `build.xml`. This file contains all the build instructions for Ant. Ant will look for this file by default. To begin the build, simply type `ant` (make sure you're in the folder with the `build.xml` file). Depending on the speed of your machine, it may take up to ten minutes to build the whole thing.

Once this is completed, the directory `opencmsCVS/build` will contain all of the classes for OpenCms, as well as all of the auxiliary files. To package everything into a WAR file, run Ant again with the WAR target:

```
>ant war
```

Now you should have a sparkling new WAR file in `opencmsCVS/build/opencms.war`. You may now deploy the WAR as explained in Chapter 2.

Generating Javadocs

The Java `javadoc` tool provides an easy way to build HTML-formatted API documentation from the sourcecode of a Java application. (For more on Javadoc, see `http://java.sun.com/j2se/1.4.2/docs/tooldocs/javadoc/index.html`, the Javadoc manual.)

The OpenCms Javadocs are an invaluable reference for developers wishing to create JSPs and modules. The OpenCms Javadocs are absent from both the website and the `build.xml` script. However, the OpenCms code contains plenty of Javadoc information.

To generate the HTML documentation from the OpenCms source files, add this to the end of the `build.xml` script (just before `</project>`):

```
<target name="doc" description="Run Javadoc">
    <mkdir dir="${destdir}/javadoc" />
    <javadoc packagenames="com.opencms.*"
        sourcepath="src"
```

```
                destdir="${destdir}/javadoc"
                author="true" version="true" use="true"
                windowtitle="OpenCms ${version.number} API
   Documentation"/>
       </target>
```

The following command will generate all of the Javadocs and put them in `opencmsCVS/javadoc/`. You can read the documentation now by pointing your web browser to that directory:

```
>ant doc
```

Summary

All of the sourcecode for building OpenCms is available. Using some simple tools, you can build a custom version of OpenCms from source. You can take advantage of the latest system patches—even before they are officially released—by building from the CVS repository code. You can also generate the Javadoc API documentation.

Using the OpenCms Lucene Search Module

As content grows, it becomes increasingly difficult to create a navigation system that leads every visitor to that for which they are looking. Search engines provide the users a way to locate the material they are seeking in a navigational framework that is nearly ubiquitous.

OpenCms does not include a search engine. While the developers have considered it in the past (and there are still remnants of such endeavors in the OpenCms CVS repository), they have decided that their time is better spent developing the CMS itself. At some point in the future, they may reverse that decision and include searching capabilities within the core of OpenCms, but for now, you will have to rely on modules to get the job of searching done.

In this section, I will introduce general searching technologies and methodologies and then explain how to install, configure, and use the OpenCms Lucene Module to handle searching of your site.

Searching Technologies and OpenCms

In the OpenCms world, there are two ways of searching the site. The first approach, often referred to as 'spidering' or 'harvesting', is accomplished by a small searching utility that connects to the home page of the server, reads it, indexes it, and then follows all the links on the page (rather, it follows all links that point to the same server), reading and indexing each page it encounters. **ht://Dig** (`http://www.htdig.org`) is a popular open-source search engine that works this way, and a number of people on the OpenCms developers list (`opencms-dev@opencms.org`) have reported successfully employing ht://Dig on their sites. When used on OpenCms, the indexer will read through all the links it can reach from the published page and create a search index. These search engines are, by nature, external to OpenCms, so searching with them entails either integrating them with OpenCms (e.g. writing a module that wraps searching code—partial code for this exists in the OpenCms CVS repository) or creating the cross-linking necessary to point OpenCms at the search engine and vice versa. This latter task can include porting, for instance, OpenCms templates to another template style or language. For instance, ht://Dig's search client (**htsearch**) uses a simple set of HTML templates to draw its search results.

This method of searching works well for sites that are statically published (that is, OpenCms renders the content once, and then the files are served as static HTML). It is also good if the search engine needs to include in the index content that is not in OpenCms. However, there are also drawbacks. By default, the indexer will index navigation bars, header fields, and template information—material that is not likely to be useful to the person searching the site. You can work around this by adding special comments to your sourcecode, but that can get cumbersome to maintain.

Additionally, this sort of external searching doesn't work directly with OpenCms, so it can't make use of CMS features like permissions, metadata (like the **description** or **keyword** properties) or file-type information.

The second approach to searching OpenCms is to use an OpenCms module to do the searching. This approach solves the problems I listed above because it runs directly in the CMS. With access to all of the information about content, it can intelligently build an index, as well as employ CMS concepts when it searches for files. The rest of this chapter will examine using the **OpenCms Lucene module** to handle indexing and searching the CMS (`http://opencmslucene.sourceforge.net`).

About the OpenCms Lucene Module

I first became acquainted with OpenCms just after the 5.0 release. Before that, I had worked on a wide variety of CMS systems—commercial, custom, and open source. While I liked almost everything about OpenCms, I realized early in the process that the applications I was working on would require a facility that OpenCms lacked: a search engine. Thus, I began writing the OpenCms Lucene module, taking the well established Lucene Java library (`http://jakarta.apache.org/lucene/`) and writing the necessary extensions to make it OpenCms aware.

After I completed the module, I released it to the OpenCms community (with the permission of the company for which I initially did the work), and a number of people expressed interest. Before long, a number of developers were contributing patches. After one developer, Stephan Hartmann, made some tremendously beneficial contributions, he and I decided to move the entire project into a public workspace so that the OpenCms community as a whole could develop it. As of this writing, the 1.5 version of the module has been released.

Obtaining and Installing the Module

The OpenCms Lucene module is at `http://opencmslucene.sourceforge.net`. Using the Module management application in the administration view, load the module into OpenCms (for more information on loading modules, see Chapter 3).

The module includes documentation in the folder `/system/modules/net.grcomputing.opencms.search.lucene/docs/`. Consult this directory for any changes and information beyond that which is included here.

Configuring the Registry

OpenCms uses an XML file, called the registry, for storing complex configuration information. While it is possible to use a custom XML file for storing Lucene parameters, by default, the module uses the OpenCms registry, located in `$CATALINA_HOME/webapps/opencms/WEB-INF/config/registry.xml`. Locate that file and open it in the XML editor of your choice. In this file, you will need to define how Lucene should go about indexing your site. Here is an example:

```
<?xml version="1.0" ?>
<registry>
<system>
<luceneSearch>
   <mergeFactor>100000</mergeFactor>
   <permCheck>true</permCheck>
   <indexDir>/opt/luceneindex</indexDir>
   <analyzer>
     org.apache.lucene.analysis.standard.StandardAnalyzer
   </analyzer>
   <subsearch>true</subsearch>
   <project>online</project>
   <docFactories>
       <docFactory enabled="true" type="page">
       <class>
         net.grcomputing.opencms.search.lucene.PageDocument
       </class>
       </docFactory>
       <docFactory enabled="true" type="plain">
          <fileType name="plaintext">
            <extension>.txt</extension>
            <class>
              net.grcomputing.opencms.search.lucene.PlainDocument
            </class>
          </fileType>
          <fileType name="taggedtext">
            <extension>.html</extension>
            <extension>.htm</extension>
            <extension>.xml</extension>
            <!-- This will strip tags before processing -->
            <class>
              net.grcomputing.opencms.search.lucene.
                                   TaggedPlainDocument
            </class>
          </fileType>
```

```
      </docFactory>
    <docFactory enabled="true" type="binary">
       <fileType name="PDF">
         <extension>.pdf</extension>
           <class>
             net.grcomputing.opencms.search.lucene.PDFDocument
           </class>
         </fileType>
         <fileType name="Word">
           <extension>.doc</extension>
           <class>
             net.grcomputing.opencms.search.lucene.WordDocument
           </class>
         </fileType>
       </docFactory>
       <docFactory enabled="false" type="jsp">
         <class>
           net.grcomputing.opencms.search.lucene.JspDocument
         </class>
       </docFactory>
       <!--
       <docFactory enabled="false" type="news">
         <class>
           net.grcomputing.opencms.search.lucene.NewsDocument
         </class>
       </docFactory>
       <docFactory enabled="false" type="forum">
         <class>
           de.wfnetz.opencms.modules.forum.ContributionDocument
         </class>
       </docFactory>
       -->
       <docFactory enabled="false" type="XML Template"/>
   </docFactories>
   <!--
   <contentDefinitions>
       <contentDefinition type="news">
         <class>
           com.opencms.modules.homepage.news.NewsContentDefinition
         </class>
         <initClass>
           net.grcomputing.opencms.search.lucene.NewsInitialization
         </initClass>
         <listMethod name="getNewsList">
           <param type="java.lang.Integer">1</param>
           <param type="java.lang.String">-1</param>
         </listMethod>
         <page uri="/news.html?__element=entry">
           <param method="getIntId" name="newsid"/>
         </page>
       </contentDefinition>
       <contentDefinition type="forum">
         <class>
           de.wfnetz.opencms.modules.forum.
              ContributionContentDefinition
         </class>
         <listMethod name="getSortedList">
           <param type="java.lang.String"/>
         </listMethod>
```

```
        <page
          uri="/forum.html?forumtemplate=viewcontributionentry">
          <param method="getId" name="conid"/>
        </page>
      </contentDefinition>
   </contentDefinitions>
   -->
   <directories>
      <directory location="/">
        <section>Root</section>
        <subsearch>true</subsearch>
      </directory>
   </directories>
</luceneSearch>
<!--
   - END lucene config
   -->
</system>
</registry>
```

The preceding example is a stand-alone registry file. Sometimes a stand-alone file is useful, but usually, the `<luceneSearch/>` element and all its contents are placed inside the main OpenCms registry, located in `$CATALINA_HOME/webapps/opencms/WEB-INF/config/registry.xml`.

> When you include the Lucene configuration in the main registry file, do not add the `<registry/>` and `<system/>` elements again. Doing so will cause exceptions. Simply copy the `<luceneSearch/>` element and its contents somewhere inside the `<system/>` section of the existing `registry.xml` file.

The rest of this section provides details on each element. While that information is useful for tuning and extending the module, many users will be able to get away with using the module with the configuration file I have provided (make sure, though, that the directory referenced in `<indexDir/>` exists and is writable by the servlet engine). If you wish to use the news and forums modules, you will need to uncomment the `<contentDefinitions/>` section and the `<docFactory/>` elements with types `news` and `forum`. Make sure to restart the servlet engine after modifying the `registry.xml` file.

Global Parameters

At the beginning of the `<luceneSearch/>` parameters, there are several global configuration options.

```
<mergeFactor>100000</mergeFactor>
```

`mergeFactor` is currently not used. However, it is reserved for future use as a way of passing merge factor data into Lucene.

```
<permCheck>true</permCheck>
```

`permCheck` is also unused, but reserved. In future releases of the module, it will allow you to override Lucene's attention to permissions in the CMS.

```
<indexDir>/opt/luceneindex</indexDir>
```

Lucene stores indexing information on the file system (not the VFS). The `indexDir` parameter tells Lucene where to store the index. Note that this directory must exist before Lucene runs the indexer. The preceding example is for UNIX-style file systems. Windows file systems will need to specify the drive letter as well. This value must always be an absolute path.

```
<analyzer>
  org.apache.lucene.analysis.standard.StandardAnalyzer
</analyzer>
```

Lucene uses **analyzers** to break down documents and create index files. By nature, analyzers are language dependent, and Lucene supports many different languages. For English, the module uses the `StandardAnalyzer`. Analyzers are part of the Lucene code itself, and are not at all modified by the OpenCms Lucene module. Consequently, any analyzers that are supported by Lucene will work fine with OpenCms Lucene. For more information on Lucene analyzers, go to the Lucene home page: `http://jakarta.apache.org/lucene`.

```
<subsearch>true</subsearch>
```

`subsearch` determines whether a folder's subfolders are also indexed. This setting provides the default behavior for Lucene, though individual `<directory/>` settings can override this.

```
<project>online</project>
```

Currently, the only project that can be searched is `online`. However, future releases of the OpenCms Lucene module will also allow indexing of other projects.

Document Factories

After the global parameters come the document factories (`<docFactories/>`). In the course of this book, we have come across a number of different document types that OpenCms supports: Page, JSP, Plain, Binary, and others. Document factories tell the OpenCms Lucene module how to parse and index each type of document in the CMS. The simplest example of this is the `<docFactory/>` element for Page documents:

```
<docFactory enabled="true" type="page">
  <class>
    net.grcomputing.opencms.search.lucene.PageDocument
  </class>
</docFactory>
```

In the `<docFactory/>` element, the `type` attribute indicates *which* type of resources this factory should index (`page`, in this case). The `enabled` attribute determines whether this factory should be used (`true`) or not (`false`).

> There can only be one docFactory per type. There is no facility for setting multiple docFactories and selectively employing a specific docFactory under a specific set of circumstances.

The class referenced in the <class/> element (net.grcomputing.opencms.search.lucene.PageDocument here) will be invoked every time the indexer encounters a document of the specified type. So, this document factory specifies that when the indexer encounters a document of type page, it will use the PageDocument class to index that document.

The document factory for plain documents is much more complex, since the information stored within plain documents is not rigidly structured. Consequently, the document factory uses **extension mapping** to determine how best to process the information in these documents:

```
<docFactory enabled="true" type="plain">
  <fileType name="plaintext">
    <extension>.txt</extension>
    <class>
      net.grcomputing.opencms.search.lucene.PlainDocument
    </class>
  </fileType>
  <fileType name="taggedtext">
    <extension>.html</extension>
    <extension>.htm</extension>
    <extension>.xml</extension>
    <!-- This will strip tags before processing -->
    <class>
      net.grcomputing.opencms.search.lucene.TaggedPlainDocument
    </class>
  </fileType>
</docFactory>
```

In the document factory for Plain documents, multiple file types (<fileType/>) can be specified. Each file type has a name (used for logging), a set of extensions (represented in <extension/> elements), and a class for processing the document. An extension is a dot (.) followed by any number of characters that indicate the type of information in the file type. If a dot is omitted in the configuration, it is automatically prepended when the file is read. Thus it is not possible to match files that end in _html or -mytext. Only the dot is a recognized extension delimiter.

When the indexer encounters a file that matches this document factory's type (Plain), it will get the extension of the file and see if it matches any of the extensions for each file type. If it finds a match, it will use the specified class to process the document. For example, if the indexer finds a document of type Plain named myfile.txt, it will find a match in the file type plaintext, and will then process myfile.txt using the net.grcomputing.opencms.search.lucene.PlainDocument class. The PlainDocument class will simply index the entire contents of the file, assuming that the file contains no markup and is just plain text. However, if it encounters `myfile.xml`, it will match the `.xml` extension to the file type `taggedtext`, so it will use the `net.grcomputing.opencms.search.lucene.TaggedPlainDocument` class to process the file. The `TaggedPlainDocument` class assumes that the file contains HTML or XML tags and ignores all the tags when indexing the file.

The OpenCms Lucene module also supports indexing of a couple of binary types, notably Adobe PDF and MS Word documents. Here's a sample configuration for indexing these two formats:

```
<docFactory enabled="true" type="binary">
  <fileType name="PDF">
    <extension>.pdf</extension>
    <class>
      net.grcomputing.opencms.search.lucene.PDFDocument
    </class>
  </fileType>
  <fileType name="Word">
    <extension>.doc</extension>
    <class>
      net.grcomputing.opencms.search.lucene.WordDocument
    </class>
  </fileType>
</docFactory>
```

Similar to the plain document factory, this will check the extensions of any documents of type binary. If the extension is `.pdf`, the file will be indexed by the `PDFDocument` class. Likewise, if the extension is `.doc`, then `WordDocument` will be used.

In the preceding example registry, both JSP and XML template document factories are disabled. Generally, this is a good idea. The OpenCms Lucene module operates on the files in the CMS. It makes no attempt to render JSP or XML template files before indexing (the assumption being that these files are dynamic, and hence should not be indexed). If enabled, the document factories for these types will simply strip out all the JSP or XML tags and then index the remaining text, and this is not very useful.

Along with the core types defined in OpenCms, Lucene can index any document that has a **content definition** (see Chapter 5). In the example you just saw, document factories exist for both **news** and **forum** types. Both these utilize custom content definitions, and for that reason, both require entries in the `<contentDefinitions/>` section.

Content Definitions

The `<contentDefinitions/>` section provides the OpenCms Lucene module with the information necessary to instantiate and access content of types defined in custom content definitions. Here is an example for the content definition of the popular 'News' module:

```
<contentDefinition type="news">
  <class>
    com.opencms.modules.homepage.news.NewsContentDefinition
```

```
    </class>
    <initClass>
      net.grcomputing.opencms.search.lucene.NewsInitialization
    </initClass>
    <listMethod name="getNewsList">
      <param type="java.lang.Integer">1</param>
      <param type="java.lang.String">-1</param>
    </listMethod>
    <page uri="/news.html?__element=entry">
      <param method="getIntId" name="newsid"/>
    </page>
  </contentDefinition>
```

In the `<contentDefinition/>` element, the `type` attribute defines *which* type is being defined (note that this should match up with the type attribute of the `<docFactory/>` element). `<class/>` indicates the class that extends `com.opencms.defaults.A_CmsContentDefinition`. The `<initClass/>` element specifies a class that can initialize an instance of the content defined in the `<class/>` element. The news module, for instance, requires an `<initClass/>` to initialize its database connection pool. Other modules, like the forum module, do not need any particular initialization before the indexer runs.

If you create a module that needs initialization before it can be indexed by Lucene, you will need to create an initialization class that implements `net.grcomputing.opencms.search.lucene.I_ContentDefinitionInitialization`.

The `<listMethod/>` element defines how the module should get a list of resources of the given type (often, content for modules is handled by an API other than simply using `com.opencms.file.CmsObject`). The name attribute contains the name of the method to call on the class specified in `<class/>`. This method should return a `java.util.List` object.

The `<param/>` elements define the Java object type (`type="java.lang.String"`) and value for the parameters required by the `<listMethod/>`. Here's the `<listMethod/>` section from the preceding example:

```
<listMethod name="getNewsList">
  <param type="java.lang.Integer">1</param>
  <param type="java.lang.String">-1</param>
</listMethod>
```

This translates to the following code:

```
newsInstance.getNewsList( new Integer( 1 ), new String( "-1" ) );
```

The `<page/>` element is used to construct the URL that the OpenCms Lucene module will use to refer to the object. It also takes one or more `<param/>` elements that define how to get identifiers (`method="getIntId"`) and then the names it should use to append the identifiers to the arguments list of the `uri`. In the case just discussed, if the 'news' content definition `getIntId()` method returned `1234`, the indexer would generate the link `/news.html?__element=entry&newsid=1234`.

Directories

The last section of the registry contains information about *what* folders are to be indexed.

```
<directories>
  <directory location="/">
    <section>Root</section>
    <subsearch>true</subsearch>
  </directory>
</directories>
```

When the indexer runs, it will read the contents of every folder specified in `<directory/>` elements and add the files in that folder to the index. The `location` attribute specifies the VFS location where the indexer should start. In the example above, it is set to the root (/). With this setting, everything will be indexed except the contents of the `/system` folder (which is protected and will never be indexed). Since this `<subsearch/>` element is set to `true`, the module will traverse the entire directory tree, not just the current folder. The `<section/>` element provides a name that the logging system uses for reporting purposes, but it has no special significance.

This configuration is a simple way to index the entire site. However, more complex configurations, consisting of several `<directory/>` elements can provide a way of strategically indexing the site while protecting sensitive information.

Finishing the Registry

If you modified the `$CATALINA_HOME/webapps/opencms/WEB-INF/config/registry.xml` file, you will need to restart the servlet container to pick up the changes. Also, make sure that you create the directory referenced in the `<indexDir/>` element. Set the permissions so that the servlet container can write to the file.

> If you do not have the News or Forums modules installed, comment or remove those sections from the registry.

Running the Index Manager

The index manager (`net.grcomputing.opencms.search.lucene.IndexManager`) is responsible for creating the Lucene index files. The easiest way to run it is using the `net.grcomputing.opencms.search.lucene.CronIndexManager` class provided with the module. `CronIndexManager` is usually configured to periodically regenerate the index files, picking up and indexing new content.

To configure `CronIndexManager`, go to the administration view and click on the Scheduled tasks menu. Add an entry to run the `CronIndexManager` task every day. The following example runs it at 1:15 in the morning daily:

```
15 1 * * * admin Administrators net.grcomputing.opencms.search.luc
ene.CronIndexManager createIndex=true
```

Note that the entire command *must* be on one line.

The cron entry is separated by spaces. There are nine slots in the cron entry. The first five determine *when* the cron script will be run. They are minute (0-59), hour (0-23), day (1-31), month (0-11), and day of the week (0-6). Note that the day parameter does not use a zero index, while the rest do.

> In the 5.0 version of OpenCms, there is a bug in the way the minute value is handled. The task will not be run if the minute value is set to zero (0).

The asterisk (*) value indicates that no value is set for the slot. Since the file is space delimited, every slot must either have a value or an asterisk.

The next two slots are for the user and group respectively. Running the module as a less privileged user will constrain the operations that the Lucene index manager can perform, and in some cases can prevent the index manager from creating an index. The next slot takes the entire name of the class to be run. In our case, it is `net.grcomputing.opencms.search.lucene.CronIndexManager`. The `CronIndexManager` may take two parameters, `createIndex` and `registry`. `createIndex` needs to be set to `true`. This will force the index manager to completely recreate the index. In future versions, the `false` value will allow you to incrementally maintain the index, adding to it, but not completely rebuilding it each time. Currently, though, setting it to `false` could result in duplicate entries in the index.

The second parameter, `registry`, allows you to specify an alternative registry file to use, such as the stand-alone registry file included at the beginning of the *Configuring the Registry* section. When this parameter is specified, the contents of this stand-alone registry file will be used instead of the configuration in `$CATALINA_HOME/webapps/opencms/WEB-INF/config/registry.xml`. The `registry` parameter requires a full (absolute) path to the configuration file. If no registry parameter is set, the default OpenCms registry file (`$CATALINA_HOME/webapps/opencms/WEB-INF/config/registry.xml`) will be used.

The parameters must be divided by commas, not spaces. Thus, a parameter string with both parameters would look like this:

```
createIndex=true,registry=/opt/tomcat/webapps/opencms/WEB-
INF/config/lucene.xml
```

> OpenCms 5.0.x JavaScript is often optimized for IE. Various versions of alternative browsers (notably Mozilla-based) may function incorrectly.

> In the case of the scheduled tasks menu, older versions of Mozilla cannot process the JavaScript to display the cron table. For that reason, you may need to use IE to edit the cron settings.

At the appointed time, OpenCms will run the `CronIndexManager`, which will in turn generate the index files.

> For testing the `CronIndexManager`, you may find it useful to schedule the index to be built immediately. Once your testing has confirmed that things are working, you can reschedule the task for a more appropriate time.

To view the output of your search results, go to the Logfile Viewer in the administration view and look for the `IndexManager`'s log output. It should look something like this:

```
=====IndexManager=====================================================
=======
[27.01.2004 23:20:10] <opencms_info> Analyzer:
org.apache.lucene.analysis.standard.StandardAnalyzer
[27.01.2004 23:20:10] <opencms_info> Extension map exists to handle
plaintext
[27.01.2004 23:20:10] <opencms_info> Extension map exists to handle
taggedtext
[27.01.2004 23:20:10] <opencms_info> Page DocumentFactory loaded
[27.01.2004 23:20:10] <opencms_info> IndexManager: indexing /
[27.01.2004 23:20:10] <opencms_info> IndexManager: indexing
/playground/
[27.01.2004 23:20:10] <opencms_info> IndexManager: indexing
/playground/de/
[27.01.2004 23:20:10] <opencms_info> IndexManager: indexing
/playground/en/
[27.01.2004 23:20:10] <opencms_info> IndexManager: indexing /release/
[27.01.2004 23:20:10] <opencms_info> IndexManager: skipping /system/
[27.01.2004 23:20:10] <opencms_info> IndexManager: 10 documents are
being processed
[27.01.2004 23:20:10] <opencms_info> IndexManager:  Index has been
optimized.
[27.01.2004 23:20:10] <opencms_info> Done
=====IndexManager=====================================================
=========
[27.01.2004 23:20:10] <opencms_cronscheduler> Successful launch of
job com.opencms.core.CmsCronEntry{20 23 * * * admin Administrators
net.grcomputing.opencms.search.lucene.CronIndexManager
createIndex=true,registry=/opt/tomcat/webapps/opencms/WEB-
INF/config/lucene-registry.xml} Message: CronIndexManager rebuilt the
Lucene index on Tue Jan 27 23:20:10 MST 2004
```

The above output provides a record of the `IndexManager`'s actions, including the directories searched and the number of files indexed.

> After editing the scheduled tasks table, you may experience an error where the task fails to run, and OpenCms complains that the cron table is corrupt. This can happen if there is a blank line in the scheduled tasks table. To fix it, go to the Scheduled tasks screen and delete the blank lines in the table.

You may also want to verify that the index files were written to file system. Look in the directory you set with the `<indexDir/>` element in the registry.

```
jericho tomcat # ls /opt/lucene/opencms/
_a.f1  _a.f3  _a.f5  _a.f7   _a.fdx  _a.frq  _a.tii  deletable
_a.f2  _a.f4  _a.f6  _a.fdt  _a.fnm  _a.prx  _a.tis  segments
```

These files contain Lucene's optimized search data. Essentially, every time the index manager is run, it rebuilds or updates these files.

The data has been indexed and is now ready to be searched.

Searching with Lucene

With the index files created, we now turn our attention to adding searching capabilities to our site. The OpenCms Lucene module includes some built-in tools for expediting the implementation of search features. To begin with, we'll use the `simple_search.jsp` element that is included with the OpenCms Lucene module.

We will begin by creating the search results page. That way, when we create the search form, we will know where to point it. Create a `search-results.jsp` page in the `/playground/` directory and set the `template` property to point to the main JSP template. All this template will need to do is include the template header and footer as well as the `simple_search.jsp`.

```
<%@ page session="false" %>
<%@ taglib prefix="cms"
  uri="http://www.opencms.org/taglib/cms" %>
<cms:include property="template" element="head"/>
<div style="display:table; padding: 5px;">
<cms:include
file="/system/modules/net.grcomputing.opencms.search.lucene/elements/
simple_search.jsp"/>
</div>
<cms:include property="template" element="foot"/>
```

The `simple_search.jsp` will do all of the work for us. The next thing to do is create an element that contains the search form. I have chosen to create an element because it is likely that I will want to reuse that same component in multiple places. In `/system/modules/com.example.site/elements/`, we will create an element called `search-form.jsp`, which looks as follows:

```
<%@ page session="false" %>
<%
// If a param q is found, it is placed in the text box.
String qval = request.getParameter("q");
if(qval == null) qval = "";
%>
<form method="GET" action="<cms:link>/playground/search-
results.jsp</cms:link>">
  Search:
  <input type="text" name="q" value="<%= qval %>"/>
  <input type="submit" value="Go"/>
</form>
```

The scriptlet at the beginning is checking to see if there is already a value for the GET parameter q (the query). If there is, then the existing query is placed in the search text field (the `<%= qval %>` is synonymous with `<% out.println(qval); %>`). Otherwise, the value is left empty. Note that I used the `<cms:link>` tag in the form action to point the form to the `search-results.jsp` page.

Now, all that needs to be done is include the search form into the main template, thereby displaying the search form on every page:

```
<%@ page session="false" %>
<%@ taglib prefix="cms" uri="http://www.opencms.org/taglib/cms" %>
<cms:template element="head">
  <html>
  <head>
    <title>
      <cms:property name="title" escapeHtml="true"/>
    </title>
  </head>
  <body>
    <div class="search" style="float:right; border: 1px solid
                                    gray; padding: 5px;">
      <cms:include file="../elements/search-form.jsp"/>
    </div>
    <div name="menu"
      style="float:left; border: 1px solid gray; padding: 5px;">
      <cms:include file="../elements/example-navigation.jsp"/>
    </div>
    <h1>
      <cms:property name="title" escapeHtml="true"/>
    </h1>
</cms:template>
<cms:template element="body">
  <cms:include element="body"/>
</cms:template>
<cms:template element="foot">
  </body>
  </html>
</cms:template>
```

The highlighted portion in the code indicates the new include. From any page that uses this template, I can now type in a search term, and the OpenCms Lucene module will search the indexes for the term. The result should look something like this:

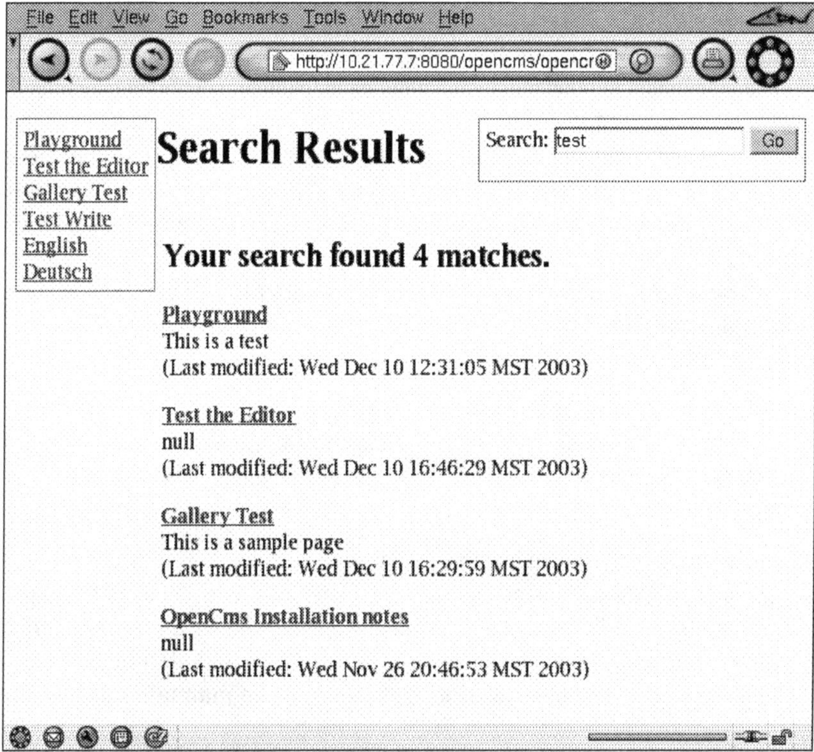

Each item in the search-results list displays the **title** (linked to the resource), the **description**, and the **last modified** date. The `simple_search.jsp` does not do much checking of the data. Consequently, when a search result does not have a description, the results page prints `null`. Also, you may have noticed that the text input for the search form shows the query, `test`. That is the result of the scriptlet in the `search-form.jsp` element we just created.

While the `simple_search.jsp` may cover basic searching requirements, it is possible to create a much more sophisticated search engine using the utilities provided both by the module and the Lucene API itself. The `net.grcomputing.opencms.search.lucene.SearchHelper` class provides facilities for running simple searches as well as getting the information necessary for constructing sophisticated Lucene index searches.

Hacking the OpenCms Lucene Module

Like the rest of OpenCms, the OpenCms Lucene module is open source. The sourcecode for the module is available from the OpenCms Lucene website (`http://opencmslucene.sourceforge.net`).

The most common need is to extend the indexer to index a different kind of document format or content definition. Essentially, all this involves is retrieving the text that needs to be indexed and telling Lucene what the indexed information should be called. This can be done fairly easily by implementing `net.grcomputing.opencms.search.lucene.I_FileDocumentFactory` for new file types or `net.grcomputing.opencms.search.lucene.I_CdDocumentFactory` for new content definitions. Some content definitions may require initialization, which is done by implementing `net.grcomputing.opencms.search.lucene.I_ContentDefinitionInitialization`. There are examples of both sorts of document indexers (for files and content definitions) in the module's sourcecode.

On the searching side, the `net.grcomputing.opencms.lucene.SearchHelper` class exposes a search interface for scriptlets to implement. Sophisticated searching code implemented in Java classes may find the `SearchHelper` class useful in retrieving data about the search indexes.

For generating the index, the main starting point is the `net.grcomputing.opencms.lucene.IndexManager` class, which reads the registry, builds a list of resources to be indexed, and then executes the indexing mechanisms. A number of patches and extensions have been submitted and included into the official sourcecode. If you write a useful extension, pass it on to the maintainers. We like contributions.

Summary

The OpenCms Lucene module provides a fast and integrated method of searching the OpenCms repository. Built for customization, it can be integrated into an existing OpenCms installation with a minimal amount of effort.

Index

A

B

C

D

E

F

L

M

N

O

P

T

U

V

W

X

www.ingramcontent.com/pod-product-compliance
Lightning Source LLC
Chambersburg PA
CBHW060529060326
40690CB00017B/3426
9781904811046